# THE CHILDREN OF SOWETO

# The Children of Soweto

a trilogy by

## Mbulelo Vizikhungo Mzamane

Longman

Longman Group UK Limited,
Longman House, Burnt Mill, Harlow,
Essex CM20 2JE, England
and Associated Companies throughout the world

First published in Longman Drumbeat 1982
First published in Longman African Classics 1987

Set in Baskerville
Produced by Longman Group (FE) Ltd
Printed in Hong Kong

ISBN 0 582 01680 0

# Contents

*Acknowledgements*

Thanks to:
Tsietsi Sr., Khotso, Barney, Sechaba, Duke, Paddido, Neo, Sydney, Mickey, Shakes, Sipho, Tsietsi Jr., Nina, Anna, Tshidi, Monica, Dithole, Bella, little Queeny, Tilly, Lolo, Tsitsi, Hector, Marjorie, Connie, Sonti, Thoko, Strike, Esau, Dumi, Motsumi, Tefo, 'Moso, Jack, Lucky — and others too numerous to mention, whose story this is. But they know themselves.

And also to:
Sam Shakong, Thato Bereng, Ntombi and Lepetu Setshwaelo, Lulu and Lulama Morrison, Gillian and Malusi Balintulo, Mpho and Njabulo 'Jigsaw' Ndebele, Pethu and Mongane Serote — for their stimulating friendship and their incisive political insights.

And to:
Moteane Melamu for introducing me to the pleasures of literature and for his expert guidance during my period of apprenticeship.

And:
Many, many, many thanks to Nthoana and our children — Nomvuyo, Thamsanqa and Nonkosi. *Ndithi ningadinwa nangomso! Le kamoso!*

To:
Mandlenkosi Langa, Lefifi Tladi, Mafika Gwala and others for permission to reprint their poems.

For Tat' uJoe, and all the black children and parents of
our beloved fatherland

it were us, it is us
the children of Soweto
langa, kagiso, alexandra, gugulethu and nyanga
us
a people with a long history of resistance
us
who will dare the enemy
for it is freedom, only freedom which can
                  quench our thirst —
we did learn from terror that it is us who
                  will seize history
our freedom

Mongane Wally Serote, from 'No More Strangers'

# Glossary

*Abefundisi abadla emhlambini* (Nguni): Priests who sponge on their flock.

*Akadinwa ukukhuluma lomuntu* (Zulu): This person doesn't tire of talking.

*Amadodana* (Xhosa): Elders of the Methodist Church.

*Amagoduka* (Xhosa): Migrant labourers.

*Asseblief* (Afrikaans): Please.

*Asiyazi leyo* (Nguni): We don't know that one.

*Azingafi ngamvu inye, bantwana bami* (Zulu): Don't let all the sheep die on account of only one, my children.

*Boerewors* (Afrikaans): Sausages.

*Dit is genoeg* (Afrikaans): That's enough.

*Dit is lewe* (Afrikaans): That's life.

*Einklek* (Tsotsitaal): Actually.

*Ek gaan was* (Afrikaans): I'm going to wash.

*Emalahleni!* (Zulu): In the coal!

*Fana* (Nguni): Short for 'umfana', boy.

*Gatas* (Tsotsitaal): Policeman.

*Gazaat* (Tsotsitaal): Give money for a common purpose.

*Gebruik* (Afrikaans): Use.

*Hambani niyolala nina* (Nguni): You go and sleep.

*Hay' khona* (fanakalo – Childish blubber often used by white employers to address Blacks): No.

*Hay' inkunku nje loontwana* (Xhosa): No, that lad is just (as innocent as) a fowl.

*Hulle gat, man* (Afrikaans): Their arses, man.

*Ibandla* (Nguni): Congregation, assembly, group.

*Imbongi* (Nguni): Praise-poet.

*Inyanga* (Nguni): Medicine man.

*Ithi sibone* (Nguni): Let's see.

*Izilungele nje yona* (Xhosa): He's a good lad.

*Izobapokela* (Zulu): Its ghost is going to haunt them.

*Jou donder se kaffir, kaan jy nie praat nie?* (Afrikaans): You bloody kaffir, can't you talk?

*Jy moenie kak praat nie* (Afrikaans): Don't talk shit.

*Kaffirboetie* (Afrikaans): Negrophile.

*Ke'ng?* (Sotho): What's the matter?

*Khuluma isiZulu wena, asizwa* (Zulu): Talk in Zulu, we don't understand you.

*Kodwa amabhunu eniwakhathalele ngani nina lana?* (Zulu): But why should you be so concerned over the fate of these Boers?

*Kodwa thina sibabolekelani imali yethu abantu abanje?* (Zulu): But why do we lend our money to such people?

*Kodwa, wena ubumusa kuphi lomuntu?* (Zulu): But where did you think you were taking this person to?

*Kragdadigheid* (Afrikaans): Brute force, as opposed to diplomacy.

*Kunjani* (Nguni): How are things; How are you?

*Kwagwala akulilwa* (Xhosa): Cowards never weep (Proverb); said of a person who avoids conflict.

*Kyk net daar!* (Afrikaans): Just take a look!

*Laat ons line* (Tsotsitaal): Let's go.

*Laititjie* (Tsotsitaal): Diminutive of *laaitie*, small boy.

*Lezinja!* (Nguni): You dogs!

*Lifaqane* (Sotho) . . . *difaqane* (Tswana) . . . *umfecane* (Zulu): Nineteenth-century internecine wars among South Africa's indigenous people.

*Los julle die arme dronkies* (Afrikaans): leave the poor drunkards.

*Maar* (Afrikaans): But.

*Majita* (Tsotsitaal): Gents.

*Makoti* (Nguni/Sotho): Bride.

*Makwedini* (Xhosa): Plural form of *Kwedini*, small boy.

*Malombo* (Venda): Literally, spirits; jazz sound fusing traditional Venda/Pedi rhythms with modern jazz idiom.

*Mayenziwe intando yakho* (Xhosa): Your will be done.

*Mbaganga* (Tsotsitaal): Township jazz; also called *Kwela*

*'Me* (Sotho/Tswana): Mother.

*Mfowethu* (Zulu): My brother.

*Miering* (Tsotsitaal): Money.

*Mkatakata* (Tsotsitaal): Trouble, fiasco.

*Moegoe* (Tsotsitaal): Stupid fellow.

*Molimo* (Sotho): God.

*Morena oa ka* (Sotho): My lord, master.

*Moruti* (Sotho): Priest, teacher.

*Mtshele ngemoto phela, ndoda* (Zulu): Tell him about the car, man.

*My ma hoor my* (Afrikaans/Tsotsitaal): I swear by my mother.

*Nangomso* (Xhosa): Even tomorrow (may you lend me assistance again!)

*Ndambula* (Tsotsitaal): Beer made from sorghum.

*Ndithi nyamalalani niphele* (Xhosa): I say, clear out of my sight.

*Ngoana* (Sotho): Child.

*Nkosi yam'!* (Zulu): My God!

*Ntate* . . . pl. *bonbate* (Sotho): Father.

*Ora nna?* (Tswana): Do you mean me?

*Rangoane* (Sotho): Husband to your *Mangoane* (maternal aunt); paternal uncle.

*Rockshin* (Tsotsitaal): Chaos, cacophony.

*Sebefuna nokuskepa amatichere manje* (Tsotsitaal): Now they even want to abduct teachers.

*Shiya* (Tsotsitaal): Forget it; from the Nguni, 'leave it'.

*Siculeni manje?* (Zulu): What shall we sing now?

*Simanje-manje* (Patois): Modern generation.

*Sithunywe yibo* (Zulu): We've been sent by them.

*Sizakucela ibandla laseWisile khe lizokubhedesha nalo* (Xhosa): We'll request the Wesleyans to come forward and make their contribution to the ceremony.

*Sizothini?* (Zulu): What can we say?

*Skokiaan* (Patois): Alcoholic concoction brewed illegally.

*Staan-staan* (Tsotsitaal): Sexual intercourse standing up.

*Sy's net een van hulle kaffir kommannissie hoer-meide* (Afrikaans): She's just one of their Kaffir communist whores.

*Umanyano* (Xhosa): Union, e.g. Mothers' Union.

*Umbhedesho* (Xhosa): Dance, ceremony.

*Umntana' sekhaya* (Xhosa): Literally, child of our house; brother or sister.

*Umshumayeli* (Xhosa): Preacher.

*Umsingizane* (Nguni): Wire grass, used to weave hats.

*Uthi umlungu kwenzenjani?* (Zulu): The white man says, what is the matter?

*Utshwala* (Zulu): Liquor, alcohol.

*Umvangeli* (Nguni): Evangelist.

*Uyakubiza umlungu wakho* (Nguni): Your white man is calling you.

*Uyaphi?* (Nguni): Where are you going to?

*Verligte* (Afrikaans): An 'enlightened' white person.

*Voetsek!* (Afrikaans): Mild insult.

*Wampatshaza* (Zulu): He got the better of him (verbally).

*Wat het jy daarso?* (Afrikaans): What do you have there?

*Woza-Woza* (Zulu): Literally, come-come. Medicine used by shebeen queen to attract customers.

*Yishiye khona la* (Zulu): Leave it right here.

# Book One

My Schooldays in Soweto

Relations between Pakade, Phakoe and us were always cordial and informal, which could not be said for our relationship with the other teachers. Only the ill-fated Nkululeko, when he joined our staff, came anywhere near Pakade and Phakoe in our esteem. Yet they could be very exasperating too.

There were several factors which set Pakade and Phakoe apart. For one thing they drank like twin sponges. Small wonder they never seemed to have enough ready cash. Their unquenchable thirst even led them to borrow from the students. We liked them, though; they had very few hang-ups.

My father, who was the local Anglican priest, spoke most disparagingly of both. They were lapsed Anglicans from whom he had long since ceased to ask for church dues, which were many years in arrears. My mother, a trained teacher herself though she had decided to follow her other profession, nursing, spoke equally strongly against 'these shameless men who disgrace the profession by their unexemplary behaviour' whenever they passed our house from Shirley Scott's, swaying from side to side like herdboys driving wayward goats. In fact, very few parents had good words for those two. But to us they were the best teachers we'd ever had.

Pakade was popularly know as S'gubhu, in acknowledgement of his drum-shaped tummy, which gave him a chiefly deportment. He liked to joke about being of Pondo royal descent. But none of us dared to call him by his nick-name in his hearing, although he knew it all right. He was built like a light heavyweight and often boasted that he'd been boxing champ at Lovedale and Fort Hare during his schooldays. We could tell he wasn't telling the truth because his efforts at shadow-boxing would have made even a novice laugh. He always came to the gymnasium (which was really a disused store-room), where our school team trained, to coach. We had to grudgingly admit that his theories were indeed sound. But when it came to practice! He liked to demonstrate his craft in the classroom. When he gave us exercises in Afrikaans grammar, as we worked on in our exercise books, he'd turn his

3

back to the class and start shadow-sparring in one corner of the classroom. He had no more grace than a cow. He held up his fists like a country boy parrying blows with sticks, which prompted some of the boys to shout, '*Meneer*, you don't put up your hands that way like a pair of *knobkierries*.' Whereupon he'd turn round to address whoever had passed the remark. '*Makwedini*, you may laugh, ha! ha! ha! because you see me *sendi* – out of shape,' he would say, affectionately patting his public opinion, as we termed his tummy. 'You should have seen me in my heyday when I was still boxing champ of the Eastern Cape.'

'Before long he'll be telling us that he also fought for the South African title,' Khulu would whisper to us in his usual self-effacing manner, with one hand covering his mouth.

'*Hawu*! It's no longer just Lovedale and Fort Hare,' Monty, who liked to tease him most, would say aloud. 'And in what division were you champ, *meneer*?'

'Go find out from your fathers, *makwedini*,' he'd say.

Since none of our fathers had been boxers in their youth or had been to school at the same time as our much younger teacher, we usually left the matter at that. But once I asked my elder brother, who had also been to Fort Hare, whether Pakade had ever been a boxer. My brother, who very rarely spoke more than ten words all put together to me, momentarily raised his eyes from the book he was reading, contemptuously exclaimed 'Mff!', and went on reading.

Both Pakade and Phakoe were notorious cowards. The other day, for instance, our school went to play at Alexandra township. The games finished late, so that we even had to call off the debating contest. We were held up further by having to wait for other students. Most of us were already in the bus. The PUTCO driver who had brought us was becoming impatient and so turned for help to Pakade and Phakoe, who were the staff members with us. Pakade went out to see what was delaying the rest of the students. No sooner had he stepped out of the bus than a girl from our school called out to him for help.

Some small-time local *tsotsi* was detaining her. Trusting to his position as a teacher, Pakade turned to her rescue. With the speed of lightning, the Alex lad drew a butcher knife from under his belt, its blade glittering menacingly in the dark. Pakade made an about-turn and took to his heels, the girl close behind him and their tormentor in hot pursuit. Near the bus, quite close to the door, Pakade slipped but the girl managed to jump into the bus. His pursuer closed in on him. As he slipped, Pakade missed the door and ran on, round and round the bus, calling Phakoe's name.

Whether from fear or alcohol we could not tell, Phakoe was past hearing. His tiny frame seemed to sink deeper into his seat and nothing would induce him to leave his sanctuary.

'We can't just stand here and watch,' one of our boys said. '*Sebefuna nokuskepa amatichere manje!*' We all agreed it was unfair to want to hijack our girls and then terrorise our teachers as well. The boys nearest the door leapt out of the bus and chased the young thug away. Several other Alex hooligans, lounging about or holding our girls by force, took fright and ran away.

From several such incidents Pakade and Phakoe had gained their reputation. So that it greatly amused us to see Pakade at his daily work-outs or threatening to beat us. 'I'll beat you up, *makwedini*,' he would say.

'*Nobani?*' the boys would ask, insinuating by that question that he needed more than Phakoe's assistance to beat us.

'You boys just won't believe that I used to be the best in my division in the country,' he said.

'Now, if you'd told us you'd been an athlete, why, that's much easier to believe', Monty said.

Sometimes Pakade dropped his guard, as it were, and told us frankly that '*Kwagwala akulilwa.*' And who among us would deny the truth of that statement, especially in our township where every passing day brought its toll in human life and saw the untimely death of one brave resident after the other, from the treacherous blades of township *tsotsis* or in the hands of vicious agents of authority? We knew all that only too well and didn't really need Pakade to tell us that the families of the cowardly had fewer occasions to mourn their lost sons or daughters.

At school the majority of us deeply resented being taught Afrikaans. We preferred to communicate in our street dialect, called *tsotsi-taal*, the *lingua franca* of black youth in South Africa, in which we violated every known grammatical construction, formulated a few rules of our own, spiced its vocabulary with words of our own coinage, and generally wreaked such havoc on its idiom as to make it almost unintelligible to its original speakers.

In class Pakade's fertile imagination transformed everything it dwelt upon, including the drabbest material of the Afrikaans language and culture. Somehow he managed to make the subject, especially its literature, come alive for us. He possessed an essentially satirical mind and his peculiar blend of humour brought even the most absurd situations featuring blacks, with which literature in that language abounds, into very sharp relief. We saw the Afrikaner, as reflected through his literature, as paranoid and egocentric in the extreme. Here were people recreating the black world in their own image, without bothering to find out whether this corresponded to the objective reality outside their minds.

Pakade also taught us to relate literature to our everyday experiences and to our conditions as Africans. We applied what we read to assess the attitudes of others towards us and their own assumptions about themselves. It amazed me to discover just how much of a writer's most hidden prejudices can filter through essentially literary material, like the angle from which he chooses to approach his subject, the thoughts and words he puts into his characters, even through the unspoken word, the suppressed thought and the unvented emotions. We had the feeling of infiltrating deep into enemy territory and came back with our heads bulging with new insights. The most ridiculous African characters in Afrikaans literature were made to look what they really were, lampoons in very poor taste.

For comparison Pakade made us read other writers on Africa. We noticed the same tendency among white writers of English expression, although here we found the same prejudices couched in more guarded terms. But the tone of condescension, of paternalism was unmistakable. Always the African character in these novels, whether in exotic tribal regalia or ill-fitting Western costume, came through as a being with whom we had nothing in common, except the colour of our skins.

We threw ourselves into reading way beyond our prescribed texts. Our only cause for regret was that we couldn't lay our hands on many of the African writers Pakade told us about because they had been banned. In discussing such writers he would preface his remarks with: 'If anyone of you is foolhardy enough to write down what I'm about to say during exams, don't blame me when you fail.'

But then for most of us in his class more was involved than just passing exams. However, we knew very well that for examination purposes we needed to modify our views drastically. We had not been brought up in the township for nothing, so we understood Pakade's remarks very well. You might say the technique was essentially one of survival for us. Our ability to supply dumb answers, to turn into obsequious samboes, to transform our whole personalities instantaneously when conditions so dictated — these qualities had been nurtured in us very early in our youth, in our daily intercourse with the white man, as caddies at his golf courses, carrier-boys at his markets, illegal hawkers of sweets and peanuts in his trains and pilferers of sundry goods from his supermarkets. Pakade had been so successful with us that even at the height of our anger against the compulsory introduction of Afrikaans as a second medium of instruction in some subjects at all African schools, it never occurred to us to object to Afrikaans literature as such, which portrayed us in such an unfavourable light. Only his irresponsible drunkenness annoyed us at times.

Phakoe was the introvert one, but no less likeable than Pakade. Never much of a talker at any time, he became

7

completely dumb when sloshed. Only his constant smile indicated that he'd not yet sunk into complete unconsciousness. He was very gentle and I never knew him to lose his temper except once, when we hid his liquor. We called him Stadig, not only because of his slow manner of speaking but also because of his infinite patience. He taught Maths. It was said of him that he could even make Kgopo's daughters follow the most intricate of arguments in proving the most complicated theorem, even if they were certain to have forgotten the first step by the time they came to Q.E.D.

Kgopo was our Headmaster. We never really got to know him well, certainly not while I was still at school. He was a man of few words and we all thought him rather aloof. Mrs Masiza, the Deputy Head-teacher, who seemed to be irritatingly everywhere at once, and other senior members of staff took turns in conducting morning assembly. Kgopo only appeared when there was some special announcement to make concerning an inspector's visitation to our school or some such forthcoming attraction. He was thus firmly associated in our minds with high policy matters. I only began to see him in a slightly different light (and I was already living in exile then), when I read in the newspapers that he had resigned his job, the first Head-teacher to do so, in protest against the government's intransigence in educational matters and their constant harassment of his staff and his students.

Kgopo's two daughters had dropped out of school after several unsuccessful attempts at J.C. No one was allowed to repeat more than twice. They were now studying for matric by correspondence. Phakoe earned extra cash as their private tutor. In our uncharitable moments we sometimes speculated about which of their parents the Kgopo girls had taken after.

'They say Mrs Kgopo never went beyond Standard Six,' I said, volunteering the information I had picked up from my elder brother in his more communicative mood.

'In their day that was the highest standard a woman could aspire to,' Khulu said. 'That can only prove that the girls didn't take after her. Besides, we can't measure anyone's intelligence by the length of their stay at school.'

I knew that was very true. I could count many former school-mates, infinitely more intelligent than I could ever claim to be, who had simply dropped out of school earlier. Those of us who went on to complete high school did so largely because our parents could afford the money to send us to school. So I searched my mind for something more spectacular to disclose about the Kgopos.

'Kgopo has something of a history himself,' I said. 'Did you know that he completed his B.A. by correspondence under UNISA in fifteen years?'

'I'd say there's conclusive proof, if the matter was ever in doubt, of who the girls have taken after,' Khulu said.

It was undoubtedly Phakoe's proverbial patience which enabled him to go over the same material every day with the Kgopo girls and his good nature which made it possible frequently to bear the butt of Pakade's jokes. Pakade joked about his small, beardless frame, his lethargy, the manner in which he got sloshed and even about the fact that Phakoe took Kgopo's daughters for 'private' lessons. It didn't matter if we were there, Pakade talked on so that you sometimes wondered whether the conversation wasn't being carried on for your benefit.

'D'you know that there are Kgopo's spies even among members of staff?' he would ask us. This was during the formative stages of our Students' Representative Council, made up of representatives from all the township's secondary and high schools – before it was banned by the government – which we had tried to keep a closely guarded secret. But somehow those two always managed to know what was going on among us. 'How d'you imagine Phakoe became Maths tutor to Kgopo's children? For thirty pieces of silver, I tell you.'

'Don't call me Judas Iscariot,' Phakoe protested rather lamely and without conviction.

'But you are a Jew.'

'Yet if it was not for what I make on the sidelines you'd

still be drinking *ndambula*.'

'You double-dealer! I must tell Kgopo that you're in the habit of gathering information from his house and disclosing it at shebeens.'

'But I only drink with you.'

'*Ja*! At Shirley Scott's. I must tell him all that. Maybe he can hire me too. Why should you have both girls, all to your little, beardless self?' Pakade turned to us. 'D'you know, boys, he tells me everything that transpires within those four walls, outside the bedrooms, of course.' He pounced back on Phakoe. 'D'you deny that you told me of a certain boy, whose identity shàll remain unknown because of his prominence in student politics, who went to tea at their house on Sunday afternoon? What I forgot to ask is what you were doing there yourself on a Sunday afternoon. . . Don't bother to tell me now. I know you're going to say I'd asked you to go and collect your money for a quickie at Shirley Scott's.'

They spoke in this way about espionage, dropping broad hints all the time.

'Seriously, boys, you must be careful of spies like him,' Pakade concluded.

That was Pakade and Phakoe all over. They could never tell us directly what they meant. But their message came through loudly and clearly. So Phakoe had heard something at the Kgopos that could prove detrimental to our movement. Information had been leaked out by one of us. We would have to be more vigilant, perhaps swear in every member on pain of death to complete secrecy, like the Mau Mau Pakade had once told us about in a discussion of Ngugi, I think that was his name. I should remember to ask Pakade one day how the blood oath of the Kikuyu was administered.

When they spoke like this they almost made us forget what we had originally come to see them about. No doubt it had been designed, at least in part, to achieve this effect. We had really come to collect our money they'd borrowed the previous Friday. It was already Wednesday and they'd solemnly promised at Shirley Scott's that they'd give us back our R5 on Monday, without fail. It was always like that, week in and week out.

Khulu, Monty and I drank at Shirley Scott's shebeen, so-called because she only played jazz. It was one way of keeping out the township's riff-raff, who preferred *mbaqanga* and considered jazz as music for 'situations', meaning those who liked to situate themselves above ordinary township folk. She only sold white man's liquor and no *ndambula*. We enjoyed the music and came regularly on Fridays after school. Upon our arrival we perched ourselves in the kitchen and ordered a dozen quarts of Castle. The beer came cold from the fridge and not straight from dusty cardboard boxes hidden under the bed, as in most shebeens.

Pakade and Phakoe also drank at Shirley Scott's. They'd arrive later, sit in the dining-cum-sitting room and place their order, always on tick.

Upon the first sign of their arrival we thrust all our unopened bottles under the table. We also lowered our voices, in deference to their authority but really more to keep them away from our beer as long as possible.

We drank like that until – forced by the call of nature – Pakade and Phakoe came out. To get to the joint quickly, which was situated in a far corner of the backyard, they had to pass through the kitchen. They'd both squeeze into the small toilet at the same time, still earnestly engaged in conversation. If they did not stop to chat on their way out, they were sure to do so when they came back.

Phakoe would only raise his eyes in that hawk-like manner he had, a most peculiar expression which seemed to convey a variety of emotions ranging from recognition to salutation to supplication.

Pakade invariably began like this – '*Julle is weer hier, makwedini*!' said in the most friendly tone of disapproval imaginable.

What could we say to that? Of course, we'd come, as usual. But we affected the right degree of coyness. As long as the game was played according to the rules everybody was satisfied. We'd then protest our innocence by denying the very fact that we were there at all, like some character from Camara Laye. '*Nee, thiza*' – that's what we called those of our teachers whom it sounded somehow amiss to address as 'sir'. But we also referred to Pakade as 'Meneer' because he was the Afrikaans master.

'What do you mean – No?'

'We were just passing, *meneer*, and felt like a glass or so, just to quench our thirst,' our spokesman Monty said. 'It is more becoming than to drink at a more public place. And then it's not as if we came here every day. Only on very special occasions. You know us, *mos, meneer*.'

'What's the special occasion this time? Oh! no, don't tell me. I know. It's . . . .'

'Sabelo's "birfday".' Pronounced that way the word acquired a double meaning which also implied drinking. So it was always my 'birfday'.

It was amazing, the regularity with which Pakade and Phakoe went to the toilet. Khulu used to say their bladders leaked. Each time they walked past us in the kitchen we whispered, loud enough for them to hear, '*Ziyavuza!*', raising our half-empty glasses in mock-inspection as if to suggest *they* were leaking. It was another standing joke among us.

After trooping to the toilet and back several times, they stopped at our table and demanded a glass each, which we obligingly offered. That was also the signal for us to drink whatever we still had as fast as possible.

Pakade disappeared into the bedroom to go and talk to Shirley Scott but Phakoe lingered in the kitchen, smiling most amicably and saying nothing. If he emptied his glass before Pakade re-emerged, he simply shoved it in front of us to be refilled. We began to pray for the success of Pakade's mission.

Sometimes we managed to finish before Pakade completed negotiating with Shirley Scott. We then excused ourselves under the pretext of going to the toilet but that didn't help. Phakoe planted himself across the door to watch. After concluding our business in the loo we filed back to the house to wait for another chance. It was a delicate operation because at the slightest sign that we were about to leave Phakoe immediately conveyed the information to Pakade, who stayed us on until he and Shirley Scott could reach some conclusion.

She had a credit limit for all her customers, although now and again Pakade managed to convince her to go beyond her limit. If he succeeded he came out of the bedroom and motioned Phakoe back into the sitting-room. That was usually the signal for us to place another order if we still wanted more. But whenever Shirley Scott proved too tough, he would summon me to the sitting-room. Whoever had told him that I was the soft one and always loaded – some kind of gang treasurer – I could never tell. But if Shirley Scott, with her reputation for firmness, sometimes gave in to his powers of persuasion, which were quite considerable, who was I to resist him? So I always came back from these consultations some R2–R5 the poorer.

'You gave him again?' Khulu and Monty would ask, as though I'd had any alternative but to give in, or as if they'd have acted differently in my place. In fact, once, Monty asked to keep the money. I don't know how Pakade managed to make out, during our consultation, that I really didn't have the money on me, or how he decided that Monty rather than Khulu had it, but after trying to pump me unsuccessfully for a loan he called Monty. I quietly slunk back to the kitchen. When Monty rejoined us he'd parted with R10, which took us almost three weeks to recover. All Khulu could say was '*Bad-lisiwe labantu, 'strue*', to indicate that he thought someone had bewitched them. I never asked if he thought Shirley Scott was responsible. Shebeen queens were known to cast a spell on their customers with *woza-woza* and other potent concoctions to keep them hooked on their alcohol. The task of keeping the gang's purse quietly reverted to me, an arrangement which seemed to suit everyone. I really think I had my good points, too, because I only let Pakade and Phakoe have whatever we could spare them without subjecting the boys to unnecessary and in-voluntary abstinence. However, the hardest task was recovering the debt. Monday, they always said, and we all knew that could never be. We didn't really mind, as long as they paid us before the next Friday. Actually, the whole deal had come to level itself, because the amount we let them have on Fridays amounted to whatever they'd managed to pay us back during the course of the week.

Another thing about them: they never came to school soused, not until the student demonstrations had got well under way. But they had the most curious hangovers of any people I know. And the means they resorted to to cure their hangovers had us fooled for a very long time.

Pakade simply resorted to shadow-sparring.

Phakoe went about it very deviously. He brought his coffee flask to class. As he was our class teacher, he kept the keys to the class cupboard where he deposited his flask every morning. During Maths he explained whatever needed explaining and then gave us plenty of exercises, while he took out his flask and went to sit in front of the class. He would first scan our faces to see if we were all engrossed in our work, before pouring himself what looked like black coffee. When one pours out hot coffee, though, there's always some smoke which is emitted. We could easily have explained the absence of smoke from Phakoe's coffee by saying that he drank it cold. However, when he started to drink he first blew into his cup ostensibly to cool the coffee, even though it should have been cold already, while his eyes remained alert to anyone who raised theirs from their exercise books. 'Get on with your work, *wena*,' he said to anyone he suspected of watching him. When the bell rang for the end of the lesson he locked up his flask until lunch-time when Pakade joined him.

They also liked meat with atcha. There were aunties who sold fruit, eggs, fatcakes, atcha, pigs' trotters and other delicacies during break. These aunties stationed themselves at the gates. Pakade and Phakoe had a standing order with one of them, whom they squared at the end of the month, for trotters and atcha, which one of the girls from our class collected for them during short break.

Once, they ordered a whole sheep's head – 'smiley', we called it – which they kept under lock and key for three days until it began to emit a faint, unpleasant odour which kept Mrs Masiza out of our classroom for the duration of its storage. Khulu swore that the sheep's ghost would haunt them – '*Izobapokela, 'strue.*' That was after the outbreak of the disturbances, when they sometimes turned up at school fairly intoxicated. We used to call on them in our classroom fairly regularly. They didn't seem to mind the cancellation of classes and spent the whole day imbibing from their flask. However, by that time we had already uncovered the mystery of the flask in an operation which almost caused Phakoe to eat the hapless Madiba, one of our classmates, raw; the only occasion I've ever seen Phakoe go up in flames from anger.

It happened on Friday morning when Khulu, Monty and I came to class earlier than the others. Pakade and Phakoe had also arrived particularly early that day. As Phakoe was depositing his flask and packing his books in the locker, a boy from one of the junior classes came running from the direction of the office. '*Thiza*, phone call for you,' he shouted. Phakoe ran out, leaving his packing unfinished and the cupboard opened.

Monty uncoiled like a spring released and ran to inspect the flask. He bade Khulu keep watch at the door. '*Yi-brandy, ma-gents*,' he announced.

Khulu left his post and we came to sniff and taste.

The cupboard was littered with empty bottles of brandy. No wonder he never allowed the girls to tidy the cupboard, even when he didn't have his flask in there.

Monty picked up one of the empties with its lid still on, opened it and emptied the contents of the flask into the half-jack bottle. He replaced the flask, shut the half-jack and hid it under a dusty pile of disused exercise books in the cupboards. The whole operation was complete before the other students came.

The first bell had already rung when Phakoe returned and Mrs Masiza was waiting outside to take us for Biology. She was supposed to be going out with the

Headmaster, although no one could say where the rumour had started. Perhaps because she was the Deputy Head. But everybody knew that Kgopo's wife didn't even want to see where her foot had trod.

Phakoe just had enough time to stuff his belongings into the cupboard and lock it, before leaving the room.

We had Biology and then English before Maths.

During the Maths period we went through the usual process. At the explanatory stage my friends and I inundated Phakoe with rather inane questions, the longer to keep him from his customary respite. He answered all our questions with characteristic detail and patience. It was nearly time up when we let him off the hook. He wouldn't stay too long in class after making his shattering discovery, so there could be no protracted investigation.

'Now to work,' he said.

We threw ourselves to our work.

Nor did the three of us appear to be watching when he reached for his flask, sat himself at the teacher's desk and began to pour himself a drink. Not a drop came out. I wished to see the expression of utter incredulity on his face but dared not look up. But the eyes of all three of us went up when he brought the flask close to his ear and shook it, rather like someone unmechanical shaking a gadget which had stopped working and hoping for an engineering miracle.

We sunk our eyes into our books again.

Presumably when he looked up from his flask the first person he saw looking at him was Madiba, who was smiling and shaking his head from side to side.

Madiba was one of those students found at every school who seem to court disaster the way nectar attracts bees. He had a tendency to be amused at everything, which did not help to pull him out of trouble. He would have laughed at a bishop trip or at two doctors fighting with the amputated limbs of a patient. 'His fate is sealed, that one,' Khulu used to say. If we went with him to town some irate white was sure to knock him off the pavement or, attracted by his loud guffaws, some white youths intent on picking on a black for their private amusement would pick on him. An offence would be commited in Dindela while he was in Dukathole, but on making an appearance in Dindela he'd take the rap.

One good thing about Madiba was that he could never tell on anyone or disclose any information passed to him in confidence, whether under threat or torture.

When Phakoe pounced on him the whole class was startled because you couldn't have imagined two more unlikely people to cause a scene.

The bell rang but no one paid any heed to it.

'Madiba, stand up . . . Up, *jong*! Where's my coffee?' Phakoe's eyes were jutting from his jet-black face as if they wanted to pounce on Madiba and devour him alive.

'What coffee, *thiza*?' Madiba asked. An even wider grin spread over his moon face.

'*Jy moenie kak praat nie!*'

I thought we'd buy it ripe today, as the saying goes. I could not remember ever hearing Phakoe swear before.

'But, *thiza*, I don't have the vaguest idea of what you're talking about.'

Even Madiba's circus expression had vanished.

It seemed a catastro-stroke, to use a favourite expression of ours, was about to occur when Mrs Masiza, unaware that Phakoe was still in our class, budged in. It was her period again. She immediately excused herself and waited outside.

'See me after school, *my laititjie*,' Phakoe said, gathered his belongings from the table, locked them up and stormed out.

'These children can tempt an angel,' we heard Mrs Masiza telling Phakoe in commiseration. But if he heard he gave no indication.

If disaster had struck and left Phakoe crippled for life a more mournful atmosphere could not have descended over our class. So that when Mrs Masiza asked her class at large, 'What did you do to him?' nobody bothered to answer her.

By lunch-time, however, Phakoe had recovered his brandy, because when we passed the classroom, several times we saw Pakade and himself working away steadily at a pile of trotters and taking swig after swig, straight from the flask. The door of the cupboard stood ajar.

I delayed near the door but out of sight and caught Pakade's remark, vouching for Madiba's innocence on the strength of what he knew of the latter's character.

'*Hay*', *yinkukhu nje loontwana*, who just can't keep out of trouble, that's all, otherwise *izilungele nje yona*,' he said. I was giggling to myself at the comparison of Madiba to an unfortunate chicken, but stopped short at Pakade's next remark. 'I think if you gave me just five minutes with your class I could pick out the culprits. In fact, I'm not sure if we've not been watching them walking past this very room with unusual frequency . . .'

I dashed to warn the others and we stopped the parade.

After school Phakoe, looking somewhat embarrassed, came to our class and told Madiba to forget the whole incident.

'Oh! thank you, *thiza*,' Madiba said. He just couldn't resist another rejoinder. 'It was the way you were shaking the flask. It reminded me of *amagoduka* from the mines trying to repair their broken transistors that way, even if the fault is only with the batteries. *Khuhlu-khuhlu* . . . *Khuhlu-khuhlu* . . .' He joined his hands together, held them close to his left ear, and pumped them up and down, as if listening to the clickety-clack sound of metals.

But Phakoe was no longer listening as he hurried out of the classroom.

It was later, at Shirley Scott's, that he told us he knew we'd been fiddling with his property.

'When I went out to receive that call, you were the only ones I left in class. I should have known from all the imbecilic questions you were asking in class that you were up to no good. Whatever made me go for that other boy? His mother should have named him Smiley!'

'Who? Us, *thiza*?' Monty said. 'May God strike us dead if we so much as come anywhere near *thiza's* cupboard.'

'Talk for yourself, sonny,' Pakade said. 'Sabelo may

not approve of your use of the Lord's name in vain. Anyway, it is Phakoe who is going to strike you dead, not God.'

'But we never so much as touched his flask,' Monty persisted.

'I've never known liquids to simply flow out of one container into another. Slam a fine on them, Phaks.'

'Half-a-jack!'

We placed an order for half-a-jack.

'You should thank your stars Phakoe is not a vindictive person and is so easily appeased.'

Pakade picked up the brandy and they retired to the sitting-room to go and polish it off.

We played several such practical jokes on them to get even with them for all the inconvenience they often put us into to recover the loans we gave them.

Only the previous Wednesday we had been running after them for money they'd solemnly declared on the Friday before to refund on Monday, without fail. It wasn't the first time either and the pattern never varied, week in and week out. We could easily have supplied the answers they'd given us ourselves, in advance, if we'd had the mind to. In our long association with them we'd come to realise that it didn't pay bugger-all to release the pressure on them. They needed a constant reminder that we weren't the *moegoes* they sometimes took us for. They couldn't treat us as if we were raw *amagoduka* straight from Umtata or Thoho-ya-ndou just newly arrived in the city on their first contracts. We didn't vote Mangope, either.

We confronted them with great indignation during short break.

'*Meneer*, we've come to collect *laa-parcel ya-last week*,' Monty told them.

As usual we had to observe the same old courtesies. It was always 'the parcel in question'. Frankly I felt sick of all this native love for euphemisms, when all these two needed was some direct talking to and none of this *lapha-lapha* business.

'Sabelo, you're frowning,' Pakade said. 'Don't tell us

you too are holding us by your heart.'

As usual, it discomposed me to be caught entertaining such uncharitable thoughts about others. Whoever had told him that my heart was grinding with anger?

'Anybody would think that you boys had heard that the firm of Phakoe and Pakade (Pty) Ltd. was to be liquidated,' he said, 'or that Phakoe and I were about to kick the bucket.'

At the thought of their death my heart instantly flowed with sympathy. If they'd tapped me at that very moment for a further advance I'd have yielded most obligingly.

'Sabelo, come and collect it tomorrow.'

I was going to agree when Monty stepped hard on my foot.

'*Nee, Meneer*, we must have it now,' he said.

'*Oh! julle trust ons nie, neh*?'

It was typical of them to try and appear as if they were the aggrieved party. Why did he have to ask us whether we trusted them or not? All part of his subtle scheme to blackmail us by loading us with all the guilt, no doubt.

'Such a thought never crossed my mind,' Monty replied. 'On Monday it was Tuesday; yesterday it was today; and today . . . *Hay' khona*! Whites are correct, *mos*, when they say "tomorrow never comes".'

'There's one thing I like about you, Monty-boy, you're a sharp lad. That bit about "tomorrow", why, that's pure Soyinka – "Those who do not befriend Pakade today will be saying had we known tomorrow".'

I couldn't quite place my finger on it, but something in the way he said it convinced me he meant to convey something more by the quotation.

Khulu chuckled out loudly. He was the quiet one, but by far the most widely read and perceptive. His father was a sub-inspector of schools (the white man always being 'inspector'), but in a different circuit from ours, somewhere in the country where no white ever wished to go. From him, Khulu sometimes obtained rare copies of African writers' and other books. We learnt almost as much from Khulu about these writers as we did from Pakade.

'What's wrong?' Pakade asked.

'That's Ezeulu from Achebe's *Arrow of God*,' Khulu said.

'Phaks, just listen to that, listen to that. Why, you boys all need scholarships to the best African universities. Mind you, I don't for a moment subscribe to the school of thought that Cambridge is superior to Makerere or any of our other leading universities. Depends what you are after. What's there to learn in Cambridge about Africa that cannot be learnt right here at home, except to cherish her more perhaps? That was the lesson of France to men like Senghor, Hamidou Kane, Camara Laye and Ousmane – I've told you all about those. We've been brainwashed, that's all, by our erstwhile colonial masters and their liberal descendants, who today control vast areas of our economy. Phaks, what do you think? These lads are the brightest students we've ever taught. We must do something to help them escape the stagnation which this country imposes upon all of us. "Too many a flower is born to blush and waste its fragrance in the desert air." Have I got that right, Khulu? You're not very much of a talker, are you? Just like Phakoe. But don't worry, you'll be a great critic some day, a great critic, I tell you. I say, why don't we make an appointment for tomorrow to discuss this further? Phakoe and I will tell you everything you need to know about applying for scholarships to Makerere or any other university of your choice.'

If it hadn't been for Monty I don't know whether I wouldn't have been completely overwhelmed by the show of so much enthusiasm from my teacher on my account. But Monty had his head firmly on his shoulder. Khulu's interruption, too, had given him time to recover and brush aside Pakade's flattering remarks.

'*Meneer*, I'd be delighted to come and fill in those scholarship forms at any time,' he said. 'But before we make any detailed plans, what about the parcel we came for, *laa-parcel ya-last week, kaloku?*'

One simply had to give Monty his due. *My ma hoor my*! He'd crushed Pakade into cinders, cinders. *Wampatshaza* straight, as they say.

Pakade's nostrils became distended like large, ineffectual bellows. His next remarks were like throwing in the towel.

'You've got the heart of a Boer, *kwedini*!'

Monty was very light-complexioned. 'Amper Baasie' or 'Rooi Nek', we sometimes called him. When Pakade was angry with him, for whatever reason, he always likened him to a Boer. But his anger also marked his capitulation. It was his cold reasoning we dreaded, because that way he could rain' blows from all angles until you didn't know which side he'd strike from next. He could hold on for long that way. It exhausted us, this war of attrition. So that we had come to rely more and more on dropping his guard and exposing his jaw, as it were, by arousing him to a great state of impotent rage. He'd already come, swinging wildly. I knew then that we'd deliver the *coup de grâce* with comparative ease.

'It's like this, *Meneer*,' I butted in. I'd not forgotten that bit about their church dues being in arrears. Fix him, too, for always teasing me about '*abefundisi abadla emhlambini*', as if I was personally responsible for what he called the campaign of the clergy to exploit their flock. 'My father actually gave me that money to go and settle our water bill. You know where the money for our bills comes from, *mos*? But nowadays even church people want their money accounted for in full. I won't get a moment's rest until my father knows for certain what's become of the money he gave me. The deadline for water bills, as you know, is today.' That was a bit of a chance. But I didn't really think that he'd stop to ponder that the deadline wasn't for at least another week. 'Last Friday when I was supposed to have settled that bill, I didn't really think it would do any harm to let you have that money until Monday. But as today is already Wednesday . . .'

'Phakoe, d'you have some aspros?'

'I beg your pardon, *Meneer*?'

'No, I wasn't addressing you.'

'Oh! I beg your pardon. As I was saying, my father

will be exceedingly . . .'

'Okay, Sabelo, that'll do. There's no need to rub it in. I don't know why priests should be the only ones to benefit from the sweat of others. Does your father pay taxes? Oh! Never mind. There's no need to bring your father into all this. I recognise your implied threat only too well.'

Damn him! Working on my guilt, again.

Phakoe, who had gone to fetch aspros from the cupboard, returned with two. Pakade swallowed them with brandy, straight from the flask.

'All three of you, *makwedini*, behave like regular capitalists, just like your fathers. It doesn't matter that some of us pour out the waters of our souls to wash the quagmire that's in your brains. A pig always returns to the sty, Soyinka teaches. What's R5 to your families? Phakoe, how much have you got?'

'*Akadinwa ukukhuluma lomuntu!*' Khulu muttered under his breath, referring to Pakade's ceaseless chatter.

'You can search me,' Phakoe said. 'You've got all the money we have between now and month end.'

Pakade scooped into his pockets and brought out a few badly crumpled notes. He counted five and gave them to me. The remainder he returned to his pockets.

'And to think payday isn't until next week,' he muttered to himself. 'Now you've got what you wanted. Clear out. *Ndithi nyamalalani niphele, makwedini.*' (As if we could just disappear into thin air simply because he wished us to!)

'I don't want to see you, ever.'

'Did you see how much they still have?' Khulu asked on our way to Kheletsane's shop.

'R3 at the most,' I answered.

'Which they're going to blow today,' Monty added.

'I guess we'll have to place the R5 they've just given us into the floating account,' I said.

'*Kodwa thina sibabolekelani imali yethu abantu abanje?*' Khulu asked.

We digested the question but no one answered. I guess Khulu didn't expect any answer either. But what a pertinent question! Did we really have to part with our money to such ingrates and then be subjected to so much abuse afterwards?

'Khulu, that quotation, what did he mean by it?' I asked.

'Actually, the correct quote is "Those who do not befriend the white man today will be saying had we known tomorrow."' Khulu said.

'But why did he have to substitute himself for the white man? My! Some people are awfully fond of themselves,' I said.

'Just plain ignorance, I guess,' Monty said.

'No, merely another of his empty threats,' Khulu said.

I tried to ponder Khulu's remark. But failing to make sense of it, left the matter at that.

Following the warning Pakade and Phakoe had given us about the leak of information from our organisation, we warned our members to be more careful of what they said in public. There didn't seem to be anything much we could do about it if Pakade and Phakoe refused to divulge the identity of the traitor. We would forge ahead. We needed time to plan our strategy more carefully and to mobilise our various student bodies effectively. There'd be time all right for us to tell the Establishment exactly how we felt. The operative phrase for the time being was to 'conscientise' the student masses, which meant creating a complete awareness in them of the hoax that was South Africa's government policy towards us. We had no illusions about the enormity and ruthlessness of the state machinery we were poised to challenge. But hadn't it been built by men? Our success against the System lay not only in the support we could manage to rally among the students but also in the element of surprise with which we could strike.

We established various study cells and appointed several commissions on politics, culture and education. Khulu brought us books on socialist theory from his father's library, collected long before these had been banned. We devoured these most voraciously and discussed them among ourselves. From my brother we managed to borrow what books we could on history – not always with his permission – and learnt most ardently about liberation movements in South Africa and elsewhere. Soon we were bandying words about like 'reactionary' and 'bourgeoisie'; and names like Marx, Guevara, Mao TseTung and Nyerere.

But none of this came easily. Sometimes the things we read failed to make any sense at all, try as we would. My brother could barely hide his resentment at the intrusion whenever I asked him to explain anything, asking why I needed to know about such things as dialectical materialism (I remember he laughed at my pronunciation), which couldn't possibly make any sense to me anyhow at my age. He asked what difference it made to me whether Jan Van Riebeeck had met the Khoisan or the Incas when he first landed at the Cape. Nor did he bother to even look up from his book when I asked who the Incas were. I felt disgusted when I thought of how he and his friends often reminisced about their days at Fort Hare as Sons of Young Africa. (In fact, for a long time whenever they mentioned SOYA I thought of the beans.) I could never understand what made them think they were some kind of political pensioners. For all their high-faluting talk what fat good had their learned analyses and timid campaigners ever accomplished?

I also wondered about what was involved in studying Native Administration, in which he had majored, and why it wasn't simply called Administration, as in the calendar from Roma University which Pakade had once shown us. But fearing to offend him more I contemplated these things in silence. My father only glared at me when I asked him why socialist theoreticians said religion was the opium of the people. Khulu met with better luck. But he also complained that his father had either never read the many volumes which lined his shelves or had long since forgotten what they were all about. I understood Khulu very well because we had a set of very impressive looking encyclopaedias at home which I'd never seen anybody consult. When we encountered very difficult passages in our reading we copied them out and passed them on to Pakade and Phakoe and the young teacher, Nkululeko, when he joined our staff. Despite Pakade's lame protests that we wanted to put them in trouble, they explained everything to us with their usual patience and clarity.

We passed round to our members everything we read with the glee of Vrystaat Boers peddling round copies of *Playboy*, surreptitiously obtained at great risk from one of the neighbouring African states.

We always ended our meetings with the singing of old freedom tunes to new words we had composed ourselves.

It was at about this time that Nkululeko joined our staff as History master. His reputation had preceded him to our school. We had read about him in the papers. His graduation address at the University had created a great furore among the authorities and an equally great stir in the country when he attacked Bantu Education. Not that his views had been original, for many before him had condemned the system which they saw as an education for servitude. But he had had the effrontery to air his views before a highly select audience which included the Minister himself, as Chancellor of the University, and many of the policy's chief architects and administrators. Amidst protests from his fellow students, the University threw him out for his inflammatory rhetoric before he could complete his teacher's diploma. The University's Rector, an Afrikaner of liberal inclinations and *verligte* views, explained in a newspaper interview that he'd personally stake his whole career in defence of the students' freedom of thought and expression, but that it was inexcusable for Nkululeko to have chosen a position of trust and such a privileged platform to voice his seditious sentiments and thus put the University in a very false position in the public eye. The Rector added that he had personally created proper channels of communication between the students and his administration; and that Nkululeko's failure to use these representative bodies such as the Senate Advisory Council, which was made up of senior black academics who'd soon have a seat in the University Senate, constituted a serious breach of faith which he could not countenance. So that in defence of democratic procedures he'd been left with no alternative but to expel him.

When Nkululeko came to our school we received him like a martyr and doted on him from the very beginning. We invited him to come and adjudicate at our debating and disco contests; to read papers on social, economic and political subjects to organisations like the Students' Christian Movement. He joined Pakade and Phakoe as staff consultants to the various S.R.C. commissions we set up. He obliged us in all things. We admired his powers of analysis. He could hold us spellbound while he explained the basic tenets of Black Consciousness in terms which even Reggie, who was never interested in anything academic, could understand. It was from him that we first heard about the Southern African Students' Movement to which we formally affiliated our S.R.C. But generally he kept to himself (and that was for us a rather sore point). We wished he would go out with Pakade and Phakoe sometimes. Actually, later when he grew accustomed to the people around he did. Otherwise he seemed to live completely in and for his school work and would remain at school long after the others had left, poring over his books. He told us he was studying by correspondence for his honours degree with UNISA.

Nkululeko's stay with us, as you may have read in the papers, was destined to be very short. After being pulled in several times by the Special Branch he decided to flee the country and died in exile, before the student riots erupted, from a letter-bomb which bore a Geneva stamp. However, while he was still with us, apart from his willingness to assist us whenever we ran to him for help, he remained until the end a closed book to us.

If we had taken to Nkululeko instantly, there was another fellow we detested from the start who had joined our staff while we were still in J.C. Dladla was a U.T. (Unqualified Teacher) on transfer from Machadodorp. He was brought to our school to introduce carpentry. We would have resented the introduction of any subject at that stage in our careers. But to have brought in carpentry of all things, we thought, was just about the limit.

Before Dladla's arrival a new building had sprung up which we were told by the Headmaster was going to house the new departments of home economics and carpentry. When the announcement was made you could have heard the students' groans from Khumalo's butchery. It annoyed us to think that instead of building more classrooms to ease the congestion at our school irrelevant departments were being added. We had classes of up to seventy students. If it hadn't been for the high rate of absenteeism there wouldn't have been enough desks for everybody. During exams we had to borrow benches from nearby churches, despite the fact that by that time several students were sure to have dropped out of school altogether. Students in the senior classes were luckier because few students stayed on for matric after J.C. Even if the new carpentry shop was to occupy itself full-time with supplying desks there would still have been no space for those in the existing classrooms. We also used the same laboratory – originally designed as just another classroom – for Biology, Physics and Chemistry. Now instead of providing what was needed most here were the authorities wasting valuable resources and forcing us to study woodwork and domestic science – the terms 'carpentry' and 'home economics' just never caught on.

It broke our hearts almost, once the building had been completed, to see the most modern and complicated cooking gadgets being brought into the domestic science wing. Where the hell were the girls ever expected to use all that sophisticated stuff outside school? Into the other wing came piles and piles of planks, planes, vices, chisels and other related paraphernalia.

The chief inspector in our circuit came for the opening ceremony. He must have thought that he was addressing a mere bunch of school kids when he spoke to us about the need to diversify and broaden our curriculum and about the need for education with a practical orientation. We knew what all that meant. All our primary school education had been geared towards the attainment of that goal. Woodwork, handwork, domestic science, sewing, knitting, crocheting, gardening, tree-planting, sports, music – all had their place in our time-table. And I don't just mean extra-murally.

One day I'm going to write an open letter to the chief inspector to ask him to explain of what practical use he imagined music, for instance, had been to us, even to the very few who had branched off into showbiz with Gibson Kente or started their own musicals. You either had the voice or you didn't. No soul or *mbaqanga* group had any time for doh-ray-mi-fah-so. Yet at school every year we formed a junior mixed choir, a senior one and another for intermediates, a boys' choir, girls' choir and several teachers' choirs. The majority of these choirs, sixty voices strong, had to render a vernacular piece, a song in English and another in Afrikaans. Since this practically involved the whole school, it was the simplest thing for the Principal to suspend regular classes while we concentrated on polishing our various choirs for the Eisteddfod competitions.

Towards competition time classes were actually suspended while we hobnobbed from one practice session to another, that is, those who were slow-witted enough not to stay away from school altogether at such times. Further, if your school was foolhardy enough to win in any of these categories at the local level, there would be competitions at the regional level and then at the provincial level and after that at the national level – not to mention the several radio broadcasts, fund-raising concerts, farewell ceremonies and so on you could be asked to take part in. And it was almost impossible not to win at least once at some level – a most elaborately worked out system of encouragement by rewards, no doubt. But we couldn't very well proceed with our lessons while a few were away from each class, representing the school.

There was that other year when it was announced that the winning teachers' choir would compete in the Eisteddfod competition in Wales. In fact they did. The teachers' choir which won came from our township and consisted of teachers from various schools in the township. What do you imagine happens to the students when all the teachers disappear on an all-expenses-paid trip to the seaside town of Aberystwyth at the height of the British summer? It was nearly the end of the year when we got back to the classroom.

Maybe in my open letter I should also confront the chief inspector about handwork, which was also intended to equip us with practical skills. So what happened in practice? For three months we trudged the veld, picking *umsingizane* to weave hats and mats, which never got made anyhow, so that in the end one had to purchase an old grass hat which had seen several previous exams, to satisfy our itinerant school inspectors who came round each year. Handwork was the only subject that was externally examined from standard three to standard six. Don't I know what I'm talking about? I remember, as if it were only yesterday, when I was in standard six, I'd decided to play truant for the whole year in order to make a little money for myself in the usual way. Towards the end of the year my parents caught up with me – I'd failed to intercept the report for the third quarter – and so I returned to school, sat my exams, which were externalised as this was the last class at primary school (and the end of a formal education for many), and still managed to obtain a first-class pass, after procuring all the items of handwork I needed for three shillings from a boy whose school had been examined earlier.

'The truly marvellous thing about our system of education,' Nkululeko once said in a paper on Bantu Education, 'is not that the black child in this country gets a poor education, but that he gets any education at all.'

I feel somebody should have warned the chief inspector, when he came to open the woodwork and domestic science block, that we weren't children of yesterday. Pakade had been correct to assert, *mos*, that once these fellows believed what they wanted to believe about us nothing could convince them to the contrary. The fact of the matter was that to drag in stuff like woodwork into our curriculum was being extremely impractical. Look at it another way. How many times did township residents ever require the services of a carpenter? Not even a pauper was buried in a home-made coffin these days, because everybody either contributed to some insurance policy or belonged to some burial society whose members contributed fifty cents or so each week towards the funeral expenses of any member of their families who might die unprovided for. Don't we have a saying in our language that only a witch has no relatives? As for ordinary household furniture, who doesn't know where townsfolk get theirs from? How then did a carpenter make his living in an environment where everybody could afford furniture even from the most exclusive shops like Bradlows? The boys supplied everything back-door, *mos*, all of which made carpentry a short cut to starvation.

Our commission for education had studied the matter very carefully. That's when somebody, I think it was Khulu, dug out a quotation attributed to one of South Africa's former Prime Ministers, who is supposed to have said that 'there's no place for the black man in the white man's cities beyond certain forms of labour.' But pushing blacks into trades like carpentry was like asking a perfectly sane man to fetch water from some distant stream in a leaking bucket. What the vocationally inclined needed most, our report concluded, were skills in electronics, motor mechanics, panel beating – not carpentry!

'Despite job reservation,' the report read, 'industry generates its own dynamics, so that blacks with skills which can fit them into an industrial society, such as ours is, are certain to find employment or, better still, to set up shop in their own backyards. There are myriads of motor car mechanics thriving in the backyards of the township, albeit in a disorganised fashion and most certainly against the law. But who is to prevent the owner of a car from taking his car for repairs to whomsoever he chooses?'

We could have told the chief inspector, right from the beginning, that his project was destined to be a flop.

Dladla and woodwork were rendered redundant from the very beginning. Attendance at his classes became a matter of embarrassment to the more sensitive among us, when even the class monitors disappeared without trace.

Soon the Headmaster began to use Dladla in a variety of stop-gap and extra-mural capacities. If a teacher was absent, Dladla sat with his class to supervise silent study. He was also in charge of late-comers. His planks came in very handy then and he used them with sadistic pleasure.

I believe it was also at this time that he began to sell some of the planks to people who were extending their houses or wanted to build fowl-runs, dog kennels or those who simply needed cheap firewood. We passed the school one Saturday morning and saw a van with a Machadodorp registration, parked outside the wood-work shop. Dladla and another man we didn't know were loading wood onto the van.

In his second year with us he was also given Form 1 to take for Afrikaans, Scripture and Physical Training. That was the move which was to spark off the row between himself and Kgopo, one which was said to have been aggravated by Mrs Masiza's transferrence of her affections from Kgopo to Dladla. Their quarrel arose out of the annual inspection of our school.

At morning assembly on Friday the Headmaster had announced that we were to expect a panel of inspectors the following week – they always gave word of their intentions at the last minute. The Headmaster exhorted us to look and behave our best.

The announcement produced predictable results and the usual spate of activities which accompanies such news.

Phakoe complained about having to bring his class register up to date. We never took roll-call, so for the purpose of putting the record straight he asked each one of us in turn to give him the approximate number of days on which we had been absent from school. When it came to Reggie's turn he said three. But Phakoe wrote a string of 'a's against his name. 'I didn't ask you to tell me the number of days on which you'd actually turned up for school,' he told Reggie.

Reggie absented himself for days at a stretch, helping at his father's shop. He was making his third attempt at J.C.

Most of the teachers remained behind after school to bring their scheme books and preparation books up to date, so that we were leaving Shirley Scott's when Pakade and Phakoe arrived. We quickly darted out as Pakade called, 'Hey, *makwedini, kom julle hier*,' and were gone.

That day the whole school had been asked to do general spring cleaning, a task which took us the whole day. We tidied our desks and everything else in our classroom. Only Phakoe's cupboard remained untouched.

The boys in Form 1, under Mrs Masiza's supervision, walked all round the school, picking up papers and orange peels. Others worked in the small plots we called gardens, removing weeds.

'We're cleaning here but that chap is busy littering the place out there,' Reggie said from his vantage position near the window. He didn't need to clean his desk. It was tidy already.

We came to look. Dladla had harnessed a group of students who had come to school late that morning. An operation that was seemingly the reverse of what was happening all over the school was taking place there. They were spreading sawdust all around the workshop to give it a used look. A new supply of wood was being carried into the workshop. Reggie said that Dladla had borrowed the wood from Zondo, a local coal vendor and supplier of firewood. We asked him how he knew and pointed out to him that Zondo didn't stock the type of wood used in a woodwork shop. '*Oho! Shiya*,' Reggie said. He was like that. Whenever anyone pointed out the absurdity of anything he said, he simply asked you to drop the matter.

'I'll tell you one thing,' he said. 'All that sawdust is from Khumalo's butchery.' That was easier to believe because just then some boys laden with sacks came from the direction of the shops and deposited them outside the workshop.

They say that Dladla went to remind the Headmaster that afternoon that he'd been employed to teach carpentry; that he didn't mind helping now and again, especially with P.T.

The Principal told him that he'd be expected to turn up for classes, as usual, on Monday, same as everybody else, and was also expected to produce his class records on demand.

Dladla said 'Nix.'

The Headmaster told him 'We'll see,' and dismissed him.

The inspectors arrived as scheduled on Monday morning, two whites and three black subs. We immediately recognised the chief circuit inspector who had spoken at the opening of the new block.

Everybody went to their respective classrooms amidst clearly discernible tension.

Dladla kept out of the way. A boy from our class sent by the Principal to go and summon Dladla to the office came back to report that there was no one at the workshop. Aside to us he reported that Dladla had barricaded himself inside the workshop, waiting to open the doors to the inspectors only. He had looked through the windows and saw planks of all sizes neatly laid out on the work benches and the tools looked newly greased.

The black sub-inspector in charge of Scripture reported that there'd been no teacher for Form I that morning.

The chief inspector himself waited in vain for the Afrikaans master for Form I.

The Headmaster heard the inspectors out with his head bowed in shame. But after they'd left, they say he swore for ten minutes at Dladla's unfortunate ancestry before he marched to the workshop to give Dladla a piece of his mind. Such gross insurbordination had never happened at his school before. He had an impeccable record with the Department which he'd not allow an untutored country goat to tarnish.

Dladla replied that he'd grow horns first before anybody caught him teaching anything besides carpentry.

The whole school was agog with rumour and speculation.

'Poor chap,' Monty said. 'For this to happen to him just when he had every right to look forward to reaping the rewards of his long service as a faithful chorister! With his B.A. neatly tucked under his armpits and thirty years' service, His Master's Voice was surely on the verge of being made sub-inspector himself. Now that Dladla guy has blown his chances to kingdom come.'

'*Einklek*, Bophuthatswana wants him,' Reggie said. But no one paid any attention to him because we all knew how his imagination could run wild at times.

'Surely Dladla's bitten off more than he can chew this time,' Khulu said.

But nothing happened to him. Instead he seemed to grow bolder and more corrupt.

Reggie again gave it as his considered opinion that Dladla used the services of a powerful witchdoctor from Bushbuckridge.

That year our class did badly in carpentry. We all failed, except Reggie – although he failed all the other subjects. After that he dropped out of school altogether, preferring instead to help at his father's grocery shop and fish and chips.

When the results were published we asked him how he had done it.

'You'll never believe anything I tell you, *mos*,' he said. 'Anyway, Dladla has an account at our shop. My father allows him unlimited credit, as he does to all of them. We differ there. I don't know why he should venerate teachers so much. Just because they wear ties and speak English. They're all bad customers. I'm going to put an end to all that *nonsens* soon. Me, I've no time for all these excuse-me's. Anyhow, the moment I heard that Dladla had failed us all, I came to see him. I told him my father had sent me to collect all the money he owed. He told me not to worry, he'd fix everything. He said he'd come in person to talk to my father. I refused to budge, so he whipped out his mark book and wrote 50% next to my name. I left and then came back the following day. He raised my mark to 60 and when I came for the last time it was 73. I am not telling you all this so that you can go blabbing about in the township. Too many people are going around using other people's names to earn themselves a cup of tea these days!'

We all hurried to assure him that we weren't like that.

'Reg, had your father really sent you?' Khulu asked.

'No. But if I understand you well, Dladla once tried to get some groceries from our shop by promising he'd pass me if I gave him what he wanted.'

'Did you?' Monty asked.

'You ask too much,' Reggie said. 'Are you *detaictives* or what?'

'Just one last thing, Reg,' I said. 'The other day, why did you say he'd borrowed the wood from Zondo?'

'Because that's who he'd given it to in the first place. That's why. He'd hired our delivery van for the purpose.'

'It's a good thing we don't have to do woodwork beyond J. C.,' Khulu said.

'He's not doing too badly for a country *skaapie*,' Monty said.

'I'll tell you something else for nothing,' Reggie said. 'Everybody is making money these nowadays, so why not Dladla? If you ask for my opinion I think he's better off than some people I could mention who use money paid in for school fees to settle their personal accounts. You can go on feeding others with your parents' money; me, I've had enough of throwing away precious money. Anyway, we'll see what that *educationinyana* of yours is going to do for you.' He expended a great deal of energy on the diminutive form of that word, so that I became anxious he wouldn't answer me on something else I desperately wanted to know.

'The very last thing, Reg, I promise.'

'Yes?'

'D'you know it for a fact that Bophuthatswana has approached Kgopo for his services?'

'My father is the local branch Chairman of the Kgololesego Freedom Party. He was sent to deliver the message in person.'

'What do they want him as?'

'Minister for Education, of course.'

'Has he accepted?'

'No. Now that's enough. Business calls.'

Sometimes it was almost impossible to separate fact from fiction whenever Reggie spoke. Too many things just didn't seem to fit in together, so we dropped the matter.

Things came to a head sooner than we'd expected. We were in our final year matric when the Department of Bantu Education announced its scheme to have at least half the subjects in every school taught in Afrikaans with effect from the following year. Up to that time English had been the sole medium of instruction in our school. In other schools only subjects like Arithmetic, which were easy to follow in any language, were taught in Afrikaans. In a few others, where you had a perfectly bilingual staff, it really didn't matter which language one used, but always the bias was towards English, especially in the science subjects.

Midway through the first term, our education commission tabled its recommendations before the executive of the S.R.C. It was time to make a public stand, we all decided. But first we had to assess the feelings of our members. We were going to put the matter before the students in the form of a public motion, as it were. The Debating Societies in our various schools were approached to debate the matter in public in place of the usual motions like 'Town Life is better than country life' or 'A horse is better than a bicycle'. We also organised inter-school debating contests.

Somebody then suggested we approach the school board for donations towards a floating trophy – which they gave.

The contests got under way on a knockout basis. Occasionally unruly conduct broke out and tempers flared. Sometimes the audience booed the speakers so loudly you'd have imagined we were watching Kaizer Chiefs or Orlando Pirates playing an all-white side. Certain speakers were threatened from the floor. In one very hotly contested debate between Nkambule High and Matseke, which were keen rivals in everything, students from Nkambule, who had had to speak in favour of Afrikaans, came very near to being assaulted. Accusations of 'Puppets . . . System . . .' were hurled at them by students from Matseke. Eventually peace was restored at no greater price than a few bruised skulls. It was a good thing our rules prohibited the bringing in of walking-sticks, mineral bottles, penknives and pebbles, no matter how beautiful, into the debating contest hall. What else could one expect when some Form 1 students persistently asked such questions as why a side we all knew to be wrong should still be asked to express its offensive views? But that was only at the beginning, when we had to explain very carefully to them what a debate was. Still it needed much persuasion to get speakers for the other side.

We also decided to integrate our teams after the Nkambule–Matseke episode rather than insist on competing along strict inter-school lines.

Another problem we had in those earlier days was to ensure the safety of our adjudicators. Pakade refused to come again, following the public indignation his verdict aroused when he awarded the contest to the side representing the unpopular view. '*Julle is barbarians, mos,*' he complained.

In one thing, however, we failed dismally. Try as we might, there were certain expressions we could never persuade the contributors from the floor, in particular, to drop. So that expressions like '*Bliksem . . . Moer!*' continued to be heard above the Chairperson's voice calling for order. The situation was hopeless. But these were minor setbacks compared to the real advances we made.

Later we dropped all camouflage and came out in public. Students formally enrolled as members in their hundreds. In some schools the public meetings we were accustomed to holding were prohibited. Certain members of the S.R.C. executive were declared *persona non grata* on some campuses. But as inter-school sports competitions continued to flourish, so did our meetings with student leaders from these schools.

At one meeting of the executive, the Chairperson and

the Organising Secretary announced their decision to drop out of school for a while in order to organise full time. We applauded their decision, so that there's no grain of truth whatsoever in what was later reported in the newspapers that we were led by non-students, so-called 'political agitators posing as students', or that we were intimidated into boycotting the exams our leaders knew for certain that they were going to fail.

Soon our activities attracted the attention of the Special Branch. Their faces became familiar to us and we knew a great many by name. VWs with SBs inside became a regular feature at most schools. Sometimes they came to our school and held long discussions in the Headmaster's office. Someone else, a student or a teacher, would join them and spend some time in the office. At other times they parked a few houses from the school and watched us in their dark glasses. Occasionally they hauled in some student and drove away with him to the police station where he was interrogated and then released.

Inevitably, Madiba was pulled in. After him a clearer picture of what they wanted began to form: What were our grievances? Who were our leaders? What assistance did we receive from any other sources? Did we plan to disrupt classes or to engage in any other works of sabotage?

'Venter even tried, surreptitiously, to shove a R10 note into my hand,' Madiba said. 'But I pretended not to see. So he proposed, point-blank, that if I told him everything which transpired at school he'd see to it that I was amply rewarded.'

'What did you say?' I asked.

'I told him I needed time to consider his offer.'

'You shouldn't have,' Khulu said. 'Now they'll be after you again.'

'It's all six and nine to me. I'll never tell them anything.'

We came out demonstrating on a cold, wintry morning. But the authorities wouldn't have it. They set police dogs on us. They panel-beat us with police batons. They sprayed us with teargas. They came out shooting. Army tanks roared down the streets like angry hippos. The contest was too uneven. We retreated in panic, leaving the ground strewn with casualties from both sides. We couldn't match them stone to bullet. But as we retreated, we razed what we could to the ground: their municipality buildings, post offices, beer halls and bottle stores.

At our school the first building to go up in flames was the new woodwork/domestic science block.

We called for a class boycott. They could prevent us from demonstrating publicly in their streets. But we still had the right to attend classes or not as we pleased. The only advantage of a system which refused to introduce free and compulsory education for black children!

The Headmaster convened a special assembly to read us a letter from the Department of Bantu Education. They were asking us to examine the consequences of our actions very carefully. In addition each one of us was required to sign a special form undertaking to desist from any acts of wilful and malicious damage to school property and promising to abide by the school rules. Failure to comply with these instructions would lead to automatic expulsion without the right to re-admission to any school under the Department's control.

We stayed away *en masse*.

The new form was withdrawn.

In the meantime we had also called for an exam boycott.

The authorities tripped over one another and bent over backwards to get us at least to register for the exams, which were postponed to give us more time to prepare. As each deadline for registration approached and few students had come forward to do so, it was most generously extended.

So, it was that important to them to show that the System worked!

An uneasy truce came into effect. We returned to school all right, but only as a way of keeping together and avoiding individual victimisation. But it happened just the same. Our leaders who had not gone into hiding were rounded up. For a while we felt beaten.

They had put a clamp on all public gatherings, besides gatherings of a religious nature and for education purposes.

At Reggie's wedding (now a prospering businessman in his own right, having taken over the family business from his ageing father), which took place at about this time, we had to wait until the last minute for a reply from the police for permission to hold the reception in one of the township's halls – a special licence having been issued for the wedding feast to be held at his home. At the last minute permission for the use of the hall was withheld.

Clearly in such a situation we had to devise means to beat the System at its own game. We met regularly at my father's church to review the state of the nation. But effectively organisation was impossible unless we returned to school. Our strength lay in collective bargaining, so we returned to school.

Somebody even suggested we adopt the state's motto – '*Een drag maak mag* (Unity is Strength)' for our own, and so we did.

Then early one morning, not so long after we'd gone back to school, they came for Madiba again. We had gone to his house on our way to school, as usual, when we learnt of his arrest. His mother said they'd been woken up about three a.m. by the police who took him away. They said they only wanted him for routine questioning.

'Did they say when he'll be back, Mama?' I asked.

'No, my child,' his mother said. 'But I asked the same question myself and one of them muttered something to the effect that it wouldn't take more than a few days at the most.'

A further shock awaited us at school. A boy in our class who stayed next-door to Nkululeko's told us they'd taken Nkululeko early that morning. Our informant told us that he'd been woken by an unusual *rockshin* from Nkululeko's house and when he peeped through the window, they were leading him to a waiting Volksie, cursing as he'd never heard him curse before.

We held a brief meeting and decided to call an emergency school assembly, to be presided over by Monty.

Khulu was sent to ring the bell.

Several other students went round the school to request every member of staff they could find to attend.

I was sent to ask the Headmaster to come. With great trepidation I approached his office and knocked gently. He invited me in.

'Excuse me, sir,' I began, 'I've been sent to come and invite you to an extra-ordinary student body meeting which is just about to start.'

'Who by?'

'The student body, sir.'

'Why at such short notice?'

'I'm afraid something frightful has happened, sir. Some people have been arrested.'

'Members of our school?'

I nodded.

He stared at me for a while, as if figuring out something.

'Is that what's causing all that infernal din outside?' he asked at length.

I looked down.

Cries of '*Amandla*! *Unitas Vires*! *Inkuleleko ngoku*! (Freedom in our time)' filled the school.

The Headmaster rose from his seat and motioned me to follow.

Everyone had already assembled. They were waiting for the Headmaster and a few other teachers who had not yet come. But as soon as the Headmaster came the meeting got under way.

'Ladies and gentlemen, please lend me your ears,' Monty began. 'First, we would like to apologise to the Headmaster and all the members of staff here present for summoning you to this meeting so unceremoniously. But when you've heard what we have to say we're sure you'll agree it was necessary to call you all here. This is essentially a student body meeting. But we thought that as the matter in hand affects both staff and students it would be better to invite everybody concerned. Now to come to the point. We're faced with a very grave problem. Briefly stated the problem is this: Madiba and teacher Nkululeko were both arrested from their respective homes very early this morning. These are not the first members of our school to be arrested without explanation. Today it is teacher Nkululeko and Madiba; tomorrow it is going to be you and me, unless some steps are taken to curb these arbitrary arrests. So what we propose to do now, without further delay, is to appoint a delegation to go and negotiate for the immediate release of teacher Nkululeko and Madiba. I take it we're all agreed on essentials, so I shall call for nominations straightaway. Any nominations?'

Hands shot into the air.

In a very spontaneous demonstration of confidence only three names came up for nomination – 'Mr Kgopo . . . Mr Dladla . . . Mrs Masiza,' before someone proposed we close nominations.

There were titters of amusement from the students assembled, especially at the last name mentioned. Rumour had it, and news travelled very fast these days, that she'd ditched Kgopo for Dladla. We had nicknamed them 'the Love Triangle'.

'Close nominations, Mr Chairman.'

'Seconded.'

'Thirded.'

'No, no, just two more names, Mr Chairman: S'gubhu and Stadig.'

Raucous laughter around the student who had spoken. Cries of '*Au, Batho! Ag, Shame!*' from the girls' side.

'*Los julle die arme dronkies*,' someone else countered.

'But they should learn to come to assembly, Mr Chairman, same as everybody else. We've no time for guys who want to play at Macavity the Mystery cat here,' the student who had proposed Pakade and Phakoe's names persisted.

It was only then that we noticed they were both missing.

'Ladies and gentlemen,' Monty said, 'the point that's

just been made has been noted. It'll be dealt with accordingly. I can assure you. However, let's not lose sight of our objectives. We're attempting to send a peaceful delegation of our most trusted authorities to go and negotiate for the release of our comrades, not a punitive expedition. Three is a reasonable number.'

'Hear! hear!'

'Thank you, ladies and gentlemen, thank you,' Monty said. 'One last word. Nobody leaves these premises until our delegates return. But we shall not go back to class until this matter has been satisfactorily resolved. When you hear the bell again you shall re-assemble here for a report-back meeting. Once again, thanks, ladies and gentlemen. *Amandla*!'

The assembly broke up.

The Headmaster, who had been standing next to Monty throughout the meeting, summoned Monty to the office.

'Sabelo, you'd better come with me,' Monty said.

We found him with Dladla and Mrs Masiza.

'Now, what's all this about?' he asked. 'Would one of you care to explain? Let's start from the beginning.'

Monty and I exchanged glances. I nodded very slightly in his direction. He cleared his throat and told them everything we knew about Madiba and Nkululeko's arrest.

'What makes you think they've not been arrested for some common criminal offence?' Mrs Masiza asked when Monty had finished.

'In that case,' Monty said, looking at the Headmaster, 'all you can do, sir, is to ask to be told what offence they've committed.'

'All right, but suppose they've just been taken on suspicion or for questioning,' Kgopo said, 'what makes you think our intervention – which, incidentally, could have been more openly and more politely sought, without recourse to any suggestion of blackmail – what makes you think we can prevail upon the police to release them?'

'You can but try, sir.'

'Yes, but suppose the police won't listen to us? What happens if we fail?'

'I really don't know, sir, the students . . .'

'The students have vowed not to return to classes, sir,' I said.

'You mean you're going to tell them to stay away from classes?' Mrs Masiza put in.

I looked down.

'All right, you can go,' the Headmaster said. 'We'll see what we can do.'

We left to go and report to the others, who were eagerly waiting for us outside the office.

Shortly afterwards we saw Kgopo, Dladla and Mrs Masiza trooping into Kgopo's car and driving off.

We walked to our classroom where we found Pakade and Phakoe, already tipsy. We remonstrated very strongly with them. They assured us of their solidarity with us and promised to turn up for assembly next time.

'I was a campaigner myself in the old days of the great Sofasonke,' Pakade added. 'You boys wouldn't remember old Shantytown, just across the railway line from Orlando, or Sophiatown:

> *U tla utloa botsotsi ba reng:*
> *Ons daak nie ons phola hier!*

That's what we used to sing in those days of defiance. Say, Phaks, those were the days, man!'

He had a voice that must have been a delight to listen to once.

'*Heita, my bla, die ou' Kofifi!*' Phakoe enthused, equally nostalgically.

'They seem to have been at too many places all at once,' Khulu said as we left them.

'Sabelo!' Pakade called after us.

I went back. But when he tried to tap me for a loan I told him, face to face, 'Not until the crisis is over,' and left him to join the others.

Two hours later the school bell rang again.

We re-assembled amidst great jubilation, for the

Headmaster's negotiating team had managed to get Madiba and Nkululeko released. The Headmaster had brought them to school first and then driven them to their homes, amidst wild cheers from us, for a much deserved rest.

Even Pakade and Phakoe showed up at the next assembly, in very high spirits.

This time Khulu presided over the meeting. We had decided on this rotational scheme to confuse the enemy about the real leadership of the S.R.C. Even structurally we had established a hierarchy of office-bearers, known only to ourselves, whereby if anything happened to the current leadership at any given time the next group would automatically emerge to fill the gap and so on.

The Chairman briefly reported what we'd come to hear about.

'It's a very small but significant victory,' he concluded. 'We all know that there are others still languishing in police custody. It is also clear that we can't all go about Kissingerising. So again a small group will be necessary to represent us with the authorities in the next phase of our struggle. I take it we're all agreed that the same party as before should return to ask for the release of our remaining comrades. They listened to them once; they may listen to them again. We're not seeking the release of Mandela; we're not asking them to let Sisulu or Mbeki out. We only demand the release of our student comrades, who should have been here with us, preparing for their exams, like the rest of us. Meanwhile we've drawn up a list here.

The names were read out.

'If you know of anyone whose name has not been called out, please, see the Headmaster in the office immediately after this.'

Khulu handed Kgopo the list.

'Release Bozo!' someone shouted. We laughed. (Bozo, who dealt in stolen cars, had recently been pulled in for the umpteenth time.)

'More seriously, ladies and gentlemen,' the Chairman resumed, 'school is dismissed for today. At morning assembly tomorrow we shall hear the results of our latest mission. But, we will not even consider registering for exams until our comrades have been released. *Amandla!*'

Some students immediately left for their homes. The boys in Form 1 raced one another to go and resume their interrupted game of football with a tennis ball at the girls' netball pitch. The rest of the students paraded around the school, singing:

> We break up, we break up,
> We don't care if the school blows up,
> No more Afrikaans, no more French,
> No more sitting on the old school bench.
> If the teacher interferes,
> Hang him up and box his ears,
> If that doesn't do the trick,
> Dynamite will do it quick.

Pakade again called me aside.

'How much, *meneer*?'

'I just can't say how much I admire the way you boys are going about things,' he said. 'Just like the Defiance Campaign. Now, about those addresses for scholarships we once spoke about, I'd say now's the time to apply, boys. We should come together again soon. I say make it R5, Sabs.'

'Okay, next week Monday,' I said, and gave him the money.

'*Ja*, we should all meet on Monday.'

'I don't mean that. I mean the R5.'

'Oh! *Ja*, Monday, without fail. Phakoe's ship will be in on Monday.'

Not so long after, he and Phakoe left in the direction of Shirley Scott's. (It is strange how years afterwards in exile I keep on thinking of Pakade's scholarships. Was it just a gimmick that or did it hide a deeper concern?)

I rejoined the lads on the school lawn. Everybody was holding forth about what we ought to do next – the suggestions, many of them outrightly fabulous and extravagant, as varied as there were speakers. But, make no mistake about it, morale was running very high in those days.

# Book Two

The Day of the Riots

'But can't you really let me put up here for the night?' Johannes Venter asked for the umpteenth time.

'Goodness gracious, no, Mr Venter,' Sipho answered. 'Can't you understand? If you're unable to leave tonight, under cover of darkness, you have no chance of coming out alive tomorrow, in broad daylight.'

'But things may have changed in the morning.'

'Yes, for the worse. Don't you realise, sir, that those children only let us go because they know me? They may very well start boasting in the streets. And when the older ones hear the story, there's no telling what will become of us all if they find you here.'

Sipho's children peered into the sitting-room where he and Johannes Venter were talking.

'*Hambani niyolala nina,*' he said.

They darted back to the kitchen but did not go to bed as he had instructed.

'No, you just can't sleep here, Mr Venter,' Sipho said. 'We simply must think of a way of getting you out of the township with a minimum of delay. Oh! yes, I think I've got it. I'll go and report your presence to the police. They'll be able to escort you safely out of the township. I'll be back shortly. Just make yourself at home. My wife will keep you company till I return. Would you like something to eat?'

'No, I'm all right, thank you.'

'Okay, some tea then. Won't be long, sir.'

Sipho hurried into the kitchen. His wife, Daphne, and their children were huddled together around the coal stove like a brood of chickens.

It was blustering wintry weather. The wind howled and lashed violently against the windows. Gushes of cold air entered through the numerous cracks on the walls, especially where the walls met the roof. The ill-fitting door was stuffed with paper and cloths to keep out some of the cold air.

Daphne was listening to the children's accounts of the day's events when Sipho entered. He closed the door after him.

'Will you stay with him until I come back?' Sipho said.

'I'll go and call the police.'

'He can't sleep here,' Daphne said.

'I'm trying to see to it that he doesn't,' Sipho said.

'*Kodwa wena ubumusa kuphi lomuntu?*' Daphne asked.

Sipho thought what an unfair question it was. How could she conceivably ask why he'd brought Venter, as though he'd had any choice in the matter?

'Please, let's not go into that now,' he said.

'Where will you find the police?' she asked.

'Where else? At the police station, of course. That's what they should be doing, protecting people instead of mowing down our children.'

'*Baba*, they burnt down the police station this afternoon,' Sandile said. He was their eldest son and was ten years old.

Sipho looked at Daphne. She nodded.

There was a loud knock at the door.

Johannes Venter sprang to his feet and made for the kitchen. He stood trembling at the door.

'Excuse me, there's someone knocking,' he said. 'D'you think they've come for me?'

'*Nkulunkulu wam'*!' Daphne exclaimed. 'What did I say? There's only one thing we can do now,' she continued in Zulu. 'You've got to hide him outside, in the coal box.' She quickly sized up Johannes Venter from head to foot. 'He's not such a big man. He'll fit in all right. Quick, we've no time to lose. Get him out before whoever is knocking comes round to the back door.'

They were talking in whispers.

Johannes Venter was shaking uncontrollably. How did one live under such constant threats? He was made to feel even more forlorn by being left out of the conversation which went on in a language he didn't understand. Nor did he feel the least reassured by being ignored each time he asked to be told what they planned to do with him. Was he going to be surrendered to the mercy of those savage children they'd met running riot in the streets? Why hadn't he simply dumped Sipho at the entrance to the township and driven home to his wife and children? But how could he have known that he'd be trapped in this infernal place?

'Risky! But I can't, for the life of me, think of anything else, besides simply letting him out through the window,' Sipho said.

'My God! Do you want a white corpse in our yard in the morning?' Daphne asked.

'No, no, not that. I guess your plan will do. But don't open the door yet. While I get him out, you and the children create as much fracas as you can. Get them to sing something at the top of their voices. And start shouting to whoever is at that door that you're coming. Take your time opening that door.'

'What shall I ask them to sing?'

'Oh, anything. "Rock of ages" or something.'

'But they don't know that one.'

'Get them to sing something else they know then.'

'I know what we'll sing.' It was Nomsa, their five-year old daughter. 'Let's sing that new song Sandile and Sizwe taught me today, the one I heard the Black Power (only she pronounced it "Powder") children singing when they came back from fighting the police. Sandile and Sizwe were there, *baba*. They were all shouting "Black Powder! Black Powder!" and "Amandla! Amandla!" Start it, Sizwe.'

'I don't know which one you mean,' Sizwe said. 'There were many songs we sang today.'

Sizwe was two years older than Nomsa. He and Sandile went to school in the township. During the day they had been involved in a demonstration, together with children from other primary and secondary schools in the township. They marched through the streets, singing old liberation songs and others they had composed themselves, to protest against the enforcement of Afrikaans as a medium of instruction in certain subjects throughout African schools. The students planned to converge at the township's largest soccer stadium to voice their opposition to the scheme.

The police met them in the streets, before they could reach the stadium, and asked them through loudspeakers to disperse. They told the students that in terms of the

Riotous Assemblies Act, which the children had never heard about, they were breaking the law by staging a protest march without obtaining permission from the police first.

'You are here. Give us your permission then,' someone in the crowd shouted. And the chant caught on, 'Give us your permission then.'

'Legalise *dagga*!' someone else shouted. There was loud laughter but no one took up the shout.

The police then used teargas to try and disperse the students. Far from scattering about in a disorganised fashion, the students soon developed a technique for containing the teargas. Armed with cloths and buckets of water requisitioned from nearby houses, they covered the canisters with wet cloths as soon as they hit the ground. In this way many of the canisters were prevented from exploding. Thus unable to break the march the police resorted to shooting. At first they aimed above the heads of the crowd, but as the students surged forward resolutely they fired at their front ranks. Some students retaliated by throwing stones at the police. In the ensuing scuffle a few people were injured, including some police and onlookers, and several children were shot dead.

Incensed by the police action the students ran riot.

'Amandla! Power!' they shouted, with clenched fists raised in the air.

'We'll burn down all their buildings . . . Away with the abominable System!'

Working in groups which struck their targets almost simultaneously, the students acted too fast for the police who had come out in large numbers, leaving the police station virtually deserted. While the police were engaged in trying to contain the disturbances which flared up at various strategic points in the township, a group of specially deployed students caught an unsuspecting skeleton staff at the police station itself and set the buildings on fire. Elsewhere they burnt down the municipality offices and other buildings associated with the township's administration board, like the post offices, beer halls and the fire department. Some schools and libraries were also burnt down.

There were many whites whose daily business brought them to the township. These included employees of the administration board, commercial travellers and people working for voluntary agencies which operated in the township. Many delivery vans bearing the names of white companies were stopped in the streets, overturned and set on fire. Buses received the same treatment. In many cases their black drivers and conductors scuttled into nearby houses, then retired to their homes or their favourite shebeens to drink the bus company's earnings. Some whites caught in this way were killed, among them a doctor who ran a voluntary medical scheme for children in the township. His body was found in a rubbish bin. Another superintendent in one of the administration board's offices who was watching the battle between the police and the students unaware of any reason why anyone should wish to harm him, was also killed.

A dangerous spirit, such as Sipho and Johannes Venter had experienced in driving through the township, still gripped the streets.

'Sing then,' Sipho said to his children.

'Just a moment, please, I'm coming,' Daphne shouted.

'Start it, Sizwe,' Nomsa said.

'Sing!' Sipho said.

Sizwe and Sandile started simultaneously, on different keys. Nomsa joined in, adding to the discord:

> *Mhla sibuyayo! Mhla sibuyayo!*
> *Mhla sibuyayo! Mhla sibuyayo!*
> *Kuzokhal' uVorster,*
> *Kubaleke uKruger . . .*

'No, no, no, not that one!' Sipho said.

The children fell silent.

'Come on, sing!' Sipho said.

'*Siculeni manje?*' Nomsa asked.

'Just sing, anything. Now go:

> Rock of ages cleft for me,
> Let me hide . . .

'*Asiyazi leyo*,' Nomsa said.

'Okay, if you don't know that one, sing something you know then,' Sipho said.

Sizwe suggested they should sing '*Amabhunu ayizinja*'.

'Not that one either, not that one. Can't you sing anything without dragging in Boers? Okay, just go on talking then. Louder . . . Louder, I say!'

The knocking continued.

'I'm coming,' Daphne said.

'It's okay, Mr Venter,' Sipho said. 'Just follow me and do as I say. This side, please.'

Sipho carefully opened the back door and edged out, with Johannes Venter following closely.

The coal-box stood in a corner of the backyard, near the toilet. Sipho had built it himself by joining sundry planks together. It had a lid with a padlock which was locked every night before the family went to bed. When empty the box was large enough to hold two children playing hide-and-seek and therefore indifferent to any temporary inconvenience.

They made for it.

Sipho felt inside with his hands. It was half-full of coal. There were also some dirty rags, old newspapers, firewood and an axe. He brought out the axe.

'Climb in here, Sir,' he said.

Johannes Venter saw the adjacent building and hesitated.

'Why can't I hide in there?' he asked.

'Sir, the toilet would be the most obvious place for any search party to look in,' Sipho answered. 'Get in quickly.'

Johannes Venter climbed in gingerly. Sipho helped to catapult him in, head first.

'Lie on your side.'

He did so. He folded his knees, brought them up to his chin and encircled them with his arms. He could feel the sharp edges of the coal and the splinters of wood through his body. He wondered how long he'd remain interred in there.

Sipho thrust the axe in his hands.

'You may need this,' he said.

'My friend, please, don't leave me buried in this place for long,' Johannes Venter said in a faint voice.

'I'll get you out as soon as I possibly can.'

The lid came over Johannes Venter's body. He sobbed a little and then remembered he must get hold of himself. He tried to fix his mind on his family. When his death was reported to his wife, would she be overwhelmed with grief? How would his children manage being left fatherless so young? He offered silent, incoherent prayers which encompassed just about everybody and everything he held dear. He cursed his fate which had landed him in this dark pit. His company should have placed him in the office. He should have pressed for an early answer to his application for a transfer. He hated travelling which often kept him away from his family for days on end. Not even their clandestine outings to Botswana with Sipho could quite compensate for this sort of inconvenience. He had last seen his family on Monday, no, on Sunday evening really, because he had left very early on Monday while they were all asleep, and today was Wednesday night. Would he ever see them again? He tried to recall his wife's face but her image had become too dim. His head ached where he had landed on the coal. And then suddenly he felt drained of all strength. A sense of unreality assailed him. It was strange the way his body felt less and less a part of him. His whole body started to tremble. He no longer had the will or the strength to control himself. His head reeled round and round. He thought he heard footsteps receding into the distance. His teeth were chattering badly. He tried to shout, but his breath was leaving him and no sound came out. A deep, deep darkness, such as he had never known before, descended over him.

After shutting the lid Sipho felt pressed. He walked into the toilet and unzipped his fly. Only a few drops trickled out. It had been a false alarm. He flushed the cistern and walked out. He washed his hands from the tap next to the toilet and walked back to the house, whistling.

He stood at the door to listen. There were several voices speaking all at once. A man's voice could be heard above the rest. Sipho sighed audibly and walked in. It was his friend, Eddie, who had come with his girlfriend, Meikie, a nurse at the local hospital.

'*Heit! Fana*' Eddie greeted. 'I learn your white man has decided to live with us in the township. Wish I could exchange places with him!'

'Shucks! Eddie,' Sipho said and flopped into a chair. 'Why couldn't you just tell us it was you? *Kunjani Meikie*?'

Meikie returned the greeting.

'How could I have known you'd gone multi-racial?' Eddie asked.

'It's no laughing matter,' Sipho said.

'Where's he?' Eddie asked.

'Come with me,' Sipho said.

Eddie followed him out.

They came to the coal box and Sipho said, 'It's all right, Mr Venter, it's only some friends.'

He opened the lid.

'Mr Venter, you can come out now.'

'Maybe he bolted out,' Eddie said.

'He's here all right,' Sipho said.

Johannes Venter did not stir.

Sipho shook him hard several times, then turned to Eddie. 'Lend me a hand,' he said. 'I think the poor guy's passed out.'

They carried Johannes Venter back to the house and placed him on the sofa in the sitting-room. He was covered with soot like a township coal vendor.

Meikie was quickly galvanised into action. She asked Daphne for a basin of cold water. While Daphne went for the water she unloosened Johannes Venter's clothes.

'Careful of breaking the Immorality Act, sweetheart,' Eddie said.

'I think it's just shock,' she said. 'Nothing much to worry about. He should be able to come round on his own soon.'

'What do you intend to do with him?' Eddie asked.

'I don't know,' Sipho answered. 'I thought I'd get the

police to escort him home. I guess I'll have to drive him myself. Some kids saw us come here. I'm afraid the story may soon leak out. Will you come with me, Eddie?'

'You must be joking!' Eddie said. 'Ask Meikie what it's like out there. Just a street away there are bonfires all along the road. And it's not just old tyres they're burning. Meikie and I just came back from town by taxi about an hour ago. Listen to me, we've seen a bit of what's happening out there and we didn't like it a bit. Look, I was born in this township. I've never seen it so angry, I tell you. We were held up no less than three times and not just by the police either. They're confining their activities to the outskirts of the township, harassing guys without passes, as usual. It was also reported over the radio that, with the police station razed to the ground, the army has been called in to deal with the riots. But for the time being those kids have established a virtual government in this township. And you ask me to go and risk my neck out there! Why, I don't even call that a risk. It's outright suicide. Let's talk about something else. Did you hear that similar disturbances have also flared up in Nyanga and Langa townships in Cape Town and New Brighton in Port Elizabeth? All police and army leave has been cancelled. This looks like being bigger than Sharpeville, man. Do you remember how the people scuttled like rats into their holes before those bazookas?'

'But if we can avoid all the roadblocks,' Sipho continued, 'we did it when we drove here, we could probably dump this guy with the police or the army.'

'And be pulled in to show them who the leaders of the riots are? Forget it, man. Besides, you can't even get that far without bumping into the students. Listen, chum, our taxi-driver told us that there are checkpoints on all the roads leading in and out of the township – and there isn't an infinite number of those, the Boers have made sure of that, for more effective control! These checkpoints are manned by the students themselves, on the look-out for whites and sell-outs. And they are very thorough. Have you heard what they did to Chabeli and Rathebe!'

'Tell us what happened, Eddie,' Daphne quickly put in.

Chabeli and Rathebe were both prominent members of the township's advisory board, 'veteran boardmen' the newspapers called them.

The advisory board's function was to make the views of the people known to the authorities. But few township residents supported it, so that its elections never drew more than five per cent of the electorate. Nevertheless, the government never failed to point out that the advisory board was the only democratically elected body to represent African opinion. The usual low percentage poll was attributed to the fact that Africans were as yet unaccustomed to the intricacies of democratic procedures. They were still apprentices to civilisation in general and needed the guiding hand of the white man. The alternative, in the Prime Minister's own words, was, 'too ghastly to contemplate.'

When the students had first made known their opposition to the compulsory introduction of Afrikaans as a medium of instruction, Chabeli and Rathebe had been most vociferous in their condemnation of the students. They denounced them as misguided idealists, living in the past rather than looking forward. They were quoted in the newspapers and over the radio as saying that the students were cutting their own throats. They were shutting their eyes to the reality of their own situation and failing to take advantage of such opportunities as their parents had been denied in their days, when African schools were still in the hands of irrelevant missionaries and lackeys of the British empire. They said that the demands of modern commerce and the need to foster better race relations and promote peaceful co-existence in such a plural society as ours in South Africa, with two official languages, rested not only on the African's knowledge of English but also on his proficiency in Afrikaans. In an interview with one Afrikaans newspaper Chabeli pointed out that the importance of English had been gradually eroded in the last fifteen years since South Africa had left the Commonwealth, and that Afrikaans was definitely the language of the future which it would benefit his people to master.

Chabeli, a former primary school Headmaster, was the Chairman of the local school board to whom the students first presented their petition, so that the board could pass it on to the appropriate authorities. Chabeli called the students presumptuous ingrates who had to be protected from cutting off their own noses to spite their faces. As an educationist of long-standing, he told the students, he knew what was good for them. How did they hope to take their rightful place in a future constellation of southern African states without an education which was at least as good as their former masters? He ended up by tearing their petition in front of members of the S.R.C., a group of elected student representatives from the township's various secondary and high schools who had brought the petition.

The advisory board under the chairmanship of Rathebe, to whom the students went next, treated them with similar scorn.

Rathebe, a bulky man with a drooping stomach, was one of the township's wealthiest men. He owned a string of businesses in the centre of the township. But it was generally rumoured that he was merely a front for some Indian and white businessmen. He made no secret of his support for government policy which was geared towards providing African businessmen with unlimited opportunity for expansion in their homelands, without unfair competition from English-speaking money-mongers. His outspoken views enabled him to win further concessions from the authorities to expand his business in the township. Through the representation of Africans like himself the government had agreed to grant leases of ninety-nine years to a certain category of Africans in the urban areas. He was very often invited to parties for businessmen of all races and entertained very lavishly himself. Only recently he had played host at the township's only hotel to a group of visiting white M.P.'s. He and Chabeli received wide publicity from the news media which referred to them variously as 'township tycoons', 'non-white socialites', 'black moderates' and 'civic leaders.'

The advisory board was in session when the unrest broke out in the township. Resolution after resolution was passed condemning the students, their teachers and parents. 'When we were boys,' Rathebe summed up from the chair, 'it could never have happened. In those days teachers did what they were paid for and every parent knew the folly of sparing the rod. Let it never be said of us that when the moment came we, in this chamber, were found wanting; that we exchanged our sacred destiny, our sanctified station in life and our duty to posterity for cheap popularity; that we sacrificed our convictions and consciences on the altar of expediency. Let us stamp out these cantankerous elements from our midst, unwitting tools of certain well-known agitators, no doubt, once and for all.'

There was deafening applause from the other councillors.

Late that afternoon reports reached the advisory board's council chambers that arson and looting had broken out in the township, and that some children had been shot dead.

The parents among them immediately thought of their children; businessmen thought of their property.

The board's deliberations were cut short in the middle of an important debate about the site for a new cemetery, many of the members arguing that the site chosen by the authorities was best suited for the proposed African Development Bank and the first African-owned supermarket. The chairman was in the process of circulating the plans, drawn up by members of the African Chamber of Commerce of which he was president, when the disturbing news came. He called for an adjournment.

Chabeli and Rathebe were driving home together when they were caught in a roadblock near Rathebe's shops, where he hoped to check first if all was well. He never got the opportunity.

Roadblocks were common in that area from traffic cops checking on stolen cars, unlicensed ones, cars with no roadworthy certificates, pirate taxis, taxis carrying overloads and mobile criminals of all descriptions.

When their turn came Chabeli and Rathebe discovered that it was only a bunch of school kids, still in their school uniforms.

'What the hell do they think they're up to?' Chabeli asked.

'Exactly what we were discussing,' Rathebe said.

'I'll bloody well teach them who I am,' Chabeli said and stormed out of the passenger's seat. 'You there, remove your little arses from the streets.'

'Look who we've got here, chaps?' one of the students shouted.

'Yes, you know me very well. I don't brook no shit from disrespectful nincompoops like you. Who do you think you are? Just what nonsense is going on here?'

Rathebe, jangling the keys of his new BMW, left the car idling and came out to check. Standing next to Chabeli, he quickly assessed the situation and felt that he didn't like what was happening, not one bit. He hoped Chabeli had enough sense to know when it was time to stop poking one's fingers in and out of the mouth of a growing lion cub which one had been keeping for a pet.

'This is more than our fair share of luck, chaps,' the same student said.

A growing number of students and some onlookers gathered round them.

'Just who the hell do you think you are?' Chabeli asked.

'It's the blokes from the Useless Boys' Club,' some other student said, deliberately provoking laughter by twisting the first letters of the name the advisory board had newly acquired when it became officially known as the Urban Bantu Council – as a step towards granting the township full municipality rights, the government had said.

'Just handle them with kid gloves, old boy,' Rathebe whispered. 'I smell gunpowder here.'

'I'd stop all this bull-shitting if I were you and go home,' Chabeli said. 'Today you've brought nothing but shame and dishonour to yourselves and your people. Now be off with you all!'

'Listen who's talking about "shame and dishonour"!' another student said.

The others roared with laughter.

'Easy now, old chap, easy,' Rathebe whispered. 'No need to blow off like that. Leave all this to me. I know exactly how to handle this.'

He appealed for silence from the students and then spoke.

'Listen to me, my children. You know us very well. We are your people. If there's anything we can do . . .'

But neither Chabeli's swaggering talk nor Rathebe's pleas had any effect on the students. Rathebe was easily caught as he tried to dash for the comparative safety of his shops across the road. A suggestion to burn his shops, however, was drowned in the general excitement. Chabeli was brought down on his haunches with several blows to his head from a hosepipe.

The two men were made to squat and frogmarched to Rathebe's house, about a mile and a half away. The students clapped all the way to shouts of 'Hop! hop!', while others sang 'We are marching to Pretoria'.

When they ultimately got to Rathebe's house his ample frame was dripping with sweat. Chabeli's lanky body felt cramped all over. Neither man could stand on his feet. The students lifted them to the air and hurled them across Rathebe's high fence. They landed on Mrs Rathebe's bed of roses.

'What happened to their car?' Sipho asked, as he peeped through the window to see if their car was still parked where they had left it.

'A group of kids jumped in and drove around until it ran out of gas,' Eddie said.

'That's what they nearly did to us,' Sipho said.

'And yet you're hell-bent on driving this guy!' Eddie said.

'How's he doing, Meikie?' Sipho asked.

Meikie and Daphne bent over Johannes Venter.

As Johannes Venter slowly regained consciousness, he

saw several pairs of eyes peering intently into his face. The eyes terrified him at first. Where had he seen just such eyes before? He tried to place the faces before him without success. He raised his head from the soft pillow and felt a throbbing pain in his head, like some king-size hangover. He felt a scorching thirst. Soft, solicitous hands were pushing him back on the pillow, gently but firmly. There was a hubbub of voices in the strange room. Finally his roving eyes lighted on Sipho's face. He felt a slight reassurance. He vaguely recalled that they were on tour together. But what were all these other faces doing in his hotel room, if that is what it was? And the black women, were they the ones Sipho had promised to organise?

Suddenly an unreasoning fear took a savage hold on him. With very painstaking effort, rather like a man trying to piece together a crazy jigsaw puzzle, he tried to recall the preceding events, culminating in that evening's horrific events.

They were returning from a long trip in the north-western Transvaal. Sipho had to drop first in the township before Johannes could proceed by himself to his own home in Mayfair. How much more convenient it might have been if Sipho, who did most of the driving anyhow, dropped him in town first! But company regulations had to be observed and they forbade Sipho to keep the company car overnight. As the manager had pointed out, Africans were unreliable and always abused the company vehicles left in their charge. There was Sipho's own case, for instance, when he had been allowed to keep the company car once because something, though it was very difficult to say exactly what, seemed to put him apart from the rest of them. And then what happened? The next morning he came to work, without the car, and then tried to sell the manager that cock-and-bull story about the wheels of the car having been stolen while it was parked outside his gate. True enough, the car had been found stripped of all the wheels outside Sipho's house, but only a fool would believe that Sipho himself had not sold the tyres. Only there was no way of proving that. That was the smart streak in them. It needed a white man who understood them very well to harness their native qualities for the good of society. For instance, the manager had decided to retain Sipho. But never again was he to keep the company car overnight. Since then they'd had no problems with him. He was very good at his work, too. Of course, you couldn't expect perfection from them. All the same he was undoubtedly the best of the lot. Not that white salesmen never put company vehicles to private use. But they did so with more circumspection.

To return to Sipho's case. When put on an inventory paper his strengths surpassed his weaknesses, to use the manager's analogy again. As for Johannes, he could never really make up his mind about Sipho. The man frankly puzzled him. Take the case of his qualifications, for instance, which every white man would have displayed with pride. One day after another long trip, Johannes had chanced on Sipho's certificate displayed on the wall when he helped him carry his luggage into the house. Sipho had a B.A. degree from the Bantu university of Fort Hare. Johannes excitedly promised that he would break the good news to their manager, with a recommendation for Sipho's promotion to full salesman, in charge of their whole district. Instead Sipho had begged him, and he had seemed in earnest about it, never to divulge the information to anyone. Johannes thought that there was certainly some grain of truth in what was said about the Bantu being temperamentally unsuited for positions of authority and responsibility. Otherwise how could anyone with ambition and inititative argue that he preferred the position he held to prospects of promotion based on his educational qualifications? It didn't make sense either what the man had said about previously having been sacked from several jobs for being too educated! But then Johannes had not pursued the matter because for his own part he had a certain respect for this man upon whom he had come to rely more and more.

Sipho was officially Johannes Venter's co-driver.

Together they did country and covered the whole north-western region of the Transvaal to the border of Bechuanaland – it was now called Botswana, though only heaven knew what was wrong with Bechuanaland, the land of the Bechuana! But he liked Botswana. They often drove across the border to spend a night or two at the Holiday Inn in Gaborone, just as they had done the night before. You could have any number of black women in Gaborone. Nobody gave a hoot there. And Sipho certainly knew his way about. Johannes Venter thought of how he had come to rely on Sipho more and more in his work. Sipho spoke all the languages of the people among whom they worked; while Johannes Venter could never understand a single word of Bantu; sometimes not even when they spoke English. In the African villages they covered Sipho took complete charge and Johannes Venter did business with the scattered white communities of predominantly Afrikaans-speaking people in the area. But for the African market, the company might as well have given up its north-western operations long ago.

Darkness was setting in when they approached the township. A large hue of red illuminated the sky. It was like Guy Fawkes' day in mid-June. The jubilant native spirit, Johannes Venter thought. What on earth could they be celebrating?

'What day is this?' he asked.

'Wednesday,' Sipho answered.

'I know that, what I mean is, what's all the excitement about?'

'I don't have the slightest idea. Looks like the chaos we usually have on New Year's Eve. I don't like it a bit. Maybe we'd better use the side streets.'

Sipho swung the car to the right hand and they plunged into the middle of nowhere. It amazed Johannes Venter how these people were ever expected to find their way through such randomly laid out and poorly-lit streets. Talk of mushrooms! The matchbox houses seemed to have been simply planted amidst rocks and debris. There were potholes as deep as children's swimming pools, right in the middle of the road. Sipho deftly avoided these and picked his way with the skill of a master navigator. And always a street or two away they could see tall flames and hear wild shouts. The scene reminded Johannes of the Kaffir cities one read about in history or in the novels of Rider Haggard, in those days of glorious savagery under the old Kaffir kings; of brightly illuminated homesteads on festive evenings, when fires were kept alight the whole night through to keep away wild beasts.

They seemed to have been driving for ages, into the deep night, across puddles of foul-smelling stagnant water, over piles of rotting rubbish which provided countless interesting smells for the half-starved mongrels that prowled the area, when their car came to an abrupt halt.

Countless little eyes, like the eyes of so many cats, glared at them from the dark.

'What's all this?' Johannes Venter asked.

'I think we've had it,' Sipho whispered. 'Listen, don't panic. My house is only a few yards up the road. I'm well known in this area. It's only a couple of kids, but you'd better let me do all the talking. I can recognise quite a few of them. They often come to play with my kids.'

The note of urgency in Sipho's voice transmitted itself to Johannes Venter.

Their car was surrounded by a crowd of jeering, yelling children. They jerked the car up and down, from rear to front and again from side to side, as if to capsize it.

Johannes Venter's fear mounted. What did they want?

Sipho's voice reached him in plaintive tones. 'Better do exactly as they say,' he said. 'It'll soon be over.'

Many small fists were thrust through the window on Johannes Venter's side.

Small voices piping instructions at him in English: 'Clench your fists like this (difficult to see how in the dark) . . . no, your right fist . . . Now, say "Power!" . . . Louder (somebody'll pay dearly for this) . . . That's not loud enough (Gentle Jesu meek and mild!) . . .'

'Move closer to me, they want to come in for a ride,

only they've promised not to take us beyond this street.'

Johannes Venter obeyed without question.

His door swinging open.

A swarm of wildly cheering pickanninnies, singing with so much gusto it hurt Johannes Venter's ears; some on his lap, others sitting restlessly beside him; some packed close together in the back seat; others hanging to the sides of the car, precariously perched on the bonnet and on the roof.

The car, moving at a funeral pace, seeming to sink under the weight of its human cargo, up and down the street, up and down.

Sipho's voice, mingled, with the voices of the little ones: pleading, imploring, explaining, persuading.

Then, as suddenly and as inexplicably as they had come, the children disappeared into the thick, treacherous African night.

They drove the few remaining yards to Sipho's house in silence.

Once in the house Sipho explained to Johannes Venter that a riot had broken out in the township. The children they had just met were on their way to join their elder brothers and sisters along the township's busy streets.

Sipho spared Johannes Venter the knowledge that several whites had already been killed in the streets of the township. He was to learn of all this, and the reasons for the outbreak of violence, from newspapers and the radio the following day.

Johannes Venter was jolted by a further realisation that he couldn't possibly hope to come out of the township alive that night if he tried to drive home by himself. And Sipho, understandably enough, refused to accompany him. What made his situation even more hopeless was that Sipho wouldn't hear of Johannes Venter spending the night at his house. What was to become of him?

Then Johannes Venter remembered that he'd been thrust into a coal-box earlier. How had he come out? No matter, he was out and alive.

Voices in some strange language reached his ears.

Only this time they were soothing, less menacing and more reassuring.

'He will get better by and by,' Meikie said.

'We've only one hope,' Eddie said.

'What is it?' Sipho asked.

'We've just got to lie low,' Eddie continued. 'Those students can't be in the streets all night.'

'But they saw us come here,' Sipho said. 'They know he's here. They only need to pass our house and see that car again. What happens if we're raided?'

'They'd have long come by now,' Eddie said. 'Anyhow, maybe that's just a risk we must take. Otherwise, if he tries to drive away by himself, then by my mother, who lies out there in Croesus, he won't get beyond this street. And, as I've already been at so much pains to explain, we can't drive him out of the township, at least not as yet.'

'He's still too weak to be moved anyhow,' Meikie said.

'But he's not sleeping here,' Daphne said. '*Kodwa amabhunu eniwakhathalele ngani nina lana?*'

Daphne again, Sipho thought. What the hell gave her the impression that they were more concerned with Johannes Venter's safety than with their own? If the worse came to the worse, they'd still have to thrust him out through that door to his would-be executioners, if necessary. But that was no reason not to try. He didn't want blood in his hands, not even that of a white.

'What do you suggest?' he asked.

'Keep him here until the streets are quiet,' Eddie said, 'then drive him home.'

'Daphne?'

'*Emalahleni!*'

'Oh, please listen, Daph,' Meikie said. 'We can't send him out there in the cold again. He'd die of exposure.'

'You all think I'm just being a heartless hag, don't you?' Daphne said. 'Have you stopped to consider what will happen if he's found here? I've my responsibility to my family, that's all. I must think of what's going to happen to my children first.'

'Don't misunderstand me, Daph,' Meikie said. 'A

mother's first duty is to her children.'

'Exactly!' Eddie said. 'He nearly passed out for good in that coal-box where you want us to send him back. Do you want a dead white discovered in your yard?'

'All right then, if you think you know what you're doing,' Daphne said. 'But I still don't think it's any of my business to look after whites at the expense of my own children.'

She walked into the bedroom, followed by the children. Their excitement and curiosity exhausted, they were now ready to go to bed.

'Actually, she's right,' Meikie said. 'Why must we expose the children to unnecessary risks? Daphne and I and the children can all go and put up at our place, can't they, Eddie dear?'

'Why not?' Eddie said.

'Oh! that's very considerate of you, Meikie,' Sipho said. 'But I'm afraid that won't be necessary. Eddie is right, if nothing's happened to us so far, nothing is likely to happen now. Let's go back to Eddie's suggestion. There are certain problems of a practical nature. We drive Mr Venter to Mayfair when all is quiet. How do we come back? You know, Eddie, I'm not allowed to keep the car.'

'Hold it right there!' Eddie said. 'You surprise me, man. Here we are, ready to risk our necks for your *baas's* sake. Why, man, he'll have to trust you for once. We won't walk back after we've dropped this fellow in Mayfair. You tell him that. Fortunately your car doesn't have the company name on its side. They're burning all such cars which they can lay their hands upon. There was one large Standard Bakery van we passed on our way from town, burning on its side. There were children beside it, munching bread and cakes. I also heard that a group suspected to be thugs broke into a bottle store and made away with most of the liquor. Which reminds me of what brought me here. All this talk about the riots has made me clean forget my purpose in coming here. Meikie, can you bring along that parcel? Might as well hold a proper vigil.'

'It's right here beside me,' Meikie produced a sealed bottle of K.W.V. from her handbag. 'Actually, I don't know why I didn't think of this before, but a stiff tot of this brandy will do him some good.'

She measured Johannes Venter a stiff one and passed it on to him.

He swallowed it gratefully and felt its warmth sinking into his tummy. He was feeling much better.

'Just relax, sir,' Sipho said. 'You're among friends and you need to conserve your strength now, nothing'll happen to you.'

Something in what Eddie said didn't reassure him so much. What new ordeal was in store for him now? What did he need reserves of strength for? He looked longingly at the bottle of K.W.V.

'What have you decided?' he asked.

Sipho outlined their plan to him, but left out the bit about the car, so that Eddie had to remind him.

'*Mtshele ngemoto phela, ndoda,*' Eddie said.

'But my friend and I will have to drive back in the company car. I'll bring it with me when I come to work in the morning.'

'My dear Sipho,' Johannes Venter said, a smile illuminating his face for the first time, 'I can assure you that's perfectly all right with me. You know me, my friend, I don't stand for these company formalities. And I don't mind telling you this right away. I've never seen eye to eye with the manager over this matter of who may or may not keep the car. After all when we're in Botswana . . .'

'If you agree then, well, that's the end of the matter,' Sipho said.

Johannes Venter made up his mind there and then to recommend Sipho for promotion with immediate effect, to take complete charge of the whole north-eastern circuit, because he, Johannes Venter, was through with it. They'd either move him into the head office or he was going to look for another job. But either way, he was through with travelling, even if it meant having to forfeit some of the forbidden pleasures of Botswana.

Sipho thought what a narrow escape it had been. Supposing his wife had been listening? And there was no telling yet whether she'd overheard them or not. Why did Venter have to blabber so about their visits to Botswana? Sipho never confided his escapades in Gaborone to anyone besides Eddie. His wife hardly knew that he had a travelling document.

'Will you join us for a drink?' Eddie said, pouring out the drinks.

'There's nothing I'd appreciate better,' Johannes Venter said. 'And thank you, my good sir, for all your generosity and this good lady's, not forgetting your wife, Sipho. I just don't know how to thank you enough, Mr . . .?'

Sipho made the introductions, grateful for the way Eddie had expertly steered the conversation from its disastrous course.

'I guess I'll join Daphne in the bedroom,' Meikie said. 'But, please, make sure you don't drink until you forget to drive Mr Venter home. The students will be out in full force tomorrow. I fear we're on the brink of a major catastrophe. Don't forget your business, please.'

Which is what almost happened!

With the brandy nearly finished, Eddie decided to remind Sipho and Johannes Venter that it was about time they left. Both men were so tight that it took Eddie close to thirty minutes to convince them that they had to go. He couldn't have accomplished that much even, if Daphne hadn't emerged from the bedroom to tell Sipho that as far as she was concerned Johannes Venter would have to spend the remaining part of the night in the coal-box, and that Sipho could follow him there, if he liked. That shook Sipho to his senses. But Johannes Venter, who didn't follow the conversation, kept prattling on about the fact that he didn't really mind where they put him up for the night because he now felt very much at one with them. He wasn't one to stand on formalities, he kept on, and Sipho would have his promotion yet, because he, Johannes Venter, was through with commercial travelling, Gaborone or no Gaborone.

It was 3.15 a.m. when they dropped him outside his house – as a precaution they'd put him in the boot – and drove back to the township.

Sipho didn't show up at work that day.

# Book Three

The Children of Soweto

We buried him on Sunday. There were several other funerals being held all over the township that Sunday, funerals of others who had died in the shootings earlier that week.

His death had come as a great shock to me. Life was difficult to imagine without him. In class he had always sat next to me. We lived in the same street. We had grown up playing marbles, spinning tops and flying kites together. Our street team had dominated the other street teams we played against in our football challenge matches, in the dusty township streets, where treacherous holes were worse than the most hard-tackling defender. He and I had formed such a deadly combination as strikers that we had been nicknamed 'the terrible twins'. We had been inseparables. I remember as though it were only yesterday how hurt I felt the day he took out his first girlfriend, Violet, to Harlem Cinema; and how on our way back he had asked me to travel home, alone, while he saw Violet to her home. We had fought rival street gangs with *bog-draads*, made up of wires intertwined to make them thicker, scout belts, bicycle chains, slings and stones as members of the same gang. We had gone together to caddy at the golf course or to carry at the market. We had attended the same schools right from our days at the lower primary school, and many were the days we had played truant together in order to explore the complex network of tunnels which connect the township's water and sewerage pipes. We had suffered harassment and intimidation in the hands of the Hazel gang side by side. We had risen together to positions of prominence in the S.R.C. and none could claim to have been more dedicated and committed to our cause than we were. His death came as a great shock to me because I could not remember a time when he had not been by my side.

It was a chilly Wednesday morning in the middle of June.

Looking back in time we can usually tell to the very minute when it all started; the day Dingane's forces were routed at Blood River, the day of Bulhoek, Sharpeville and so on. Some of the manifestations, we later discover, had been in evidence for days, months, generations previously. The whole of the preceding summer had evinced all the symptoms and been full of omens, but we never noticed until after the event. With the wisdom of hindsight there are some people who can tell us they saw it all coming; who remember feeling inexplicably depressed the whole of that preceding week; whose very dreams, interpreted retrospectively, had been ominous visions of the future. Looking back in time, we can usually find the exact moment when a new epoch began, whereas when it happened it was simply just another day indistinguishably linked to others. Such was that fateful morning in the middle of June.

We were marching along the main road, some three streets away from ours, when we encountered them. They stood across the road, blocking our way. We had been marching resolutely through the townships, with children from other schools, gathering yet more others as we proceeded. Boys and girls aged between ten and twenty. Students from Orlando High, Musi High, Naledi, Sekano-Ntoane, Morris Isaacson, Orlando West, Zola, Madibane, Eiseleen, Jabulani Junior Secondary, Tladi Junior Secondary, Molapo, and Thesele. Along with them thousands of primary school children. The march had been organised to demonstrate our opposition to the imposition of Afrikaans as a medium of instruction in our schools.

Addressing us first in Afrikaans and then in broken Zulu, they tried to order us to disperse. But we had grievances which could no longer wait. We surged forward, aiming to sweep them out of our path if they would not give way. By now our frenzied numbers had swelled and swelled. We shouted '*Amandla!*' (Power), '*Inkululeko ngoku!*' (Freedom in our lifetime) and 'One Azania, One Nation!', as we marched on, our clenched fists held high. The air resounded with menace. We sang. Our song drowned the remonstrative voice issuing from the loudspeaker. We shouted our defiance in song:

*Asikhathali noma bes'bopha*
 We don't give a damn, even if
  imprisoned
*Sizimisel'inkululeko.*
 For freedom's our ultimate goal.


He and I and student leaders from other schools, carrying denunciatory placards against the System, were marching in front.

Suddenly from just ahead of us there was a great rumbling noise. Several times the thunderous explosion came, as if the very roof of heaven was collapsing over our heads.

Pandemonium broke loose as we scampered for protection from the nearby houses, he and I and a handful of others hurling stones as we retreated.

He stumbled and fell, with an anguished cry which pierced through my heart as surely as if it had been the Roman soldier's sword.

'They've hit me,' he cried and collapsed to the ground like an empty sack of potatoes.

Khotso Duiker and I tore ourselves from the retreating crowd and crept on all fours to where he lay.

Khotso was our Treasurer in the S.R.C., which was made up of student representatives from all the townships' secondary and high schools. He was dedicated, level-headed and tough. He often spoke of an Italian novelist he had read called Giovanni Guareschi, by whose code of conduct he tried to live. 'Even if they kill me,' he'd say, 'I will not die.' In the days preceding our big Wednesday demonstration, when the SBs had tried all sorts of intimidating tactics to compel our S.R.C. to disband, he had been in and out of police detention, ostensibly for routine questioning, countless times. It didn't seem as if anything could ever dampen his enthusiasm or undermine his commitment.

'Hold him on the other side,' I said to Khotso. We struggled on, with him between us, to the safety of the nearest yard.

The shooting had lasted for seconds perhaps, but it

had seemed like ages. To be sure, I had expected to be blown to pieces at any moment. But nothing as dramatic happened.

We handed him across the fence to some students who had preceded us to MaVy's yard and jumped in after them.

'Bring him over here,' I said.

Khotso rolled his school blazer on the ground close to the wall. We lowered him to the ground with his back to the wall.

'Where does it hurt?' I asked. Only then did I notice the streams of blood oozing through his fingers as he held his hands clasped to his tummy.

'Khotso, keep an eye on him,' I said. 'I won't be long.'

'All right, folks, some of you go from house to house to see what help we can get,' I heard Khotso saying to the others as I darted away.

I leapt across the fence to the next yard, across the next street, through another yard to the next one and then into the street, until I reached his home. His elder sister, Sindiswa, was cleaning the sitting-room floor when I burst in through the front door. Their parents were at work. She and her brother were their only children. Upon my entrance she quickly sprang to her feet.

'What a fright you've given me!' she said with both hands clasped to her heart. 'With all that nasty shooting going on outside I'm scared to even step out of this door. It's as if something terrible is going to happen any time. What on earth is the matter?'

'Sis' Sindi, we've got no time to waste,' I said. 'Please come with me.'

'But why, what's wrong?'

'I'm afraid something frightful has happened to your brother.'

'Oh! no, he's not been killed, has he?'

'No, no, no, not that.'

'Where's he then?'

'Come, you'll see.'

I led the way out. Sindiswa followed close behind, her knees red with floor polish.

She tried to pump out more information from me, but I was somewhat too dazed to give any coherent explanation as we trotted back, through side alleys and backyards, to where I'd left the others in MaVy's yard.

MaVy herself, who ran a spot (which is our euphemism for a drinking joint) at her house, was already there.

MaVy was a buxom lady in her fifties. She was called MaVy after her eldest daughter, Violet, who had been my friend's sweetheart when we were still much younger, before they parted. The story of MaVy's family was public knowledge. Violet had been forced to leave school after Standard Six to work in order to supplement their family income. He and Violet began to drift apart the moment she left school. I was not at all sorry to see them break up because, among other things, she had taken up with the Hazels, a knife-happy gang of merciless thugs who reigned over our township with an iron hand. They terrorised school kids by taking all the money we brought to school for lunch or waylaying us when we were sent to the shops by our parents. The Hazels had bluntly told him that if he carried on with Violet, they'd cut him to pieces. I convinced him, though he was adamant at first, to drop the affair. I'm not sorry that I did, for there are moments in the townships when it is folly to play brave. The ego has no actual physical proportions.

MaVy had not known anything about Violet's affairs. She was too busy figuring out how to feed her husband and their six children. Her husband, whom everybody simply called MaVy's husband, had been out of work for more than three years. Before then he had been a factory hand at Vulcan's in Croesus. His right hand had been caught in a machine and chopped off. Vulcan's paid him R500 in compensation money. They also paid for his treatment and the cost of fitting him with an artificial hand. After leaving hospital he set out to blow his money like it was made of soap bubbles, so that very soon there wasn't a cent left. That made him go back to work. But Vulcan's was laying off several factory hands made redundant by the introduction of new machines. Moreover, the operation of the new machines required higher skills than blacks were allowed in law to possess. MaVy's husband began to besiege the Unemployment Bureau until he thought he'd never see the day when he didn't have to rise before five every weekday and take a train to town to go and line up outside the offices of the Bureau, with multitudes of other job-seekers, for a job which never came. He soon abandoned these fruitless efforts and took to drink the way a cat takes to milk. As far as his family responsibilities were concerned, he simply drifted into blissful oblivion and euphoric apathy.

That was when Violet left school and abandoned herself to shebeen-crawling and the orgy of weekend-long parties with the Hazels, on money they had forcibly extorted from kids or by mugging people returning from work on Friday evenings with their pay-packets bulging. She always brought her own earnings home intact. On that score her mother had nothing to complain about. If on most Friday and Saturday nights Violet didn't sleep at home, it was more than her mother could have been reasonably expected to know. She was now running a shebeen, which did a thriving all-night business, particularly at weekends. As her own business expanded, she left her job as a domestic servant in Parktown. On the Wednesday of the shootings she had witnessed the shootings from her window, which overlooked the main road. She had seen us flock into her yard and when the shooting stopped came out to attend to the injured.

When we arrived, Sindiswa threw herself into the small crowd of students who had gathered round her brother. One look at him, propped against the wall, his face ghastly pale and contorted with pain, and she burst into a most heart-rending wail.

'*Wu! Umntana' sekhaya*,' she cried, 'they've killed him, they've killed him!' She threw her hands into the sky and held them clasped on her head.

When his eyes lighted upon hers, he affected a smile but said nothing.

'My child, we must rush him to the hospital immediately,' Ma Vy said. She was kneeling beside him. 'In the meantime let us move him into the house.'

Sindiswa then did a most unpredictable thing. Like a woman possessed, she picked him up and carried him in her arms, as if he were a baby. She staggered a little but moved resolutely towards the gate facing the main road, which was deserted except for the police and some newspaper reporters.

A piebald township mongrel, lethargically scratching fleas, stood watch beside the gate. It looked up momentarily at Sindiswa and immediately lost interest.

She walked out of the yard, with tears streaming down her cheeks.

'*Yeyeni bo!*' MaVy exclaimed. 'Where's she taking him to?'

'I think she's going to get a taxi, auntie,' I replied softly.

'But we can't allow her to go alone.'

Khotso and I trooped after Sindiswa at a discreet distance, while MaVy and the others watched us apprehensively. We walked on with a great sense of foreboding. We expected the police to unleash a thunderbolt at us at any moment.

A few policemen detached themselves from the rest and came towards us. Many reporters, their cameras flashing, rushed forward despite efforts by the police to hold them back. I saw two policemen grab a black photographer like so much dirty washing, rip out the film from his camera and crush it under their heavy boots into near-pulp. But some of those photos, with Sindiswa carrying her dying brother in her arms, like a pilgrim bearing some sacrificial offering, found their way into the world's leading newspapers, as we were to find out later when we went into exile.

With our ugly presentiments still undiminished, Khotso and I closed ranks behind her.

The mongrel, still lounging unperturbed at the gate, did not so much as raise its head in our direction.

'Sis,' Sindi, let's put him down while we wait for transport.'

I sat on the pavement and invited her to rest him on my lap, which she did, with Khotso's help.

He was breathing with increasing difficulty. A faint smile played on his lips, but furrows of pain showed on his forehead and in his eyes. His wound was no longer bleeding freely. MaVy had tied a piece of cloth torn from one of her sheets round his tummy.

'*Wat makeer met hom?*' A white policeman asked when they reached us.

'*Uthi umlungu kwenzenjani?*' a black police sergeant called Hlubi translated.

Hlubi was the most dreaded policeman in Soweto. His name spelt blind terror. He was rumoured to be fearless and ruthless to the point of recklessness and sadism. Stories about him were legend. One story had it that enemy bullets turned to water before him and gun barrels puffed harmless smoke. Some said he could also turn into a black cat and stalk unwary criminals like a cat after mice. And once in their midst he would again assume human form. They said that during his annual leave he always went home to Soshangane to be strengthened by the most powerful doctors of that land of illustrious *inyangas*. In Alexandra township in the days of gang warfare between the Msomi gang and the Spoilers, when Hlubi was still a young private on the rise, they say he once came between the rival gangs, who were taking snipe-shots at each other across opposite ends of the street. The gangs switched targets and aimed at him. He stood there while bullets sailed harmlessly past until, their ammunition exhausted, the gangs fled. At the Back of the Moon, where the gangs used to drink during their momentary periods of truce, which could be as short-lived as each gang leader's state of sobriety, they used to post sentries all round the joint and around the police station to spy on the movements of the police. Despite such precautions Hlubi would suddenly appear, as if from nowhere, and blow his whistle to summon the other police, waiting in their squad cars and black marias a few streets away, to come and collect their haul. And not a single one of his victims ever managed to escape. In this way he came to be attributed with the distinction of having broken the Msomi gang and the Spoilers almost single-handed.

When the era of vicious gang warfare subsided in Alexandra, he was transferred to Newlands to help smash the criminal squads which had begun to rear their ugly heads in Western Native Township, Newclare and Sophiatown. With the help of the *knobkierrie*-wielding Zulus he smashed most of the gangs there, too, and unleashed a spate of atrocities such as the townships had never seen before and probably the whole of black Africa since the *lifaqane* wars. He used to accord special favours to Zulus coming to seek work in Johannesburg by arranging for them to obtain work-seeking and residence permits without difficulties (they then had no problem in finding a room, mainly in the newly opened hostel in Mzimhlophe), in exchange for their help in clubbing down any youth they met in the streets. The Zulus composed a new battle cry which sent cold chills down every young man's spine. They used to shout *'Ngashay' ikepisi kwaphum' utsotsi'*, meaning there's a *tsotsi* lurking beneath every cap so hit every man wearing a cap, you can't go wrong. Ayres and Smith experienced a sudden slump in their sales figures. As the township's youth wouldn't take all of this sitting down, a running battle developed between the Zulus and themselves, which called for more effective organisation from all sides.

Various mobile stores soon emerged all over the townships and did a roaring business in three-star knives, baby browns, knuckle-dusters and, for the very poor, socks loaded with sand, broken bicycle chains and *bog-draads*, very cheap but effective. The 'Russians', a gang of blanket-clad Basotho mainly from Newclare, who always moved about with their long sticks hidden under their blankets, brought them out in the open and fell upon both groups indiscriminately. Every other group hitherto uninvolved began to put out their battle regalia within easy reach. The Pedis, famous for their prowess with bare fisticuffs, went on a preventive rampage. This also put the Mpondos on a war footing, who drew out their *ntshumentshus*, made of thin but strong wires the size of bicycle spokes, which killed without

85

drawing blood or causing any superficial injuries. Their more peaceful cousins, the Bacas, who had made the gumboot dance famous and were employed by the City Council as nightsoil men, began to wreak havoc upon the townships with their *sjamboks* and buckets. There are many who have ascribed this outbreak of violence to Hlubi's squad. Hardened criminals who have survived their jail sentences bow their heads and lower their voices whenever they describe their treatment by Hlubi.

'What's the matter with him?' Hlubi repeated the white policeman's question.

Sindiswa simply blew, so unexpectedly the policemen were left gaping. Looking back, I believe her outburst then had something to do with the manner in which she was later hounded and harassed by the police, so that when she could no longer take it, she skipped the country, although to the best of my knowledge she had remained largely apolitical, unless joining in the singing of a few freedom songs at her brother's funeral and raising her fist in the black power salute, along with thousands of other mourners, can be construed as engaging in politics. Anyway, it cost Sindiswa dearly, including a broken nose.

'You have a bloody nerve!' she said. 'First you kill my brother, then you ask what's the matter with him!'

'Sis' Sindi, please calm down,' I said.

'You're nothing but common murderers!'

She spat venomously on the ground and paused for a while, as if savouring her unspoken poisonous thoughts.

'You!' She pointed to Hlubi and other black members of the police force, her eyes wet, her voice tear-stained and her expression virulent. 'You would shoot your own children for a miserly thirty pieces of silver. I could peel you like peaches and God himself would call it justice. You're incomplete; the human parts of you are missing. *Sies*!'

I was beginning to think that a taxi would never come or that if it did it would come too late to be of any use.

Up and down the street police were diverting traffic off the main road, I noticed with added despondency.

His breath was beginning to fail him. Despite the chilly weather sweat showed on his forehead.

Just then, to my infinite relief, Bra P. arrived in his BMW.

The police had allowed him through.

Bra P. was in many ways so enigmatic he might have been a character straight out of Cannery Row. He was held in awe and respect by both the old and the young of Soweto, although precisely on what his reputation rested nobody could say. But in their infinite wisdom, born of the most gruesome and excruciating experiences, township folk have grown to trust the rumoured word more than the printed one. The evidence of their own instincts, sharpened and refined by the demands for survival, carries more weight than the most thoroughly researched and carefully prepared programmes of the S.A.B.C. which claim to deal dispassionately in facts. Only a few facts were known about Bra P. and the rest was pure conjecture. However, the people knew, as if by intuition, that no legend, no matter how bloated in its subsequent editions, ever grew out of nothing. Bra P.'s life-style seemed to give a lot of credence to some of the things that were said about him. His wife had died many years ago, when we were still children chasing around tennis balls in the streets. She had left him no children and he had never remarried. He was decidedly one of the most well-to-do people in Soweto, with a passion for expensive German cars. Indeed, this could be said to have been his only form of indulgence for he neither drank nor smoked, nor was he known to ever chase after women. He owned the latest BMW model and a Mercedes 280 SL.

Bra P. was what the legal *gurus* usually describe as ' a native of no fixed occupation', although as far as anybody could tell he had never been pulled in for vagrancy or charged under the Influx Control regulations. He had a clean police record and exhibited remarkable smoothness in his operations and with his tongue, which in normal times would have enabled him to choose between the most popular pulpit in any parish and a seat in parliament, rising in either case to become a prince of the church or to the highest executive position in the land.

He had been born in the early days of old 'Kofifi', when African politicians, priests and pick-pockets lived cheek-by-jowl with Indian pacifists and Chinese philosophers. His relationships and contacts with people of other races and in every profession dated to those days in old Sophiatown. Bishops of certain churches anxious to avert looming schisms within their churches, politicians wanting to heal imminent rifts within their parties, government officials desiring to quash serious scandals implicating them in corruption, gangsters seeking the most effective methods of eliminating opposition – all had been known to seek advice from Bra P. Neither the restrictions imposed on others by the Group Areas Act nor the Job Reservation laws circumscribed his freedom of movement or association. But in other directions he had been hemmed in by all kinds of legislative constraints for so long that he had come to consider them as a kind of protective hedge. His association with crimes of every description was accepted as normal and admirable by township residents. From his early youth he had led the kind of gangsters you read about in Dugmore Boetie's Sophiatown sagas of which the Hazels of our time are but a poor apology and imitation. Everything he touched invariably turned out to be against the law as surely as if he'd had the Midas touch.

Bra P.'s prosperity was somehow connected to the fact that he had rejected the theories of honest labour and private ownership of removable property almost from infancy. He was master of every criminal technique in existence connected with larceny, fraud, robbery, safe-cracking, house-breaking and theft. He was reputed to be engaged in certain nefarious dealings with every big crime syndicate from Springs to Randfontein. His influence, which was rumoured to be quite considerable, was said to stretch as far as the diamond city of Kimberley and the *dagga*-growing districts of Pondoland and the Maluti mountains. In this regard it was also noted that he had once beaten the daylights out of a certain prominent but presumptuous journalist who'd had the effrontery to publish an exposé of organised crime on the Rand in which Bra P. was said to be implicated and to feature prominently. The same journalist had previously been showered with accolades for his daring revelation of the abuses of prison labour, of Africans convicted of petty offences under the pass laws, by white farmers in the potato-growing district of the Eastern Transvaal. But success, like the *skokiaan* many drank in those days – and the reporter in question was known to drink like a fish – can sometimes go to the head. As many people pointed out, not without fear of the wrath which such recklessness in the name of enterprising journalism could unleash on the heads of many innocents, it is one thing to expose the true and proven enemies of the people and another to turn in one who is black and struggling like yourself. And that is how the people tended to view a certain category of criminals who were known to behave sometimes like wilful children thwarted from achieving their fixed purposes, but who otherwise never terrorised the townships unless somewhat frustrated in their dealings when their blind rage, like a tornado, could strike everybody.

Bra P. had never been known to react violently in public; people who knew him preferred to keep it that way. But not so the journalist concerned. He filed a case of assault with the police and let it be known that he'd die defending the freedom of the press. It didn't matter that people told him that, after all, it was a white press. The reporter in question died a few weeks later, coming from a drinks party, of multiple stab wounds, and the murder was never solved. So that his case against Bra P. had to be thrown out of court for lack of evidence. A second more spectacular and devastating part of the article promised for the next issue of *Drum* never saw publication. But such rumours as the reporter had floated clung to Bra P., like the halo from an artist's impression of the archangel Michael.

Others said that no policeman dared to lay his fingers on him.

Bra P. was also a keen sportsman, had played centre-half for Sophiatown Rovers, and was now honorary President of the National Professional Soccer League, by virtue of having been one of its first major sponsors when it was formed, before white industrialists caught on to the bandwagon. He was behind the first soccer match between a white professional team and a black side, when Germiston Callies played Orlando Pirates in Maseru, and those in the know ascribe many of the advances made in multiracial sports in the country to his untiring efforts, especially behind the scenes. This alone made him a very important figure in the life of the township, where sport rivals politics in importance and is only rivalled by shebeens in vying for the undivided attention of township residents. Generally he was considered to be a greater celebrity and exercised more influence in our lives than either the Minister for Plural Relations, Sports and Culture or Soweto's Mayor, Mr Rathebe.

Bra P. had been directed to us by a group of students sent by Khotso to seek help. They had dashed about pleading with everybody they knew who owned a car to rush our injured friend to hospital. Many people with cars had gone to work, but the few who could be found were unwilling to meddle in a case which appeared to involve the police. Next to death itself what township people dread most are the police. You can never get anyone to lend you a hand in a case which shows all the likelihood of involving the police, no matter how remotely; just as you can never get anyone in their right senses to help you with those other minstrels of death known in township parlance as *tsotsis*, who kill as easily as it takes to say '*Voetsek*'. Between the police and the *tsotsis* it is difficult to decide exactly who rules the township – very often both have very well-defined spheres of influence and a kind of no-man's zone where they strike terror into the stoutest hearts; both are backed by a massive state machinery which would definitely recoil upon itself if it were to know the truth about the extent of its own involvement. Only one kind of being can be said to tower above the police and the *tsotsis* and is the spiritual mentor and the physical sustainer of both these groups. He is not the State President either, but is the man who consorts with both groups, from whom they derive their real powers. He can bring down the highest placed officers in the land at the drop of a hat and can break the most vicious gang of *tsotsis* as if they were made of so many twigs. Bra P. was just such a man.

He was strolling towards the main road to see what all the *rockshin'*, as he called it, was about, when he met the students who had been sent to organise transport, and without the slightest hesitation offered to help. They told him where to find us, so he sent them back and went for his car.

He stopped a few yards from us, came out of his car and walked towards us. He recognised Sindiswa immediately. She was still 'damnalising' the police, as township folk would say. Bra P. knew almost everybody in our township by name. As for us, we had grown up right before his very eyes, as they say.

'Sindi, get into the car, *asseblief tu*,' he said.

'Bra P., they've killed my brother, they've killed my brother, they've ki . . . lled him!'

'All right, all right, Sindi. Just come with me. Let's get the lad to the hospital. He's not going to die.'

He put his right arm around her shoulders and gently but firmly led her away. He opened the front door for her to get in.

She obeyed but continued to shout – '*Lezinja*, they've killed my brother, they've ki . . . lled him.'

Bra P. came back to help me and Khotso carry our friend into the car.

'How is he, boys?' he asked.

He stopped to take a closer look at him and asked – '*Kunjani*, Muntu?'

'*Yesslik!*' he moaned softly to himself.

He looked up at the police. His eyes narrowed, just a little, and his mouth twisted, ever so slightly.

We carried our friend to the back seat of the car and there laid him to rest.

'I'll need your help, boys.'

We needed no urging. Khotso and I got on either side of him in the back seat.

Muntu died on the way to hospital.

We waited in the bedroom at Bella Mohlakoane's home for the others to arrive. Khotso, Bella and myself. We had finished relating to Bella the circumstances of Muntu's death. Each one of us was now lost in his or her own thoughts.

In our organisation Bella was Deputy to Khotso. She was the third of five children, all girls. Her eldest sister was married in Dobsonville. The second eldest was at the University of Turfloop. Two years previously she had walked out of Turfloop, along with several hundreds of other students, in protest against the expulsion of certain student leaders for organising and participating in a pro-Frelimo rally, which the government had decided to ban a few hours before it was due to take place, to celebrate Mozambique's independence. But they were later all readmitted to the University, except for those who decided to stay away permanently. She's the one who was in prison, when we skipped the country. Of Bella's remaining sisters, Tshidi was in her final year J.C. and Queen was in Standard Six.

Their father was serving a life sentence in Robben Island. He had been accused of furthering the aims of a banned organisation, of conspiring to overthrow the government by violent means and of many other charges, twenty-two in all. He was found guilty on all the charges brought against him, except the main two. The two which were dismissed were the recruitment of people for military training and arranging for these recruits to leave the country illegally. The last two charges had arisen out of letters found in his possession. These letters, which were produced as evidence at his trial, were actually letters of application for his eldest daughter to schools outside South Africa and to various overseas scholarship-awarding bodies. In connection with this, a prominent member of the liberation movement in exile had written to offer his assistance in securing the girl a scholarship once a place had been found for her in a school outside South Africa. Several schools in Botswana and Swaziland had accepted her, but she was refused a passport.

During the trial the State tried to prove, on the strength of another letter written by Mr Mohlakoane, after her daughter had been refused a passport, accepting a place for her at one of the schools, that once her application for a passport had been turned down Mr Mohlakoane planned to send her out of South Africa illegally. He was also cross-examined closely about his reasons for choosing that particular school for his daughter where the Headmaster, a former South African, was a known political associate of Mr Mohlakoane's. To substantiate the latter fact the State whipped out its records of the Treason Trial of 1956 in which the accused, the Headmaster of the school concerned, together with more than a hundred others, had appeared on charges of high treason. All the accused in the case, after four years, had been acquitted. A whole other case was built up around the fact that the exiled leader who had offered to obtain a scholarship for Mr. Mohlakoane's daughter was, in fact, the military supremo of the liberation movement in question. In throwing out the State's case on these remaining two charges the presiding judge did not fail to point out that the State had failed to prove its case against the accused, *prima facie*. However, the learned judge continued, he had no doubt in his own mind that the conduct of the accused had been in all cases conspiratorial, seditious and ill-intentioned in the extreme. After pointing out a few loopholes in the existing legislation, he sentenced the accused to a life-term on the remaining twenty charges.

Bella's mother worked as a City Council nurse at the clinic in Orlando. She was a good-natured, affable lady in her mid-fifties, who bore her cross with the dignity of a madonna. Her house had become our secret rendezvous. I once asked Bella whether her mother didn't really mind having us at her house and what she thought of all our discussions. My own parents often told me to take my politics with me to hell. Bella told me that her mother never probed into the activities of any of her children, consequently they were all very open to her about everything they did. She usually received all their intelligence without comment, save on those issues on which they specifically sought her advice. Her own history of involvement and her organisational ability were vast. She was involved in various self-help projects, which ranged from simple church bazaars to being a consultant to Kupugani, a country-wide feeding scheme for the alleviation of malnutrition. Although she hadn't appeared alongside her husband and other prominent leaders in the Treason Trial, she and her husband had been very instrumental in our township in launching the Defiance Campaign four years previously. With other ladies like Lillian Ngoyi she had also organised the women for the great anti-pass demonstrations of the fifties when the government extended passes to women. After the demonstrations, in which the women from as far as Sekhukhuniland and Zeerust came out very strongly against the new measures, the government had promptly shelved the scheme, at least for a while. She had already served one five-year banning order imposed on her after the shootings at Sharpeville in 1960, but the government had subsequently decided to lift her ban. It was hard to see the uncompromising activist and fire-eater in her. To us she was simply Bella's mother, who smiled often and said very little; the midwife who trooped the streets of the townships at all sorts of awkward hours with her little black bag, bearing a baby for some fortunate family.

Duke was the first to arrive. He was carrying a newspaper under his armpits.

'*Heit! majita*. Hi! Bella,' he greeted.

'*Heita*,' we responded.

'Sorry I'm late. Haven't the others come yet?'

'Does it look like we're hiding them under the bed?' Bella asked.

'*Ja*! Things are really tough, when even your comrades turn against you,' Duke said.

'*Waat het jy daarso*?' Khotso asked.

'Just a copy of *The World* I bought at the corner as I

was coming here.'

'*Ithi sibone,*' I suggested.

Duke unfolded the newspaper. The headlines hit me like a fist: RIOTS BREAK OUT IN SOWETO. In smaller print was written: Police Shoot to Quell Rioting Students. We read on, with our heads huddled together:

The planned student demonstration against the enforcement of Afrikaans as a language of instruction in all African schools broke out into an ugly riot in Soweto this morning. Students braved the chilly weather and turned out in their thousands to march through the streets of Soweto, carrying placards bearing various anti-government slogans. At the start of the demonstration the police were alerted by one of the Principals of a school emptied by the marching students. They immediately sent a small detachment of the crack anti-riot squad, a newly formed paramilitary wing in charge of riot control, to the scene of the disturbances.

According to Colonel Fierce, Divisional Commander of police in Soweto, 'The students started hurling stones at passing cars. The police moved in to restore order. When the students paid no heed to the police order to disperse, the police fired warning shots in the air. But the students, in a dangerous frenzy, continued to surge forward and hailed more stones at the police. When their warning shots went unheeded the police, whose restraint had been taxed to the limit, had no option but to fire at the rioting mob.'

From Colonel Fierce's report the order to shoot was only given after all the other methods of mob control had failed. The police, Colonel Fierce said, were justified to shoot for their own protection.

In a telephone interview with one of our reporters the Minister of Police, Mr Jimmy Parkes, has blamed the riots on agitators belonging to certain prohibited organisations committed to the violent overthrow of the government. He warned against Communist infiltration and promised that the State would not hesitate to act with all the power at its disposal to crush the Communist-inspired onslaught against the forces of law and order. 'The Bantu knows his place, and if not I'll tell him,' he added. 'The Bantu always sings "We Shall Overcome", but I say *we* shall overcome.'

Asked to comment on the number of students killed in the shooting Mr Parkes said, 'They leave me cold.'

He also reiterated Colonel Fierce's statement and said that according to his information the police, both black and white, had conducted themselves with the greatest measure of patience in the face of the greatest measure of provocation.

Our reporters also interviewed two officials of the Department of Bantu Education. Deputy Minister Johannes Onsskwiel, Chairman of the Broederbond and the brains behind the introduction of Afrikaans, told our reporters that, 'It is in the Bantu's own interest that he should learn Afrikaans. And where government builds schools and pays subsidies, is it not their right to determine in which language pupils must be taught?'

The Chief Inspector of Bantu Education in the West Rand, Dr Eiselen, frankly confessed that he was puzzled. 'Have you ever heard of 13-year old children striking?'

Blaming the student uprisings on agitators he said: 'The public does not realise that there are many people who want to spread unrest in South Africa. I don't know who is behind the strike – but it is not the children.'

Two policemen were injured in the scuffle. Official figures released estimate the number of students killed at 114. Minister Parkes said about 30% had died from police bullets and the rest in faction fights among blacks themselves, from stabbings and from bullets of a calibre not used by the police.

'*Hulle gat, man*!' Bella's voice broke in.

'How the hell can they say we are to blame for our own deaths?' Khotso asked. 'Did these students kill themselves?'

'Shit, man!' Bella said and stomped out of the room.

The front page also carried a picture of students in their school uniforms with clenched fists raised to the air in the black power salute. Two placards showed in the picture. One read: AFRIKAANS IS OPPRESSOR'S LANGUAGE; the other one said: IF WE MUST DO AFRIKAANS, VORSTER MUST DO ZULU.

There were more pictures in the next page of students running helter-skelter with police dogs hot on their heels.

A report in the second page carried the news of the death of Dr Edelstein, who ran a voluntary medical scheme in Soweto. His body was discovered in a rubbish bin outside one of the yards in the township. Another report on the third page was about the Superintendent of White City Jabavu. When shooting broke out he had come out of his office to watch. He must have thought that the battle was just between the students and the police. He couldn't possibly have imagined that his own life was in mortal danger, as he stood with his African aides outside his office to witness the one-sided running battle between the students and the police. He was hit on the side of his face by a flying missile. Dazed and incredulous, the Superintendent was caught on the *stoep* and killed on the spot.

The newspapers were very selective and incurred our deepest mistrust, although some did ultimately modify their stance. When I later saw that evening's *Star* I was amazed to read the same facts, albeit in greater detail, as we had seen in *The World*; same pictures and everything.

The following morning the *Rand Daily Mail* carried slightly more facts and pictures. There were more interviews with white officials in government and in the police force. The Deputy Minister of Bantu Education was interviewed at length. And although the editorial called for his resignation because of his intransigence – he was even nicknamed 'Dr No' – the full text of his statement was given prominence in the centre spread of the paper. The views of blacks were represented by officials of certain church organisations, civic leaders on government-approved bodies and some Bantustan chiefs, one of them a former educationist and sub-inspector of schools. For the rest the strongest criticism was reserved for the Minister of Police for his 'regrettable' utterances when he had said that the deaths of the students had left him cold. The statement was seized upon with sickening regularity by all the other English language newspapers as an example of bad tactics on the part of the government.

On the actual number of whites killed on the day of the riots, as anybody from Soweto will tell you, there are thousands of whites in Soweto at any time of the day: whites employed as petty bureaucrats by the West Rand Administration Board (which runs the townships), whites in charge of various construction projects, whites in various other supervisory capacities, salesmen, businessmen, researchers, voluntary welfare workers and so on. It was simply too preposterous to imagine, as the newspapers said, that only two whites had been killed. As far as I know, not a single white caught in Soweto on that day was left alive.

All over the townships of Soweto bonfires of motor cars and delivery vans, set alight when their white passengers were stopped and dragged out, could be seen.

Along the old Potchefstroom road, which goes through Soweto, white drivers and their families travelling to the city or back were stoned. Not many managed to escape with their lives. And as the police had temporarily withdrawn from Soweto while awaiting reinforcements from the army, this state of affairs might have continued indefinitely if they had not sealed up all the entrances into Soweto and turned back all the whites driving into or through the townships.

Thereafter the incensed crowds turned their anger on the PUTCO buses. Passengers could be seen scuttling for safety, hot on the heels of bus drivers and conductors.

They say even Lee Chong, the old Chinese who runs fah fee, was badly shaken up by the crowd. Only his constant vigilance saved him from reaping the grapes of wrath.

To the people returning home from work in the city of Johannesburg that evening, the events in Soweto came as a complete surprise. As thousands of men and women poured out of Inhlazane station, one of several stations serving the Soweto complex, they were met by security police. No attempt was made to explain the situation. As a huge crowd gathered around them, in the manner of curious township crowds, the police charged with batons. Teargas was thrown but the crowd of commuters retaliated with bricks and stones, and before long older people had joined the students and youths on the streets of Soweto.

Many of these incidents were left out of the papers.

Right up to the end of the Soweto crisis official estimates of the dead and injured, both blacks and whites, as reported in the news media, differed from the figures we compiled. In general we counted more casualties than were reported in the news media.

Bella returned to the bedroom accompanied by Micky and his girlfriend, Nina, who was our Secretary. Micky was also carrying a copy of *The World*, which he was waving excitedly.

'Have you guys seen this?'

'I told you we've seen it, Micky,' Bella said.

'*Ja*, but I'm asking the others.'

'*Hawu*! Micky, they've already seen it,' Nina said.

'Why hasn't anybody asked us to tell them our side of the story?'

'Because nobody gives a damn for your opinion,' Nina said. 'Now forget it, Micky.'

'Shut up yourself.'

'All right now, cool it there,' Khotso said.

'Some people just want to be chased with a *sjambok*,' 'strues God.'

'*Ora nna*, Micky?'

'I'm not talking to you! . . . Or somebody should plant a petrol bomb at the home of just one of them, for a lesson. I can't believe that these guys who've filed in this shittish report are just as black as us.'

'I've just heard it said that they've no real say in the final form a report takes,' Duke said. 'That's the job of the editor.'

'But he's also black,' Micky said.

'They say he, too, has no control over . . . what do they call it? . . . Something like a newspaper's manifesto.'

'Editorial policy,' Khotso said.

'Yes, that's it,' Duke said. 'The editorial policy is determined by the prop . . .'

'Proletarians?' Micky asked.

'No, sounds more like "property",' Duke said. 'That's the white guys who own the newspaper, you know, like Louis Luyt.'

'He owns *The Citizen*,' Micky said.·

'Yes, they're all of a kind. Anyhow, it's these guys, the prop . . .'

'Proprietors,' Khotso said.

'Yes, they're the real owners.'

'But why then is it called "Our One and Only Paper"? We should really call upon our guys to start a truly black paper.'

'There's the question of finance, Mickey,' I said.

'Come again?'

'Money. *Miering*.'

'There are numerous tycoons in Soweto from whom they could get all the money they need, if they really wanted.'

There was no way anyone could gainsay Micky once he started talking in this way. So I looked for a way to start the meeting.

'Ladies and gentlemen, we'll just have to start. We can't wait all day for the others, when we don't even know for sure that they'll show up.'

The others agreed the meeting should start.

'I met Tsietsi on my way here,' Duke said. 'He asked me to tell you he'd be late because he has to accompany his mother to visit his brother in hospital.'

'Any other apologies?' I asked. But there were none.

'Okay, then, I declare the meeting opened. I don't want to make a speech. You all know what's happened, so there's no need for me to go into that either. We're all very sore over what's happened, but it won't do us any good to sit here eating our hearts out. We've got to show some positive thinking. I want to suggest, therefore, that the big question which this meeting must resolve is what are we to do next because the others are looking to us for some decisive action. So I'll ask everyone to kindly keep to the point.'

'Mr Chairman,' Duke said. 'While I agree with your words, I also wish to say it's no use pretending. We're just going to go on and on telling minor stories to avoid a major one, avoiding the major subject. It may be a painful subject but let's dispense with it once and for all. We've a skeleton in our wardrobe, ladies and gentlemen. The System has inflicted some mightily heavy blows on us. We've suffered very grave and severe losses. I think the Chairman is right in one important respect, we don't need to go into the details. But I want to say just this one thing, we do need to lick our wounds. Crying can be therapathe . . . terror . . . peutic.'

Micky asked what 'terrorpathetic' was, very softly, so as not to interrupt.

'Something like Dettol,' Khotso whispered back.

'There are many families tonight, all over Soweto, who

are mourning the loss of loved ones. I move that the first item on our agenda should be the problem of helping such families.'

'I second that emotion,' Micky said when Duke had finished.

Nina prodded Micky slightly with her elbow and asked if she could be allowed to speak next.

'Duke has raised a very important point,' she said. 'As I see it, this may yet turn into a very long battle between ourselves and the System. In which case we'll need just about everybody's support. One way of building up such solidarity for the battles ahead is to come to the assistance of our own aggrieved people. Not just to improve our public image, but because we believe it is the correct and decent thing to do . . .'

'As far as the funerals of our own members are concerned, Mr Chairman,' Bella said, 'I think it is only proper that we should run these ourselves, perhaps organise a mass funeral.'

'Hold on, I think we're leaping too far ahead . . .'

'I hadn't quite finished, Mr Chairman,' Nina resumed. 'In line with what Duke has already said, I wish to propose, as a matter of extreme urgency, that we set up a special fund to help all the bereaved families of Soweto as a result of what's happened. Our members must be requested to make a door-to-door collection for the purpose.'

'That's all right, as far as it goes,' Khotso said. 'But if we're talking in terms of raising funds to meet hospital, funeral and other expenses, we need to know exactly how many families have been afflicted.'

'Correct, Mr Chairman,' Duke said. 'Nobody must be left out. As we all know, some people, not necessarily members of our organisation, were hit by stray bullets from the police. They need our help, too. But the other point Khotso has just raised can be attended to in this way. When we make our rounds to collect donations we should also take down the names and addresses of all those who have been affected by the disaster. One further point. From now on there may be no time to convene a general meeting for all members, so we must spread the word through the usual channels as soon as this meeting is over.'

Then it was Micky's turn to speak. He said he had no quarrel with anything that had been said so far. Nina shouted that we had not come here to quarrel, but Micky overlooked her remark and continued. He said he didn't think that what had already been said went far enough. 'We must destroy the snake and not just scorch its head.' He said that he shared the Chairman's view about the need to look beyond the present, to see beyond what would happen after we'd bought and supplied all the Dettol that was needed.

He ignored the puzzled expressions and continued. 'There's the matter of these reporters, for instance,' he said shaking *The World* vehemently before us. 'How are we to make sure that they don't spread lies about us next time? I've already suggested one solution. I agree with the person who said that there must be complete solid . . . , you know, the togetherness thing. First, we must make next week a national week of mourning. As everybody knows, when people mourn they don't go to work. When my grandfather died my parents didn't go to work for a whole week and we didn't go to school either. Of course, for us school is out of the question now. But what I'm saying should also take care of this other question of our parents, who continue to work for whites and so on. Suspend all sports and shows as well, so that people can sit back and think a little. Then there are lots of guys who continue to enjoy themselves at shebeens, beerhalls and so on while others suffer. These drinks are made to drug people's minds so that they don't ask too many questions or do something about their oppression. We need to be one people. I also think there are far too many offices belonging to the government in Soweto. Of course, there'll be many people who won't see things our way. I remember, my grandfather used to say there are many people in this world who need to have some sense knocked into their heads. Something must also be done about blacks who serve as police, school board members, the guys in the Useless Boy's Club, you know, the Urban Bantu Circus, and all the other sell-outs, maybe our Principals and teachers, too. I could mention others . . .'

'Not so fast, Micky-boy,' I said. 'We must resolve one thing at a time. I'm sure you're right on a number of issues. But we've got to take one case at a time and plan our strategy very carefully in each case.'

A silence fell over the meeting. Micky's speech had stirred us in a strange kind of way, had stirred deep chords in us. Without realising it and in his usual blunt manner, he had just about summarised the various courses of action open to us. And in doing so he had more than spelt out the gravity of our situation as well as our dilemma. From now on there could be no two ways. Complete capitulation or a war of attrition to the bitter end.

'Does anybody wish to respond to what Micky's just said or shall we ask him to go over the main points of what he's proposing?'

'Mr Chairman, I think I've had my say. Now if I may be excused from this meeting. I've some business to attend to.' And so saying Micky rose and left.

No sooner had he walked out than everybody began to talk at once. I tried in vain to bring some semblance of order into the proceedings. Discussions grew more and more heated as other members arrived and joined us. Voices rose and fists flew into the air. I was about to throw my hands into the air, too, when Bella's mother, who had already come back from work, appeared and stood at the door. A hush fell over the room.

'My dear children, I know I've no right to interfere. You've all been under a terrible strain from the day's events. Do not let it get you down lest your enemies triumph over you. Now, if you'll agree to break your discussion for a while I'll bring you something to eat. Bella, can you come and help your sisters in the kitchen?'

She smiled most agreeably, then went out, followed by Bella and Nina.

But what else was there to talk about? So that very soon the silence was again broken as people resumed their argument in smaller groups of two or three.

Tsietsi, who was among those who had arrived late, pulled me aside and told me he wanted to speak to me outside. We went out.

It was already getting dark outside. The atmosphere was thick and heavy with smog. The cold bit into the flesh with a deadening numbness.

Tsietsi's story nearly made by bowels run and almost shattered what still remained of my equanimity. I'd been steeling myself the whole day against just such an eventuality. And so far no crack had shown through my armour. I just had to keep it that way.

'By the simple exercise of our will we can exert a power over good practically unbounded.' Where had I read that?

You've got to play this cool, I kept telling myself. There's simply too much at stake. There are too many people who are going to take their cue from you.

'Better tell this to the others,' I said to Tsietsi. We walked back into the house.

I called the meeting to order and told them Tsietsi had something to tell them which I was sure would interest them all.

'Ladies and gentlemen. I'll be brief. You all know that my brother was shot in the leg this morning. I rushed him to Baragwanath, left him there and rushed back home to tell my mother. This afternoon my mother and I went to see him in hospital. The place was swarming with cops. At the casualty department where I'd left him he was not there. They told us he'd been treated and discharged. As we were leaving, we saw a nurse who lives back-opposite to our house. She told us she'd been on the look-out for us because she'd seen my brother, handcuffed, being led away by the police. The hospital authorities, she said, have instructions to report to the police all cases admitted with bullet wounds. When we got back home our next-door neighbour told us that some police had been to our house. I've a *'mangoane* who comes immediately after my mother. Her husband is a policeman. Shortly before I came here, *'mangoane* came to our house and told us that she'd been sent by *rangoane* to tell us that the police were after me. They've been forcibly extorting confessions from all those they've arrested, mostly people picked up from the hospital, to reveal who their leaders are. My information is that sooner or later they'll be after everybody in this room. That's all I had to say.'

Dead silence.

They brought us *pap* and *boerewors*. We ate in silence.

'The only thing is for a guy to disappear to the farms until this dust storm settles down,' at length Duke spoke, wiping his mouth with his shirt sleeves. 'I've relatives at Badplaas, that's quite near the border with Swaziland. But my mother's people come from Shupingstad, close to the border with Botswana. From either of those places a guy could make a quick dash into Swaziland or Botswana once things start hotting up there too.'

'The only relatives I know of all live in Johannesburg,' Nina said.

When everybody had eaten I suggested we resume our meeting, which then proceeded to the end on a more placid note.

It was getting late and we still had to communicate our resolutions to various cell leaders, who would in turn disseminate the information to our rank and file members. So I asked Nina to read out the resolutions so that even those who had arrived late could know what had been decided in their absence.

We agreed to meet again the following day. As we couldn't agree on the venue, we decided to leave the matter hanging until a suitable venue could suggest itself.

In the light of Tsietsi's report, it was also agreed that our homes had definitely become unsafe, and that we'd have to seek alternative accommodation soon, at least until the dust storm settled down.

That night an unprecedented outbreak of arson and looting hit the townships at different places, almost simultaneously.

As darkness fell over Soweto a group of students arrived at Rathebe's filling station shortly before closing time.

Winter was in the air everywhere and the thick, dense smoke from coal fires enveloped the townships. Crowds of people returning from work or going to the shops or on some other errands criss-crossed the streets around Rathebe's petrol station and shopping complex.

As a fuel conservation measure all filling-stations closed at six p.m. Very stiff fines were imposed for breaking the regulations, although township people did it all the time whenever the price was right.

A long line of taxis were waiting their turns at the petrol pumps, a wild cacophony of horns blaring their impatience.

The students carried empty jerry-cans and waited under the dark shadows cast by the adjoining petrol building, avoiding the bright lights of the cars.

The authorities had lengthened the lamp posts of the street lights quite considerably so as to put them out of the reach of stone-throwing township vandals. But someone had already destroyed several of the street lights around Rathebe's garage and the surrounding area was cast in darkness. However, the people of the area did not appear unduly inconvenienced. They knew the topography of the area like the palms of their hands.

At length all the cars at the petrol station were served.

A Valiant pulled in just as the garage attendants were locking up the pumps. After a little bickering with the two petrol attendants the driver of the Valiant was served. A fat bribe exchanged hands and he drove off.

There were two petrol attendants who actually served the customers at the pumps. They brought the money they collected to a third man, who sat behind the till in the adjoining building, a pistol within easy reach but hidden from the public. A Zulu nightwatchman, who had just come on duty, stood sentry behind the man at the till as he counted the day's takings.

On the average Rathebe's petrol station was the target of two successful armed robberies a month, with the result that the till was emptied three times a day. There was a mid-morning take, a mid-afternoon check and the evening's haul. Rathebe had once applied for guns for all his petrol attendants plus his nightwatchman, but a licence had been granted for only one. Even the Zulu *mantshingilane* had to rely on his *knobkierie* and *assegai*. Only the other day they had found the *mantshingilane* in the morning, kneeling beside the fence. His ear lobes, which were pierced in tribal fashion, had been fastened to the fence with a padlock by a group of night prowlers who had broken into the garage and made away with some spare parts and a few tools. The man who sat at the till was Rathebe's longest serving petrol attendant and his most trusted. He had been with the filling-station for nearly twelve months. His predecessor, after an unbroken spell of ill-luck which had brought him a string of robberies on five consecutive week-ends, had finally decided to abscond with the petrol money himself.

At length the petrol attendants prepared to leave. They had just locked up everything for the night and were taking leave of the nightwatchman when the students emerged from the dark like a small invading army. They disarmed the *mantshingilane* very quickly, even before he had realised what was happening. They warned the gunman at the till that at the most he stood to fire only three rounds. 'And then after that, grr . . . r . . . tlaka,' one onomatopoeic student said enacting a violent struggle with the men.

'We don't want your money,' another said. 'We're not criminals. Just a few litres of petrol.'

It was a fortunate thing all three attendants had been brought up in the townships. What were a few litres of petrol compared with their lives? Moreover, Rathebe need never know what had transpired. They could refund every cent of the petrol they'd given away. After all, the kids were not asking for money from petrol sales already made. And to think they had devised this other method of making extra cash, which worked out very well especially in the dark as the petrol pumps had no lights! They had disconnected them themselves. Their method was very simple. When a customer came to fill up, all they did was to pour the petrol, shout out the cost and quickly bring the price on the pumping machine back to zero. If the customer demanded to see for himself on the machine how much the petrol had cost, didn't they only have to apologise very profusely to him for their thoughtlessness? Even the most enraged customer was invariably disarmed by the *fait accompli*. So what did a few litres which the students wanted really matter?

But the *mantshingilane* had other ideas. However, his colleagues did not give him a dog's chance to expound on any of his inane notions. They told him, to the great amusement of the students, to keep his objections to himself because Soweto was not Nongoma. After all, they told him, they'd take all the rap for any shortages, not him.

One of the men addressed the students. 'Just ignore this one,' he said. 'He lives out there at the hostel in Mizimhlophe and can't even tell his left shoe from his right one.'

'Fancy yourself a warrior, *baba*, eh? . . . Inkatha kaZulu, eh?' the students jeered.

'*Baba*, look here, kl . . .,' the onomatopoeic student said, flashing a knife blade before the nightwatchman's eyes and making a cutting motion round his own neck.

That silenced the *mantshingilane*.

An interesting sequel to this and similar episodes, although I'm now running far ahead of my story, was that court case which many may have read about in which Micky and a group of other students appeared at Kempton Park charged with intimidation, vandalism and participation in or inciting others to commit acts of arson against State property. Some people may still remember the nightwatchman who gave evidence at the trial to the effect that he and his co-workers had given petrol to a group of students on the night of June 16th, 1976 and on several other occasions thereafter. But the two surviving petrol attendants – their colleague, who had been the longest-serving employee among them, having left his job before the month of June was over –

had flatly denied giving away petrol for free on that or any other occasion. They had brought out a whole year's sales figures to prove their case.

The students left Rathebe's petrol station with fifty litres of petrol.

That same night in the Soweto townships of Emndeni, Zola, Naledi, Tladi, Moletsane, Jabulani, Zondi, Mapetla, Molapo, Phiri, Senaoane, Chiawelo, Dlamini, Moroka, White City Jabavu, Mofolo, Dube, Orlando East and West, Klipspruit, Pimville, Diepkloof, Meadowlands – municipality offices and other buildings associated with the System mysteriously caught fire.

Only one fire station serves the whole of the Soweto complex, so that Soweto's fire department was caught terribly unprepared. As Soweto's chief fire officer explained through the press, only that same morning he had approved several applications for leave from a number of his black subordinates anxious about the welfare of their children when reports reached them about the outbreak of the student disturbances, which had left the fire station near Jabulani with a mere skeleton staff. At least three out of his twelve fire-engines had been out of order for the last fortnight and the mechanics from the city's fire department had been promising to come and repair them ever since. When the telephone first rang to report the outbreak of fire at the two Moroka offices in Rockville, he'd immediately sent all the fire-engines there. So that when subsequent calls came through from the other municipality offices there were simply no more fire-engines to send. He had called for assistance from various other stations in the city. But the response had not been quick enough. 'Perhaps if these fires had not occurred almost simultaneously,' the chief of the fire brigade in Soweto was quoted as having said, 'we just might have been able to cope.'

An ironic twist to these events was provided by the fire-station itself catching fire.

At White City Jabavu, where a white superintendent had been killed earlier in the day, when a small batch of students arrived the municipality constables on night duty dashed out through the windows. In the process a considerable number of windows were broken, even before the students started dashing everything about. The escaped blackjacks arrived at the nearby police station in Moroka on foot. In fact, one of them actually walked all the way barefooted because he'd been busy cutting his toe-nails when the students dashed in. But by the time the blackjacks reached the police station the offices at White City Jabavu had already been gutted down.

As the students ransacked the offices at White City Jabavu for the township's records and prepared to set the building on fire, a hijacked bus, driven by a student, came rumbling in through the front of the administration building. It went up in flames with the rest of the building.

With the municipality offices went all the township's records of house allocation lists, rents and all the rest. Several months were to pass before anybody in Soweto paid rent. There were many people who'd been two, three months in arrears with their rents. When three months later everyone was asked to report to the authorities with their receipts, these people claimed that they'd lost their receipts. As a compromise everybody was then asked to pay rent from the first of June. But even then many people claimed that they'd already paid their rents six months in advance. They were asked to pay all the same and the authorities promised to set up a commission of enquiry. That was the last anybody heard of the matter.

Several people, not registered as residents in Soweto before the outbreak of the student disturbances, applied for new passes and claimed to have been so registered. They were duly issued with residence permits.

Our school and several others also went up in flames. There was a caretaker at each school who lived in a house provided by the school board on the school premises. Our caretaker was first asked if he had any relatives in Soweto. When he said he had a brother at Emndeni, which is on the other extreme end of Soweto furthest from town, he was told to take his family and go and stay with his brother, for good.

Under cover of darkness bands of people roamed the streets removing usable furniture from smashed and burnt buildings.

The attacks on the beer halls and bottle stores produced an interesting assortment of allies. The Hazels came, already prepared with petrol cans, empty cardboard boxes and a truck, the moment our boys approached the bottle store in Dube. Afterwards nobody could tell how they had got wind of what was going to take place. Micky, who might have shed some light on the matter, has remained extremely reticent ever since his trial, which had brought him within a hair's breadth of the hangman's noose. In other areas shebeen queens turned up in large numbers. On several occasions that year the students imposed a boycott on alcohol as a mark of respect for the dead who had fallen that same year. The purchase of alcohol from bottle stores in town was banned; students searched commuters returning from town for hidden parcels of liquor, confiscated any they found and gave the alcohol away in the streets. But there were shebeens which could still fall back on their June stocks. A new phrase, '*utshwala bePower*', was coined to refer to the large quantities of liquor requisitioned in the name of Black Power.

Flames over the most architecturally sophisticated structure in Soweto, the Council Chambers of the U.B.C., could be seen from all the twenty-eight townships which comprise Soweto.

We left Bella's house in a group. She saw us to the gate and bade us farewell.

'Who of you, blokes, will be going to Muntu's?' Khotso asked.

'I am, but I'd like to go and clock at home first,' I said.

'Oh, sure, we all are,' Duke said. 'In fact, why don't we all meet at Muntu's about an hour from now?'

'I honestly can't make it, chaps,' Tsietsi said. 'My Mom's worried to distraction. She wouldn't let me out of her sight, so that I had to dodge her to come here. I've got to go back and discuss a few things with her and my father.'

'What of all the people you're supposed to contact tonight to convey the meeting's decisions?' Duke asked.

'I'll do that right away and then go straight home.'

'That's all right, Tsi,' Khotso said. 'We understand.'

'I don't know if I'll be able to come either,' Nina said. 'My parents will be fuming when I get back home. I didn't prepare supper and they don't allow me to go out at night. Who's going in my direction? I'm afraid of the Hazels at night.'

'I'll walk you home,' Duke said. 'Say Nina, where d'you think Micky was in such a hurry to go to?'

'You'll soon know, all of you, before the night is over,' she said. 'He's said nothing to me, but I know. You know how secretive he is. Like the time he gave a wrong answer to an exam question because he wanted to hide the correct one. That's Micky for you. But he can't fool me. Anyhow, see you folks, whenever that'll be.'

'Honey, you sound as though when next we meet we'll all be in the next world,' Khotso said.

'Who knows?'

We parted. Khotso and I went together. He lived in the street next to ours.

'Let's touch Shakes' place first,' he said. 'He's my number one contact man.'

But when we got there Shakes was not at home.

'He was here only a while ago,' his granny said. 'And left without saying where he was going to, just when I thought I'd send him for my snuff. Perhaps if you boys are going anywhere near the shops you might . . .'

'Unfortunately, granny, we're not,' Khoto said. 'We're going to the home of one of our friends who was shot dead by the police this morning.'

'I see, my child. My ears can no longer hear properly. I heard there was a lot of shooting going on in the location. Nobody's been able to tell me yet why they shot the little ones. What had your friend done?'

'Nothing, Granny.'

'Nothing?'

'Would we do anything against the law, granny? . . . And now we must be off. Remain well, granny.'

'Go well, my children.'

Khotso bumped into me as we made our way out of the house.

'Who's next?' I asked when we reached the street.

'Neo.'

Neo lived only three houses away.

He was finishing his supper when we arrived. He quickly wolfed down what remained of his food and followed us out.

'Hey, *wena*,' his mother shouted after him, 'don't forget what I just told you. Don't go beyond that gate.'

'Okay, Mama, I heard you.'

'You just came in the nick of time, gents,' Neo said when we got to the gate. 'My parents have been preaching at me so much my ears are almost blocked. To hear them talk you'd think there was something worth preserving. If they'd devoted more of their time to the overthrow of the System first instead of trying to carve themselves a comfortable niche in this faggot-ridden country, we wouldn't have been in this mess. My father, for instance. He's sore because on his way from work they stopped his car and searched him like a low-down *dagga* smuggler. Looks like they've thrown a cordon round Soweto. But he should have made his stand decades ago and nobody would be treating him like a common criminal today. Instead what's he done? Spent a lifetime accommodating himself to the System. What's so precious about his slave chains, anyway? It isn't as if they were valuable bangles . . .'

It was obvious Neo's repression had only worked to build up a well of resentment inside him. When he had spoken on in this vein for a full ten minutes, he came to a sudden halt.

'Have *bo*-Micky left already?' he asked.

'Ahem . . . *Ja*, Micky left before the meeting was over,' Khotso said.

'*Kyk net daar*! I hope they don't imagine a fellow's trying to chicken out. I just couldn't shake off my parents.'

'That's all right.'

Khotso went on to outline our plans.

'How soon d'you think you can get away?' he asked.

'No problem. I'm not going back there. As for communicating all this stuff you've just told me, why, I should imagine everyone I need to tell this to is at this very moment at the assembly point. I'm coming along with you right away.'

'Well . . . ahem . . . we're not going to the . . . er . . . assembly point just yet. We have a few other things to attend to . . . er . . . right away.'

'I understand. Such a pain in the arse, my parents! Okay, see you later, gents.'

Neo shot off like a bazooka.

'Think that Micky is up to any good?' Khotso asked.

'Your guess is as good as mine,' I answered.

'He had no right not to confide in us. He should have tabled his plans before the executive for approval, like everthing else. It's dangerous for anyone to act so unilaterally like Rhodesia's rebel leader Ian Smith.'

'Why really bother, chap? You know Micky's the perfect anarchist and all that. What does he care for the niceties of democratic procedure? He'd probably stare at you with complete incomprehension if you so much as mentioned the phrase to him. I don't believe he trusts even his own mother. His name should go down in history with Machiavelli. It takes all kinds. But Micky's no blabbering idiot.'

'Oh! sure. But all the same I can't help feeling nervous over all this uncertainty and lack of information. I feel as if we're poised on the brink of a major disaster. Like sitting on a powder keg near a fire or living in the last days of Pharoah's reign over the ancient Jews.'

'Except that we'll never achieve our objectives through divine intervention. That belongs to biblical times. You know, chap, I don't really care for Micky's methods; I wouldn't use them myself. But I sincerely believe we need our Mickys somewhere along the line. Don't look so morose, *fana*. Come along, we must get someone to tell us what's been happening. We've been shut indoors for far too long. To tell the truth, my own nerves have been on edge, too. But what the hell! *Aluta!*'

We turned into our street so engrossed in our conversation that we didn't even hear my younger brother's approaching footsteps until he was quite close. Not that we would have recognised him from a distance. His appearance was as foreboding as a telegram. He wore a balaclava, which he hated normally because he said it made him look like a *moegoe*, and an old army overcoat which had once belonged to my father, its lapels pulled up to his cheeks. I remember how as a kid I used to imagine that army overcoat as containing a thousand, tiny, unerasable bloodstains of soldiers killed in the war. The idea persisted long after I'd discovered my father had only been a cook in the army at a camp for recruits near Pretoria, thousands of miles from the nearest front. In his attire my younger brother had about him the air of Boris Karloff or Peter Cushing in a horror movie filmed live, with no stunts but the real thing.

'Vukani, what on earth's the matter with you?' I asked when I had recovered from my initial shock, a little anger now rising inside me. 'Why are you dressed up like that?'

'A good thing I found you both, together,' he said. He rubbed his hands together in the melodramatic manner of Richard Widmark. 'Gee! It's freezing out here, but I also needed this garb for a disguise. The place is crawling with cops, man.'

'Cut out that Hollywood act. What d'you want?'

'I've been on the look-out for you in the streets since before sunset . . . We can't talk here. Let's move over there, out of the light.'

'For goodness sake, man, will you try and make some sense?'

However, we followed him into the shadows, along the fence of the nearest house.

'See that car at the end of the street?' he resumed. 'Not Mthombeni's old crock . . . the other one, the whitish Volksy? It's been parked there since four o'clock.' He dipped his hands into the pockets of the overcoat and brought out a shrivelled, dirty little piece of paper. 'Here, I noted down the registration number. O.A. 5603. Now, tell me, why would guys from Bethlehem want to come and park in the middle of Soweto for four hours?'

'You tell us.'

'There are two guys in there, with dark glasses on, who must be SBs. They've been watching every movement in this street and taking down notes. They've also got a radio in there from which they've been relaying messages.'

'How d'you know all that?'

'I've been past them twice already. Not in this disguise. I've had to change three times. Don't worry, they couldn't have known who I was. In one of my disguises I even came right up to our house, asked Mommy for a glass of water, and she didn't recognise me until I was on my way out. But I didn't look back even when she called after me.'

My brother was just made for theatricals, but at that moment he seemed determined to outdo even himself.

Next he turned to Khotso. 'Your mother was at our house looking for you. They've been to your house as well.'

'Have they been to our house?' I asked.

'Two groups already, not counting the SBs at the corner. We thought we'd warn you both to take care when coming back home.'

'Who's at home?'

'No one, they've all gone to Muntu's. I guess those guys have a secret camera hidden somewhere and have been photographing everybody going to Muntu's. But no matter, they couldn't identify me in a thousand years.'

'Are there many people there?'

'Oh! It's simply crowded with people.'

'Good, now listen very carefully and stop your prattling for a while. I'd like you to go back home and do something for me. Just walk across to that yard opposite. And then scale over the fences until you reach home. Don't let anybody see you just to prove how good your costume is. Understand?'

'What about Ntate Sebotsane's dog?'

Ntate Sebotsane was our next-door neighbour on the side Vukani would approach our house. He kept a vicious dog. When were were younger we used to go at night to steal peaches in his yard. One night I was high up the tree when I heard Vukani shouting from our yard – he was supposed to be collecting the peaches as I dropped them – that the dog had broken its chain and was waiting for me at the foot of the tree. Several times I tried to come down but each time the dog growled at me so ferociously it sent me scuttling up the tree. Goodness knows how long the situation might have lasted, but in desperation Vukani shouted to Ntate Sebotsane to come out and rescue me.

Ntate Sebotsane worked for the City Council's electricity department. He read the meters in those sections of Soweto which had electricity.

'He keeps it chained,' I said.

'Not on a night like this.'

'Okay, avoid Ntate Sebotsane's yard then. When you get home take Mom's overnight bag. Pick me a clean T-shirt, a pair of jockey pants, my blue denim jeans, a toothbrush and a washing rag. You'll find us at Muntu's. Got that?'

'Vukani, please, get me the same, too, from our house,' Khotso said. 'My sister, Sophie, should be able to help you. If you find my parents at home, please, tell them I'm safe but that I won't be coming home tonight.'

Vukani was off like a bolt.

We went up the next street, but not Khotso's street, and approached Muntu's house from the rear.

A bright golden hue illuminated the sky, as if the whole township was ablaze. Fires had sprung up everywhere like winter *veld* fires. From the general direction of the flames it was possible to guess fairly accurately which buildings had been set on fire.

'*Molimo*! It doesn't seem as if there's any public building they haven't set on fire, including the Barclays Bank in Dube,' Khotso said.

'What I think is even more important is for the embers

inside us to remain glowing.' The flames were affecting me in a strange sort of way, as if my very heart was on fire. 'And that, my dear Khotso,' I continued 'is our most unenviable task, to feed these embers. We've got to hold together like this.' I showed him my clenched fist.

I suddenly realised that I'd spoken with more vehemence than I'd intended. Khotso was gazing intently at my face. My hands were sweating, as they always do when I'm excited or nervous. My whole body was trembling a little. Where was my 'Mr Cool' image? I tried to pull myself together by telling myself, over and over again, that I had to show exemplary self-composure and restraint.

At Muntu's place there were two groups of people gathered in the backyard. A group of elderly men sat around a log, warming themselves. Another group was huddled round a brazier.

We approached the group of young people round the brazier. We could recognise many of them as we came closer. We stood by and listened for a while. They were discussing the day's events in subdued, solemn tones. But there was also an undercurrent of excitement which seemed to animate them, so that try as they might their voices kept rising of their own accord until one of their number had to draw their attention to the noise they were causing by whispering 'Sh' above the din. This only added to the noise.

'*Heit*! gents,' we greeted.

'Where've you guys been all this time?' 'Moso asked. 'You've no idea what you've missed. Some real Guy Fawkes, the way they say it really happened in the history books.'

'Listen, chaps,' I said. 'None of you has seen us. Understand?'

'Sure, we understand everything,' 'Moso said. 'We understand there'll be no school tomorrow but that instead we're to start collecting money, all over the location, for the dead. Tell us, we've been arguing over this for a long time, when exactly are we supposed to march on John Vorster Square. Gee! You guys . . .'

'Hold it!' Khotso said. 'Listen to this carefully, none of you guys are to talk about these things. The walls have ears. Just keep your own ears open and your mouths tightly shut. You'll be told everything at the right time.'

'Can somebody go and call Sis' Sindi for us, please?' I asked.

'Moso volunteered.

'Don't say who's calling her,' I added. 'A discreet tug, that's all. Understand?'

We waited around the brazier.

Inside the house people were singing hymns, as is the custom.

'Moso soon returned with Sindiswa.

'Where've you guys been?' she asked. 'Your mothers have almost died of worry, trying to trace your where-abouts. And, Mazwi, your father thinks you should take the first available train to his people in the Transkei.'

'He can forget it! Listen, can we talk to you for a while, in private?'

We stepped aside with her.

'Tell us, what's been happening?' I asked.

'To start off with, the police have been looking for you. There are SBs in a car up the road who've been keeping an eye on everything.'

'Yes, we saw them. But listen, Sis' Sindi, don't tell anybody you've seen us. We've got to find somewhere else to sleep tonight.'

'Where?'

'We don't know yet.'

'I think I know just where. Wait for me here.'

She disappeared into the house and came back a few minutes later with Bra P.

'What can I do for you, boys?'

Sindiswa explained our predicament.

Just then a scuffle broke out in the house, so that even from outside we could hear most of what was being said.

'What! Have you no respection for the dead?' a female voice asked, meaning 'respect'.

A male voice mumbled something.

'What the hell are you writing then?' the same female

voice asked. 'You've been shamelessly jotting down every word that's been said in this house since you arrived. Why? And drinking our tea into the bargain . . . You say this is only your first cup? Liar! Who do you think you're fooling? You've had three cups already and twice as many scones' (only she pronounced it 'sconce'). 'Do you think we're an African eating-house for every hobo in the streets? We're mourning our dead here and you're busy stuffing yourself like a pig and taking down every word that's being said in addition!'

'He's a *blerry* spy sent here by the System,' another male voice added with a slur. 'Throw him out!'

'He should be ashamed of himself, spying on other people's funerals,' a woman said.

There was another jumble of indistinct voices as everyone contributed his or her opinion on the matter.

'You say you've a free-what?' the voice of the original inquisitor boomed above the rest. 'What in God's bloody name is that?'

'*Nkosi yam*'!' Sindiswa exclaimed. 'That's Aunt Bessy. I only hope she hasn't been drinking again. Who could have come to provoke us at our funeral?'

'Wait here, boys, I'll be back in a minute,' Bra P. said.

He hurried back to the house with Sindiswa.

It was now easier to follow the conversation because they had moved to the kitchen in order not to disturb the rest of the mourners in the sitting-room and in Muntu's mother's bedroom.

'It is not right, my child, for whatever reason' – it was Fr. Molale of the local Anglican church – 'to add to the grief of the afflicted parents by pursuing a private vendetta . . .'

'*Moruti*, keep out of this. What do you know about it? Or are you perhaps another . . .'

'Bessie, that's enough.' Bra P. was being tough. 'I'll handle this. Leave our friends to me. My friend, come with me.'

'Let him leave that notebook behind,' Aunt Bessie said.

'*Yishiye khona la, mfowethu*,' Bra P. instructed the culprit. 'And come with me outside.'

Bra P. and the offender came out of the house, with the latter holding forth about his rights.

'Look, sir, I'm only doing my job. How on earth am I expected to earn my bread? Is this what we're fighting for, to take bread out of our mouths. My business here is quite legitimate, I tell you.'

'I know, *mfowethu*, I know,' Bra P. spoke more softly. 'Now, leave everything in my hands. Go home and come back tomorrow. In the meantime I'll see that I arrange a press conference for you with the appropriate people. People here are a bit touchy tonight. You must understand, they've lost a loved child.'

'But my note-book – what about my note-book? It has an important interview with the Mayor of Soweto.'

'Tomorrow, I promise you. When you come for your press conference tomorrow, I'll arrange for you to get it then.'

'But the interview with the Mayor, I've got to lodge it with the Associated Press tonight.'

'*Mfowethu*, if you're as bright as I think you are, you'll leave the matter with me. I'll tell you something else. Tomorrow I'll have a real scoop for your newspaper.'

'That's why they say we Africans are backward; we still don't appreciate the role of a free pass in an open society. The lot of a black journalist is an unhappy one. We're suppressed by the Boers on this side and hounded by our own people on the other side.'

'I agree with you entirely. Tomorrow then.'

'Our people still have a long way to go.'

'Sure, *mfowethu*.'

Bra P. went back to the house. After a while he and Sindiswa rejoined us.

'Sorry about that little interruption boys. It's that fool, Zandie, who fancies himself a freelance journalist. For the last three years he's been sending reports regularly to newspapers in Europe and America, even though not a single one of them has ever been published. I don't know which self-respecting newspaper abroad would employ his kind. No wonder they never get their facts straight!

It's all right, he's just a harmless fool. Only he'll get himself in a fix nobody'll be able to extricate him from one of these days. Last week I had to rescue him near Elkah Stadium from being panel-beaten by the Hazels because of a report he'd sent to *The Star* about some stolen cars these chaps have been selling. And the week before – it was at another funeral – he caused a similar fracas at Lefty's funeral when he insisted on interviewing Lefty's widow.'

We all gaped in surprise. Who had ever heard of a widow being interviewed at the height of her greif? And Lefty's widow at that! Bra Lefty had been one of the few original leaders who had survived the era of gang warfare between the Msomis and the Spoilers. He had recently been liquidated in mysterious circumstances in which even the police refused to be entangled.

'Where were we?' Bra P. asked. 'Oh yes, so you boys have nowhere to sleep tonight. Here's the key to my house. You can go straight there and wait for me.'

I received the key with both my hands cupped.

'There are still one or two others we've got to wait for,' Khotso said.

'That's all right. I've got my own key in case I have to leave before you. Say, I saw your parents in the house. Do they know about all this *mkatakata*?'

'We thought it would be better if we didn't add to their worries,' I said.

'They've been asking about their whereabouts the whole evening,' Sindiswa said.

'You'd better allow me to talk to them. You can trust me. All they need to know is that you're both safe so that their minds can be at rest.'

'Gee! Thanks, Bra P.,' we both said.

'See you later then, boys.'

He went back to the house, leaving us with Sindiswa.

'How have your old folks taken it?' I asked her.

'Bad. But I guess they'll be okay. *Dit is lewe, mos.*'

'There's just one thing we'd like to ask,' I said. 'When's the funeral?'

'That's being fixed for Sunday. Fortunately my father

has already contacted my uncles in Queenstown by phone. They'll be able to make it for Sunday. Our other relatives don't stay so far, so it should be easier for them to come. Well, chaps, I should be going in; they'll soon be looking for me. If that's all you needed to know . . .'

'Just one last, small favour,' I said. 'If Micky shows up tell him where to find us.'

'Okay. Good luck.'

'Thanks, Sis' Sindi,' we both said.

She went indoors.

The rest of the gang trickled in one by one, including Tsietsi. We held a conference in a corner of the yard under a peach tree. How often Muntu and I had stolen raw peaches from that tree and defied all the predictions of diarrhoea!

We told them about the latest arrangement. They in turn told us how the police had also been to most of their homes. None of them had stayed long at their homes after hearing the bad news.

They carried an assortment of paper bags with a few personal belongings stuffed in.

Soon Vukani arrived with a paper bag for Khotso and my mother's overnight bag. He had now changed into my father's overalls.

'What shall I tell Mom and Dad?'

'We've already attended to that,' I said. 'Don't worry. And thanks. You can go back home now.'

'N. . . no. There's nobody at home. I guess I'll just hang around until Mom and Dad are ready to leave.'

'Take care, little brother.'

'How d'we contact you?'

'Don't try to. I'll keep in touch. And, buddy . . . tell Mom and Dad not to worry.'

'Sure.'

'Are we all ready?' I asked the others. 'Is everybody here?'

'Except for the girls and, of course, Micky,' Duke said.

'Let's split,' I said.

As we were leaving someone started to sing 'Thina Sizwe', a popular freedom song. Other voices joined in.

The mournful strains of the song rose, timidly at first, and filled the air. The women in the kitchen picked up the song and hummed it under their breath:

> *Thina sizwe: Thina sizwe esintsundu.*
>> We, the nation: We the black nation.
> *Sikhalela: Sikhalela izwe lethu.*
>> We mourn: We mourn for our land.
> *Elathathwa: Elathathwa ngabamhlophe.*
>> Stolen from us: Stolen from us by the
>> white man.
> *Mabayeke: Mabayek' umhlaba wethu.*
>> Let them leave: Let them leave our land.

An old man we passed as we walked out of the yard was grumbling to himself about certain ruffians who wanted to provoke the police unnecessarily and bring trouble to innocent people.

All over Soweto the flames had now gathered strength, as if the whole place was one huge bonfire.

'Jesus Christ!' Khotso exclaimed with a loud sigh.

We let ourselves in Bra P.'s house through the front door and made ourselves comfortable in his spacious, sumptuous living-room.

Duke brought out a pen and a note-book.

'We might as well start drafting our circular while we wait,' he said. 'In Nina's absence I'll take down the notes.'

'Excellent idea,' I said.

'Which shall it be first?' Khotso asked.

'Can't we issue one circular to cover all the issues?' Tsietsi asked.

'Fine,' I said. 'I'll start the ball rolling. Duke, you can take down the following:

## A CALL TO ALL THE CITIZENS OF SOWETO

Listen, our parents,
It is us, your children,

Who are crying;
It is us, your children,
Who are dying.
*Amandla!*

We, the children of Soweto, hereby call
upon you all to join us in mourning our
martyrs massacred in Soweto by Vorster's
fascist stormtroopers. As a mark of respect
for the dead we call upon our people to
cancel all sporting, social and other
activities scheduled for the week-end of
June 19–20; we call upon the NPSL to
postpone all fixtures for Saturday and
Sunday; we call upon all organisers of
concerts, shows, weddings, picnics and
parties to cancel such activities; we call
upon you all to join us in mourning our
fallen heroes. United we stand; divided we
fall! *Amandla*!! *Awethu*!!!

As a mark of respect for all our dear
departed we call for a national week of
mourning from Monday June 21 until
Sunday June 27. The following 10-point
plan must be adhered to without fail:

1 All workers stay at home;
2 Nurses and doctors go on with their
   work;
3. Shops in Soweto open from
   8.00 a.m.–12.00 noon;
4 No purchases from white shops;
5 All shebeens close down . . .

The notice gradually took shape with contributions
from every one.
'D'we also need to put in any of that stuff about the
police, members of the U.B.C., the school boards,
teachers and so on resigning?' Tsietsi asked.

'No,' I said. 'Don't put in too much into a circular, otherwise it confuses. I suggest we visit them, one by one. More effective that way.'

'Frankly, I'd like to be the one to tell some of these people that,' Duke said. 'Like our big, fat Rathebe and proud, strutting Chabeli.'

'When d'we start?' Tsietsi asked.

'Tomorrow,' Khotso said.

'But they're simply too many', Tsietsi said. 'How d'we reach them all?'

'We pick out a few key blokes and make it clear to them we consider it their responsibility to inform and make sure their subordinates carry out our instructions,' Duke said.

'Where'll we have all this stuff typed out?' Tsietsi asked again.

'Better raise the matter with Bra P. when he arrives,' I said.

'And the matter of the league fixtures,' Khotso added.

'That's a touchy one,' I said. 'I mean, Bra P. has given us accommodation.'

'All the same, it's our painful duty to raise the matter with him,' Duke said. 'Nothing personal.'

The prospect made us a little gloomy and haunted us until Bra P. himself arrived. He let himself in quietly through the kitchen door.

'Have you chaps, had anything to eat?' he asked.

'Just a little, Bra P.' I answered. 'Bella's mother prepared us something.'

He went to the kitchen and soon we heard the rattling of pots.

We quickly planned our line of approach, until interrupted by his return.

He put on a Nina Simone record on his B & O stereo and came to sit on the settee. The voice of Nina Simone came through in plaintive tones. But it also had a strangely soothing effect.

'Ahem . . . Bra P., we've a coupla things we'd like to discuss with you,' I said.

'Shoot on.'

'First, we need to put out a circular. We've no typing or duplicating facilities.'

'No problem. There's a typewriter and some stencils right here in the house. Can any of you type?'

We looked at one another.

'No, but we can learn,' Khotso said.

'Good. I can show you how. Then I'll run them tomorrow at the NPSL offices. I know of a disused duplicating machine nobody can trace. But it works all right. You can also buy it when you open an office in exile! D'you want many of these notices printed?'

'Plenty, in fact, thousands, to reach just about everybody in Soweto,' Duke replied.

Bra P. appeared to consider this for a moment.

'Mh . . . I suppose it can be done. Now, tell me something. How will you distribute so many pamphlets?'

'We've the finest distribution service in the country,' Khotso said. 'Better than the G.P.O. There's not a single street in Soweto without at least one school-going kid.'

Bra P. seemed to find that amusing and chuckled to himself.

'Is that all you wanted to discuss with me?'

'N . . . no. But the other matter's more difficult,' I said.

'Let's hear it.'

We discussed our call to the people at length with him. He listened in silence. It was difficult to tell how our story affected him. Only occasionally did he raise his eyebrows in an expression which seemed to convey more surprise than either puzzlement or disapproval. Otherwise his face remained as placid and indecipherable as Lee Chong's.

After we had finished our exposition he was a long time answering.

Nina Simone continued to the end in a soft, mournful staccato:

> . . . Then you'll know and agree
> that every man should be free.

Bra P. rose to switch off the stereo and resumed his seat,

still wearing his mask of imperturbability.

'You, boys, seem to have just about every angle of this thing figured out,' he said.

There were no signs of mockery either in his face or in his voice, so that I felt my self-assurance returning a little. But the next moment I felt my self-doubt, which had begun to assail me since that morning, returning again. My heart sank at his next remark.

'You're, in fact, asking us to call off our fixtures for the next two weeks, and that includes some mid-week fixtures.'

'Bra P.?'

It's an old habit of mine, of stalling for time, to pretend slight deafness at critical moments.

'This week-end's fixtures, and then again your week of mourning doesn't end until next Sunday.'

'That's right.'

'I can't take any decision on this matter by myself. I'll have to discuss your call with my colleagues at the office. I can't say they'll be charmed by these proposals. Still, I suppose, this calls for a great act of sacrifice from all of us. But I'm only expressing a minority viewpoint . . . I'll tell you one thing for sure, boys. You're fast earning my respection, as Bessie would say. Do I leak your circular to the press? Free publicity, you know. I promised one other fool a scoop for his newspaper.'

Bra P. laughed at his own private joke.

We were elated. We burst into sudden animated conversation.

'Why, Bra P., that'd be simply wonderful . . . We can certainly reach more people that way . . . As long as they don't twist our message to suit their purpose . . . As long as they don't present us in an unfavourable light . . . No, they won't if they get our message, straight from Bra P. . . .'

'There's just one other question I'd like to ask,' Bra P. said. 'I know I've no right to ask this, but don't you think this call for a whole week's stay-away from work is simply too long?'

He must have noticed our discomfiture because he

immediately came to our rescue.

'You needn't answer that if you consider the information classified, you know, top secret,' he said and winked. 'Just an old boy's curiosity. Now, I'll see if our grub is ready, then I'll show you where you'll all sleep.'

'Can't we type out our circular first?' Duke asked.

'Not until you've eaten, Duke Ellington. Mazwi, come and help me in the kitchen.'

I followed him to the kitchen from which an appetising aroma of fried steak drifted through. We also warmed some spaghetti and baked beans and served them with bread and butter.

After we'd eaten our fill he showed us to our bedrooms first, in the upper floor of his double-storey house. Finally he got out a typewriter, a box of stencils and other related paraphernalia. After showing us how to use these he bade us good-night.

'Leave your stencils on the table,' he said as he walked out of the sitting-room. 'I'll pick them up in the morning on my way to the office. You can stay up for as long as you like. You'll find all the food you need for tomorrow in the fridge. There are also plenty of records in the house.'

It took us the greater part of the night and about half a box of spoilt stencils to type out our two-page circular.

We were woken up by Micky at about eight o'clock the following morning. Bra P. had already left.

Micky looked as if he'd not slept for a month. His eyes were as red as a *dagga* addict's. His hair stood up like a guerrilla's. There were blotches of soot on his face and clothes, as though he'd spent the whole night warming himself around a burning tyre. His thin lanky frame had the sombre look of a grave-digger's.

'Jesus Christ!' Khotso exclaimed. 'I don't think your own mother would recognise you.'

'Has she been looking for me?' Micky asked.

'She'd probably renounce him on sight if she met him in this state,' I added. 'I can't say I wouldn't sympathise with her. I suppose you've come to tell us that you slept under Zondo's coal cart?'

'It's a long story, gents,' he said.

'All the same, out with it,' Duke said.

'*Waar begin ek?*'

'From the moment you decided to declare your U.D.I.,' Khotso said.

'Come again?'

'Oh! Never mind,' I said. 'Just tell us where you've been.'

'*Ek se*, has this attack been planned, *na?*'

'I'll go and make some coffee,' I said. 'Anybody for coffee?'

Everybody wanted some coffee so I went to the kitchen. Bra P. had shown me on the night before where to find everything.

I returned with the coffee to the sitting-room where everybody had now gathered to listen to Micky's story.

He had arranged with a gang of decoys – without consulting any of us, of course – hot-headed, intemperate creatures like himself, to round up a number of equally spirited dare-devils like themselves. It was a brotherhood such as the Red Brigade would have felt proud to enlist into its youth league.

From Diepkloof to Emndeni word went round, even down dim alleys where normally only the smoke of *dagga* had free and easy access.

They assembled at pre-arranged points, chosen for their strategic importance, to await further instructions.

There are many congregations whose members would have felt severely shocked and scandalised if they'd walked out that evening and observed the motley crowds of potential arsonists, highwaymen cut-throats, looters and felons of every description, who had gathered at their churchyards under cover of darkness. Nor do I imagine anything would have outraged their religious sensitivities more than the knowledge of how opposite in character the crowds gathered at their churches were from the apostles of old. These were not lamb-like children of probity and virtue.

While the others waited at these assembly points, a select band had gone out for petrol at Rathebe's and one or two other petrol stations in Soweto. In the weeks to follow many people in the petrol business were to seriously consider shutting their filling stations in Soweto for good in order to re-open at Mmabatho, Umtata or Thoho-ya-ndou.

The petrol was distributed to the crowds at the assembly points in a borrowed van, with instructions to attack selected targets at a fixed time – it would be more accurate to say that the 'borrowed' van had, in fact, been requisitioned. Micky had enlisted the Hazels for the purpose. This is the same van they were to use to transport looted liquor to their hide-outs.

Micky made it sound as natural as breast-feeding.

'What did you do after you'd burnt down everything?' I asked.

'Who, me? I didn't burn down anything.'

'After everything had been burnt down.'

'I went to sleep.'

'Where?'

'Up the bell tower of the Nazarene church in Rockville, near the offices of the blackjacks. Lucky thing it wasn't Sunday. Imagine if I'd woken up to the din of church bells all around me! I'd probably have run to the blackjacks for help.'

'After you'd helped to destroy their offices!' Khotso added.

'How did you find us?' I asked.

'Sis' Sindi told me I'd find you here. I went there before coming here. *Maar* before that I'd been to Inhlazane and then Merafe, just to see how the fund-raising is coming up. I think it's picking up as well as anybody can expect . . . Did you know there are wild doves which sleep in the bell-tower at Nazarene? They woke me up at dawn. I'd do with some sleep right now.'

Khotso and I exchanged glances. Khotso shrugged and said, '*Ja!*'

'Go and sleep,' I said. 'We'll wake you up when we have to go.'

Micky went to one of the bedrooms upstairs in which we'd been sleeping.

Duke selected a few records from Bra P.'s collection. He played a banned Miriam Makeba record in which she sings with Harry Belafonte.

We continued to play records all morning. A great reluctance to make any move set in among us. We kept enumerating all the things we had to do, without making a move, not even to wash or eat. And so we continued to listen to records. Bra P. had the largest and most exciting collection I'd ever seen, more like the record library of a small radio station. We played Miles Davies, Louis Armstrong, Oscar Peterson, Quincy Jones, Ray Charles, Bessie Smith, Ella Fitzgerald, Sarah Vaughan and Dina Washington. We even discovered an Afro-American group who called themselves The Last Poets. They recited revolutionary poetry to the pulsating background of polyphonic African rhythms and soft, tranquil jazz. We played their record over and over again until we could recite almost all the poems off by heart.

Around 2.00 p.m. Bra P. came back.

We had still not washed or eaten, except to drink cups and cups of strong percolated coffee.

'You boys had anything to eat?'

'We were just planning to, Bra P.' I said.

We told him of Micky's arrival.

'Don't worry, I'll collect my rent money from all your parents at the end of the month,' he said. 'Slept well?'

'Like new-born babies,' Khotso replied.

'Good. Mazwi come and help me in the kitchen. I'm famished, too.'

I followed him to the kitchen. We prepared lunch of fried steak, eggs, chips and bread with tomato and onion gravy.

When lunch was ready we woke Micky up.

'Hi, Mickey Rooney, ducking cops, too, eh?'

'Hi, Bra P.'

We ate in silence, curious for news of the outside world. But if Bra P. noticed our restlessness he didn't let out anything.

After we'd eaten, Duke and Tsietsi volunteered to wash up. Only when they'd finished did Bra P. indicate he'd observed our impatience.

'Well, boys, I should imagine you'd like to know how I fared in my mission.'

A door from the kitchen led directly into the garage. He asked us to follow him. In the boot of his Mercedes we found no less than twenty packets neatly wrapped in brown paper, each containing about a thousand copies of our pamphlet. Appearing on print like that they put an even more serious stamp on our campaign, which until then had appeared rather nebulous. Here were tangibles, testimony that the struggle was on. But what I found more remarkable was the fact that they'd not been confiscated, despite roadblocks and police searches everywhere. As on the previous day, he had passed through without problems.

We unloaded the papers and carried them into the house.

We were so full of gratitude we didn't know what to say.

'This is even hotter than I'd imagined,' Bra P. broke the silence. 'D'you think you can pull off any of this stuff, boys?'

'We can't afford to sit on our laurels anymore,' Duke said. 'It's a tall order but we don't want to be defeat. . .'

'Defeatists,' Khotso completed and then added, 'We can only try.'

'I'd say this is even more daring than the Krugersdorp bank robbery through that tunnel from the cafe opposite when they made away with close to a million,' he said. But the allusion was lost on us.

I searched for something to say and said the first thing that came to my mind.

'Bra P., we just don't know how to thank you enough.'

I knew it sounded trite, even as I said it, but I felt the better for having revealed to him something of the way we all felt.

'Forget it,' he said.

He told us about the damage which had been wrought upon the government property and said that he didn't think that even the tornado which had once hit Albertina could have been more devastating. We didn't know who or where Albertina was, so we kept quiet. From the way he looked at us you could tell he thought we'd been responsible and in his own way was complimenting us. There was no point in explaining, so we let him carry on.

He also told us that the authorities had brought in the army. Armoured vehicles, as ugly and menacing as hippos, were already patrolling the streets of Soweto.

'I've never known them to bring out the army for a mere bunch of school kids, armed only with stones. Or have you, boys, already become expert in the making of Molotov cocktails?'

He passed a lot of equally obscure remarks, which I didn't think he'd quite intended for us. It was more like he was talking to himself. Finally, when we thought he'd forgotten, he broached the subject which was then uppermost in our minds.

'Well, boys, concerning the postponement of fixtures which you asked me to raise with officials of the NPSL, all I have to say is you've won, hands down. There was hardly any need for me to impress upon the members the importance of your message. The ruins of Soweto speak their own eloquent language which none can gainsay. And so they have agreed to postpone the fixtures due to be played at Orlando Stadium over the coming weekend. Not only the NPSL, but the Johannesburg African Football Association has also agreed to do the same. They'll announce their decision through the press tomorrow morning, which, incidentally, should also be carrying something about your memorandum.'

He didn't say anything about our other appeal for the cancellation of the following week's fixtures as well. But we were to discover that the NPSL had decided to switch its venue for the following week to George Goch. Our rank and file members were annoyed by the league's bid to outwit us. It didn't tally with their declared commitment to our cause, as reported in the press. Retaliation from our members was swift and decisive. It caused some soccer officials a few broken windscreens. Consequently in subsequent weeks the league had to use soccer stadiums as far afield as Kwa-Thema. Several weeks passed before professional football could safely return to Orlando Stadium.

'Now for the most ominous news,' he continued. 'Bella's been taken from her home.'

Bra P. told us how he had got to Muntu's house only to learn from Sindiswa that Bella had been taken from her home very early that same morning. He had immediately rushed to Bella's mother at the clinic in Orlando, who confirmed the news.

I believe when he saw the expression of utter dejection on our faces, he hastened to reassure us.

'There's nothing to worry about. I've been to see her already. She's being held at Protea. They've promised to release her tonight after taking down her statement. But we've another storm brewing. Here, take a look at this.' He handed us a list with about twenty-five names. 'It's the students who are wanted by the police. They say they got the names of what they call the ring-leaders from other students. I suppose there'll soon be a price on all your heads. I wish I may be the one to receive it!'

The confirmation on paper of what we'd dreaded all this time shattered our morale even more than the news of Bella's arrest. All our names were there, plus the names of several other people known to be close to us. There were also a few surprises of completely innocent people whose names could only have found their way into that list by some malevolent humour of the gods. The only consolation was that we'd been forewarned and could thus spread word to the rest to scatter. And many of those warned of their impending arrests wasted no time but fled to Botswana or Swaziland. The second great exodus of our time since the Sharpeville and Langa massacres, the new diaspora had begun.

It was only Micky who injected the right tone of defiance when we received this grim intelligence.

'I swear by my grandfather, who lies six feet underground out there at Croesus, if I'm destined for the cemetery at Doornkop, I'm taking some people down there with me,' he said.

But the rest of us clearly needed to be reactivated. We pored gloomily over the newspaper Bra P. had brought us, heads huddled together.

The very headlines were simply sickening: TERRORISTS AND VANDALS STRIKE IN SOWETO. There was a report which purported to be based on inside information emanating from certain banned underground sources. The report carried what it called a claim by a senior member of the liberation movement in exile for the responsibility of the outbreak of the student disturbances in Soweto. The claim was supposed to have been made by a member of the High Command in London. An article by a professor of political science at the University of South Africa, an authority on African resistance, expressed the view that the incidents of arson in Soweto marked a significant shift in strategy and a change of policy by the liberation movements in exile. The professor predicted an upsurge of urban terrorism as a result of the new emphasis on urban guerrilla warfare. There was also a call by an eminent member of the South African Defence Force for 'total warfare' against the communist-inspired insurgents. Another lead article by a white educationist at Wits University called for an increase in government expenditure on the education of African students. A leading economist, a consultant to the Anglo-American and De Beers companies, advocated various other concessions for urban Africans, including home ownership, the granting of more business licences to urban Africans, an injection of more capital from major business concerns for the improvement of social, recreational and other amenities in Soweto. There was no end to suggestions for cosmetic changes. And from the emphasis on Soweto one might have imagined that the lot of blacks elsewhere in the country was a rosy one. One was left wondering whether these other blacks needed to resort to similar acts to draw attention to their own plight, as indeed they did a few days later. Finally, there was speculation, in a move to preempt the schools' boycott which was anticipated, that the Deputy Minister of Bantu Education would announce the closure of schools in Soweto in parliament that very afternoon. The closure of the schools, a full week before our winter vacation was officially due to start, was already being hailed as a master-stroke to avert confrontation and a crafty move in defusing an otherwise inflammable situation which would soon cast the whole country in a major holocaust.

If Bra P.'s news had been a damper, the anger which the newspaper aroused galvanised us into action.

'*Ek gaan was*, gents,' Micky rose and headed for the bathroom upstairs.

'*Gebruik 'n* scrubbing brush,' Duke suggested to Micky, who paid no attention.

'There's another bathroom downstairs,' Bra P. said. 'Anyone else who wants to wash can follow me.'

Duke followed him.

The rest of us remained wrangling about whose turn it was to wash after Duke and Micky.

After we had all washed we told Bra P. that we were off and would be back later.

'I'm intrigued,' he said. 'A while ago I could have sworn you were all heading for the nearest border. Tell me, what d'you plan to do next? On second consideration, don't. It's more fun if I find out for myself after the deed has been done. You have your key, take it with you. You can come and go as you please, boys, though I rather think, as a precautionary measure, you want to be on the move all the time. You don't want to sleep at the same place twice. But that's all up to you. My home is your home, boys. Remember that.'

But shortly before we left, as the sun was going down, Nina joined us.

She was visibly shaken. The police had just been to her home, where they found her alone. Her parents had still not returned from work. They asked if she was Nina. Sensing trouble, she told them that Nina was her elder sister – actually she was an only child. But as soon as they had left, she stuffed a few clothes into a bag, left a hastily scribbled note on the table for her parents and left. She was still trembling. We suggested that Nina should remain behind and left, taking a few of the parcels Bra P. had brought from town with us.

The fund-raising campaign went on as smoothly as a school fete or a church bazaar, although we were later told that a few of our field workers had also resorted to some unscripted methods. I suppose the exigencies of our situation in those days often called for a lot of on-the-spot improvisation which would have certainly met with stern disapproval from charitable organisations of the more orthodox kind.

First on the ball were groups of students whom Micky had told us about and who invaded the railway stations, bus stops and taxi ranks as early as five a.m.

People on their way to work donated hurriedly rather than miss their regular trains or buses.

At the railway stations many workers, coming from behind and seeing the queues leading to the platforms moving more slowly than usual, instinctively began to search their pockets for their passes. Fearing it was a morning pass raid some who had forgotten their passes at home went back for them; others who were in arrears with their poll taxes or were illegally resident in Soweto in contravention of the Urban Areas Act and its multifarious adjuncts or those who simply didn't have any passes at all decided to turn back and try for the buses and taxis. But to their acute mortification the long arm of the law, as they imagined the cause of the disturbance to be, seemed to have reached the bus stops and the taxi ranks as well. They turned back to their homes, already working out excuses in their minds for their bosses for not showing up for work that day. Those who had hoped to contact their employers by phone found to their utter dismay that the telephone service in Soweto had been disrupted. Doctors in private practice had a busy day forging certificates of sickness.

At the taxi ranks the methods employed by the students were characteristically direct. The first taxi-driver to refuse them a donation got a flying missile through his windscreen. Taxi-drivers are a close fraternity. You hit one, you've hit them all; you pick a quarrel with one, they all gang up against you. Their communal outlook serves a basic purpose of survival and is a direct outcome of constant hold-ups, harassment by traffic cops, difficult passengers refusing to pay their fares, impossible drunkards refusing to alight at their destinations and other abuses of the taxi service. Coupled with such fraternal feelings, they've also evolved an exceedingly efficient communications system. So that when the first taxi mysteriously bumped into a rock the news travelled fast. Soweto braced itself for another gang warfare. But instead of the anticipated acts of retaliation and counter-attacks a curious bond soon developed between the students and the taxi-drivers. A great deal of the co-operation which followed between these two groups was no doubt greatly influenced and facilitated by the strong smell of burning car tyres which was still very fresh in everyone's nostrils. The outcome of such mutual understanding was that, in addition to the regular taxi fares, every passenger was required to drop an extra amount into an improvised till with which every taxi driver had been supplied by the students. These tills were collected at regular intervals at certain check-points, and new ones supplied. A number of ugly accidents happened to the passengers who resisted these new arrangements.

Similar requirements were made on PUTCO bus drivers, except that in their case the students were quite satisfied to receive a share of the actual fares the passengers had paid. A brilliant bus conductor suggested to the students that they could take all the profits if they collected and supplied him with disused bus tickets. It was a satisfactory arrangement to all because afterwards the bus conductor did not have to issue tickets which he could not account for to his employers. The method spread to other bus routes. Even primary school kids were kept busy scouring the back streets of Soweto for disused tickets, any tickets.

At about half-past eight, when the passengers boarding the trains had thinned down to a mere trickle, the students who had been operating from the stations withdrew. But in the evenings when the workers returned home they still found the stations jammed.

The students had returned. But their activities in the morning had now attracted an audience and some opposition. As the matter had already been reported by those who'd been to work to their employers, who in turn had passed on the information to the police about why so many of the city's labourers had been late or absent from work, a platoon of police reservists in camouflage uniforms had already been deployed to all the stations of Soweto, where a violent confrontation between themselves and the students soon developed. Finding their sticks and *sjamboks* ineffective against the students, the police reservists fired a few shots. To their utter horror and amazement their shots were returned, bullet for bullet. Judging from their subsequent lopsided assessment of the situation, what the police reservists, the government and the news media didn't know was that, as on the night before, the students had again attracted disparate allies from the unlikeliest sources. The Hazels and other township gangs, sensing a field day for pickpocketing, had also gathered at the stations, many of them armed to the teeth. The police reservists were easily routed and forced to beat a hasty retreat. But when the army, which had been patrolling the streets all day, appeared on the scene in their hippo-like tanks the students and their allies melted into the crowd. The soldiers sprayed the already dispersing crowd with teargas and shot into their midst, wounding a few, some of them mortally. However, by this time many of the people getting off the trains had had to donate to the student fund for the second time that day — a few more were to make it three in a row when other students came round to their houses. So that from that time onwards many people in Soweto carried piles of coins with them wherever they went.

The house-to-house campaign itself was just as successful, despite a few unavoidable hitches here and there. But the students were already becoming accustomed to extemporising.

In each house the students generally had more time to explain their mission. They were exceedingly patient especially with the aged, the disabled and the illiterate. Those who brought the pamphlets read them out to all those who couldn't see or read.

At MaVy's an argument, which threatened the continued existence of shebeens in general, developed between the students and some of MaVy's more strong-headed customers. These were mostly men to whom shebeens were places of retreat and a refuge from the hostile world. There they could dissipate all their problems and drown their sorrows; there they could buy a night's love, away from family considerations and other weighty social obligations. Here men who would have given up their wives at the point of a blade without much resistance fought like wounded tigers for the retention of their mistresses; here men who would have surrendered their children's feeding bottles without much of a struggle were prepared to stake their very lives for a bottle of beer. These were men who had become exceedingly fed-up with being hounded virtually out of existence by the *tsotsis*, but who felt as able as fish in a net to resist the evil doings of the *tsotsis*. These were men who worked hard all week, but could never be certain of reaching their homes on a Friday night with their pay-packets still intact. They had become mistrustful beings by inclination, precautious creatures by upbringing and long-suffering by temperament. But occasionally they displayed the behaviour of cornered animals, when they could defy odds and throw all caution to the wind, especially when they had been drinking. Often this turned out to be no more than token resistance, as intense and short-lived as their drinking bouts, a reckless gesture of defiance by frustrated individuals, an expression of desperation such as drowning men indulge in and a way of letting off steam. They flared up, experienced a carthartic effect to their outraged emotions, were purged and then went about their daily routine and activities. Essentially self-centred, they could hold their own in the field of polemics if at nothing else, especially when their tongues had been loosened by heavy drinking. It was in just such a mood that the students found some of MaVy's customers.

'Fuck *julle*!' a flabbergasted customer with one arm said, after they'd been listening to the students for a while. Like MaVy's husband, who was at that time too soused to give a damn, he had a wooden stump in place of his right arm which had been amputated, following an accident in a factory. He had a reputation for using his wooden arm in a brawl with the dexterity of a *knobkierrie*. 'How can we tell we're not simply being taken in for suckers?' he asked.

His sentiments received the loud approbation of his fellow revellers.

When all the excitement had died down a spokesman for the students spoke, with as much respect as he could muster. '*Groot man*, where do you live?'

'What's that got to do with you?' the man responded.

The student ignored his impertinence and appealed to the house. 'You yourselves have been eye-witnesses to all the atrocities perpetrated against us by the System,' he said.

'Whose bloody fault is it when you decide to offer yourselves as cattle fodder?' the man with the wooden arm asked.

'Let me ask you one question, all of you,' the student said. 'Is this the way you'd have reacted if one of the children shot had been yours?'

'Me, I've no child,' the man with the wooden arm said. He laughed at his own joke.

Only a few of his drinking mates joined in the laughter.

'I'll make my contribution towards the funeral expenses of any people I know in the usual way,' the man with the artificial arm said.

'There are some people who are better known than others,' the spokesman for the students said, 'who will receive all the assistance while others receive nothing. And they're not necessarily the most destitute.'

'Why should I give a damn for people I don't know? Do I look like a social worker?'

The student spoke without looking at the man with the wooden arm. A few of MaVy's customers had raised their eyes from their glasses and were watching the student with intent expressions.

'It is our collective responsibility and our inescapable duty as Africans to help all the parents who have lost their children in the struggle. We ask for contributions so that we can distribute them according to the needs of each family. We know all the people who have incurred the loss of loved ones. We shall go to them with the money you have given us out of the generosity of your hearts and say to them, "Here is a little contribution from all the freedom-loving people of Soweto, who weep with you." We shall then give them every cent we have collected; they shall all receive something from your large-heartedness.'

The little speech had a curious effect, especially upon the women in the room. They leaned towards their partners and a lot of whispered conversation went on.

'What you propose, if indeed you intend to carry out your impractical scheme, is, to say the least, most unprecedented in the annals of our history and goes against the very grain of our customs.'

'*Khuluma isiZulu wena, asizwa,*' another man shouted.

There were many people in that assembly, who, maybe because they could not follow what the man with the broken arm had been saying, like the man who had just told him to talk in Zulu, had stopped listening to him.

'Unless we learn to close our ranks against the enemies of the people,' the student continued, 'we'll always fall prey to all the hostile forces ranged against us.'

'You brought this monster upon our heads,' the man with the wooden arm said.

'Maybe what this *groot man* has been saying all along is true,' the student said, 'we don't know . . .'

'If, by your own admission, you're such ignoramuses and probably confident tricksters, too, why did you decide to pick up such grave matters which you should have left to your parents by rights? We can't listen to all this rigmarole anymore, so scram, buddies!'

'*Groot man*, we respect you, please don't spoil it. Have we said anything offensive to you? I leave it to the others to judge. Whether you like it or not, we're all in this together. In this situation in which we find ourselves – and the *groot man* can't be right to imply that we're responsible for all the violence, the excesses and the evils of apartheid – in the position in which we are, you're either for us or against us. Now, I'm going to talk to you plainly; straight talk breaks no friendship. Are you going to contribute a small percentage of that money you use to chloroform yourself with daily or not?'

'I don't parasite on anybody; I drink my own money.'

'*Maar* I don't know why we don't burn down all these shebeens as well,' another student said to no one in particular.

A man stood up, staggered towards the door and headed for the toilet. As he opened the door a strong draught blew in, bringing in all the interesting evening smells of the township. The smoke from coal fires and burnt piles of rubbish had not yet settled down. A strong smell of burnt rafters and doors still clung to the air.

MaVy's little daughter of three came and leaned against her legs. She squeezed the child gently against her and stroked her head. She explained later how at that moment ugly, vivid pictures formed in her imagination. She could see the ugly storm brewing and culminating in a vast conflagration; she could visualise her house, her furniture, her wardrobe – all going up in flames. A picture of her desperate but futile efforts to extinguish the flames, her husband slumped in a drunken stupor on the table, flashed through her mind.

She moved away from her paraffin fridge against which she'd been leaning and walked distractedly to the centre of the room, the scene of the argument.

'Shut up, all of you, and listen to me,' she said.

Complete silence descended over the gathering.

She berated the man with the wooden arm for his insensitivity in the face of death. Her other customers glared at the man being scolded as if to say, 'Didn't we warn you?' She turned to the others and told them to give something to the student fund or leave her house. No one moved. She threatened to stop serving them forthwith. Her tone was imperious; she spoke like a person dispensing the great gift of life itself. Then with a sudden change of tone she asked the students to overlook the drunken insensitivity of some of her customers in the words: '*Azingafi ngamvu inye, bantwana bami.*' She expressed her sympathy as a mother and told them how she had tried to help with the injured. At the end of her speech, she donated a few rands.

'You can afford to because all our hard-earned money comes to you,' the man with the artificial arm said.

A few customers followed her example and gave away the coins they'd received from her as change. Those with their girlfriends gave slightly more generously.

She ignored the howler with the stump for an arm. 'My children, have mercy on a struggling mother. I have children, too, so I know how it all feels. It is not my fault that I must resort to selling alcohol in order to keep my children alive. You can deal with blubbering idiots like him' – she pointed at the man with the wooden arm – 'though, goodness knows, he speaks in this way because he is drunk; you can deal with such people without removing the bread from my children's mouths or burning down my house.'

It is easier to see why the permanent liquor boycott we initiated was the least likely to succeed in the long run. To begin with we had dug out the springs, as it were, ourselves even as we struggled to turn off the taps. And then again too many of our people depended on the illicit sale of alcohol for their livelihood. We were really caught in a vicious circle. You can't do a thing like that without cutting your own people's throats. With the wisdom of hindsight it is possible to see these things.

While all this argument was going on some of the students at MaVy's had been distributing pamphlets to all her customers. They all dipped their heads into the hand-outs, trying to read by the poor candle-light. Only the man with the wooden arm had refused to take the pamphlet.

The spokesman for the students assured MaVy that she didn't have anything to fear from them. They were all enjoined, he said, towards working for what was, in the long term, in the best interests of the people. However, he warned her that if she didn't close her shebeen on the days shown on the pamphlet, they'd confiscate all her liquor and burn down her house, but only if she went against the people for her own selfish ends.

MaVy was deeply worried because she'd been looking forward to record profits, after purchasing several dozen cases of beer and spirits from the Hazels at very low prices. But she kept her disappointment to herself.

The students also warned her customers that anyone found drunk on the days shown on the pamphlets would be in for a high jump.

'Since when has this become a Muslim country?' the man with the artificial arm blurted out.

'*Groot man*, nobody can argue with you because you know all the answers,' the spokesman for the students said. 'Half the time we can't even follow what you're saying. We don't know what goes on in a Muslim country. But if we catch any of you soused after tonight, we're going to rip your guts. And that's God's truth.'

In a bid to neutralise the remarks of the man with the wooden arm, MaVy hastened to assure the students that she'd observe all their directives to the letter, even though she was sure she'd lose her customers to other shebeen queens because they'd continue to sell just the same.

'And you're damn right!' the man with the artificial limb interjected.

But the majority of MaVy's customers had long read the signs of grim determination on the faces of the students. They joined MaVy in denouncing their fellow drunkard and so helped to defuse an otherwise inflammable situation.

Through her sensitivity and foresight MaVy founded the Shebeen Owners' Association. So that in the days which followed we were able to negotiate with them for the closure of shebeens during certain periods. This enabled us to exercise a certain measure of control over drunkenness, which we deemed to have been the scourge of the black nation. Today MaVy's association has become so strong that it was recently able to negotiate successfully with the government for the legalisation of shebeens, once considered by the same government dens of iniquity. With what motives the government yielded to this appeal by the Shebeen Owners' Association is anybody's guess. Certainly people who visit us here tell us that the news was received with mixed feelings in Soweto. However, for a long time after we'd launched our campaign against shebeens the uncertainty over their future became the subject of grave concern in many quarters.

Much as MaVy had promised to comply with the student request her biggest worry, as she had said, was over unfair competition from those who chose to sell on the sly. But she needn't have worried about unfair competition. The liquor boycott which ensued lasted for several weeks. Those shebeen queens who defied the students had all their stocks confiscated and the liquor distributed to everybody within sight. Of course, business continued on the sly, as it had done even in the height of prohibition. But many people drank with moderation while they pondered over their lot as Africans. Severe punishment was meted out to those caught staggering in the streets. One of the first people caught in this state was our next-door neighbour, Ntate Sebotsane. He was found walking up and down the street, as was his custom when he'd been drinking, keeping rhythm by clapping his hands together and singing uproariously the same verse, over and over again, of his favourite hymn, '*Mayenziwe intando yakho*', and pausing periodically to deliver a sermon, which never varied, to an imaginary congregation on the Second Coming. My parents said he'd once been a lay preacher in the Methodist Church and a teetotaller who belonged to the Independent Order of True Templars (I.O.T.T.) – we interpreted the abbreviation to mean I Only Take Tea.

But that had been a long time ago. The students came across him in this pious condition and chased him up and down the street several times over, without really endeavouring to catch up with him, before allowing him to sneak into his yard, exhausted and sober. He was saved from being lynched by the fact that he was an old man and something of a distinctive feature in our street, like free bioscope. The communications system in a place like Soweto is as mysterious as magic and as rapid as light. The news of Ntate Sebotsane's treatment spread like a veld fire and, although it provoked a great deal of laughter, it was also analysed very closely in every drinking joint behind closed doors. Afterwards, whenever he was drunk, Ntate Sebotsane insisted that on the night in question he'd been accosted by the Devil himself, with green horns, and his assistants, all of them wielding dangerous forks.

Through the length and breadth of Soweto word went round and donations flowed in. Businessmen, great and small, normally reluctant to plough their profits back into the community, were suddenly seized by generous impulses. Grocers conspicuously vied with each other for the privilege of supplying mealie meal, flour, sugar and packets of tea to the nearest homes of the bereaved; coal-vendors, unsolicited, delivered bags of coal and firewood.

After secret consultations with student delegates, which lasted late into the night, black traffic cops withdrew traffic charges if the offender in each case agreed to pay an on-the-spot fine into the tin bank. The fine was calculated as a percentage of the officially prescribed fine.

Gangs of petty thieves, trouble-shooters and small-time *tsotsis*, who spent their leisure-time staff-riding on the trains or lounging aimlessly around the shops, spinning unlikely yarns about improbable acts, were suddenly moved by a crusading spirit, inspired with lofty ideals and fired with new zeal. They invaded the market stalls of Johannesburg for vegetables under the guise of carrier-boys; the City's supermarkets experienced an unaccount-

ably steep rise in their June figures for shop-lifting, unknown outside the Christmas shopping spree; itinerant
white farmers, accustomed to doing business with urban
natives at the edge of the townships on the way to town,
were robbed in broad daylight of all their produce at the
point of a knife; Jewish shopkeepers who'd done business
all their lives with honest mine labourers, to whom they
could have entrusted their till while they answered the
call of nature, suddenly found themselves with a security
problem. For the social lepers of Soweto, a flame of
charity burning brightly in their bosoms, it was a glorious game, this feeding of the distressed and destitute,
from whom they'd spent a lifetime taking away things.
They acquired a new social purpose in life. Theft without
its customary stigma (not that it ever had in the
townships, if you stole from the right people), robbery
untainted by any selfish considerations – what could be
more absolving and gratifying than this new discovery of
the saving graces of crime, of the notion of crime as a
means of social rehabilitation?

In the homes of whites, wherever there were domestic
servants in employment, groceries meant to last for three
months were used up in the middle of the second month,
even in homes where families had been on holiday at the
coast for the greater part of the period.

The police records of the time show an uncanny wave
of unsolved minor crimes in and around Johannesburg.

Avowed enemies; rival gangsters, who fought pitched
battles on sight; business competitors; political rivals,
who had not spoken kind words to each other in years;
hostile neighbours and other antagonists tacitly agreed
to bury the hatchet without brandishing it first at the
enemy, saluted each other with clenched fists without the
temptation to take a swipe at the other and sat around
open fires in the backyards of Soweto or in dimly-lit
rooms, discussing the state of the nation. Catholic dog-
matists, Protestant heretics and Zionist syncretists ral-
lied around the old banner of Rubusana's, Mahabane's
and Mzamane's IDAMASA; attended the same church
services and openly preached politics. Old Man Nxele, a

veteran of two world wars, now toothless with old age, brushed away the cobwebs from his Congress uniform, and spoke to his sons from his old homestead:

> *Bafana bami*,
> Sons,
> > *Badubula*
> > They are gunning down
> *izingane zethu*
> our children
> *eSoweto*
> in Soweto;
> > *Yini enye pho*
> > What more
> *esisayiphilela?*
> are we still living for?

A truly altruistic spirit gripped the people's minds and their hearts, and a compassionate feeling pervaded all our relationships. It was a perfect example of the collective goodness and generosity of a deeply troubled community.

Upon leaving Bra P.'s house we decided to call on Rathebe and Chabeli first.

In Soweto one didn't simply speak of Rathebe without mentioning Chabeli in the same breath. To do otherwise would have been like thinking of one side of the coin only. They were two of a kind, as complementary to each other as Abbot and Costello. They received wide and favourable coverage in the newspapers, which were trying to build them up as leaders of the community and exponents of black experience. Like Bra P. they were considered successful men in material terms, but it was more difficult to conceive of more diametrically opposite personalities.

Bra P. was a man whose whole direction and impulse were humanitarian and altruistic. No doubt he had his own idiosyncrasies and shortcomings, but these only made him more human. His public image was without blemish. He was what is called a man of the people; a popular man, in the original sense of that word. He combined the virtues of legal, social and marriage counsellor; parish priest and money-lender. Litigants abandoned their astute lawyers, with years of successful practice behind them, in the middle of their cases to go and consult with Bra P. And they never forgot that voice of providence, that moment of pure inspiration, which had prompted them to go to him. Young virgins, ready to be broken in, willing to sacrifice their only treasures, brought their sob-stories to him at all hours of the day and returned home soothed; mothers brought their wayward children with the simple injunction, 'Talk to him, *asseblief tu*, Bra P.,' and left with the satisfaction that they had discharged their parental obligations to the best of their abilities.

Bra P. had style, without really striving for effect; Bra P. belonged. He fitted into his environment like a glove in hand or a lady's nylon stockings, flesh-coloured. He had one advantage over most of our dignitaries in Soweto – he was not associated in anybody's mind with any established form of authority, institution or interests. And because he was not overtly engaged in business either, he appeared to everyone as somebody who gave without ever expecting anything in return. A person could come and borrow various sums of money from him several times, on the same day even, without feeling ashamed of himself or unduly weighed down by a sense of obligation and indebtedness. Consequently, if the money he'd lost in this way through bad debts could have been calculated it would have been found to amount to a small fortune. Yet despite his success in the world, there was nothing stand-offish or ostentatious about him. People regarded him in the same way as they'd have thought of their next-door neighbour who'd had the uncanny luck of catching the jackpot in the July handicap for three years in succession. Fortune may have smiled at him, but he was still their next-door neighbour from whom they could borrow a cup of sugar, except that, now he'd risen in the world a little, they need not return the cup in which they'd carried away the sugar.

Not that they thought he wouldn't notice the cup was missing, but they acted in the firm conviction that he wouldn't mind and might have told them himself to keep the cup if the idea had occurred to him first.

It is difficult for people in the ghetto to resist the temptation to take from their neighbour while his back is turned away. The Hazels broke into Bra P.'s car, stole his spare tyres and all his tools, and were knocking at his door the following morning, after disposing of his property to the highest bidder, to beg for his forgiveness with truly contrite hearts. In the days which followed it might have been observed that Bra P. woke up each morning with a puzzled expression to collect a brand new carburettor, a car battery, a set of shock absorbers or an assortment of other spare parts belonging to a variety of car models (which could only have been of use to a dealer in spare parts), dumped on his *stoep*. The owners never came to reclaim their goods and Bra P's garage became really cramped for space. The supplies might have continued to pour in unabated if Bra P. had not decided at a certain stage to call aside a certain Budda Slim together with Kid wa Bantwana and confide his troubles to them, carefully and delicately, so as not to hurt their feelings.

Bra P. possessed that rare quality Africans call *ubuntu* or *botho*, which is the sum total of human values as Africans understand them.

Except for their comparable wealth, Rathebe and Chabeli were the exact opposites of Bra P. – egocentric, misanthropic, megalomaniac, paranoid, power-hungry, ostentatious, snobbish, avaricious and mean. They were called *Ama-Situation* by township people because they were forever trying to situate themselves outside everyone else's social orbit; other people called them *Bo-Excuse-me* because they were always putting on dainty manners. People said of them that it was difficult to see how anybody but their own mothers perhaps could have liked them.

By some compulsive urge they were forever ready to support every government-conceived scheme and every government-created institution. As sell-outs they were probably unsurpassed and might have easily run a course for puppets if one were ever set up. They were considered stooges and stool-pigeons who paraded the fact with impunity before everyone's eyes. To consolidate their positions, people said, they might have easily sold their own grandmothers – Chabeli did, in fact, threaten to disown and disinherit his children for siding with us against the authorities. Their allegiance to any cause which did not immediately feather their own nests and enhance their own status was reputedly very shaky indeed.

They believed explicitly, almost superstitiously, in the omnipotence and omniscience of the white man. When they spoke of government they uttered the very word in reverential tones as though there was some mystical aura about the whole notion of government. In casual conversation Rathebe was inordinately fond of posing the question, 'What do Africans know about government?'; on the other hand, Chabeli might have been heard haranguing his subordinates in the office, 'Did your people invent the wheel, not to mention gunpowder?' They disassociated themselves from all radical black organisations and dismissed them as a threat to peaceful co-existence. In fact, they possessed a whole register of Nationalist platitudes – 'racial harmony', 'peaceful transition,' 'gradualism', 'the onslaught of foreign ideologies', etc.; and might have easily turned out a phrase book of official political terminology if they'd put their minds to it.

On this very subject of lexicography, it is, in fact, very interesting to note that in an address to the South African Urban Foundation, a group of influential white businessmen, set up at the instigation of white business magnates like Anton Rupert and Harry Oppenheimer after the Soweto uprisings, to improve the material conditions under which blacks live in the townships like Soweto, at their inaugural assembly Rathebe used the phrase, 'a galaxy of Southern African states', a full week before the Prime Minister announced his new diplomatic offensive in parliament geared towards the creation of ' a constellation of Southern African states'. In the same speech Rathebe also proposed that the government might consider a scheme to extend the lease on home-ownership in Soweto to ninety years, long before the government announced its decision to introduce a ninety-nine year lease.

Sowetans denounced both Rathebe and Chabeli as opportunists, careerists and weathercocks of the first order, who had spent their whole lives accommodating themselves to the System. To this end they had turned their backs on their people; they believed that all the opponents of the government were chasing shadows. They said that they owed it to themselves and their families, if no one else was sensible enough, to sit at the foot of the white man's table, if necessary, and feed off the leavings of his plate. They were inordinately fond of quoting proverbs like 'Half a loaf is better than no bread', 'A bird in the hand is worth two in the bush' and other equally trite sayings they'd managed to pick up from their white associates in their endless rounds of dinner engagements. They delivered these homilies to the community, or rather to the newspapers, with the voice of profundity, wisdom, conviction and originality. In return for certain business concessions they had agreed to take up Homeland citizenship and to persuade their people, with all the power at their disposal, to do the same.

They were regular guests of state departments and multinational companies in New York, London, Bonn and Paris – where their wives bought all their clothes. They also took the opportunity afforded by these con-stant trips abroad to meet disgruntled officials (never ordinary members) of the liberation movements in exile, whom they managed to convince to return home (by which they meant one Bantustan or the other) without fear of recrimination. And in this they spoke with the voice of Pretoria. Both of them belonged to the ruling parties of their respective homelands. In Soweto itself they were indefatigable campaigners for full municipality rights for Soweto. But others saw this as a bid to acquire semi-Bantustan status for Soweto, under Rathebe's leadership. On this platform Rathebe and Chabeli campaigned relentlessly for the acceptance by the black community of the Community Councils, which the government was then introducing in place of the old Urban Bantu Council (which we called the Useless Boys' Club). They wanted Community Councils for Soweto, they said, as a launching pad in their struggle for self-governing status for urban Africans. An open letter, signed by both of them, to the City Council of Johannesburg, the Transvaal Provincial Administration and the central government appeared in all the country's major newspapers, in English and Afrikaans, appealing for the granting of city status to Soweto. They were elected with a resounding majority to the new Community Council on a 6% poll, and became known as the six-percenters. Taken separately, as individuals, Rathebe and Chabeli were a slow poison to the people; together, they constituted a major catastrophe, a deadly combination to morale and a serious epidemic to the nation.

Rathebe was the 'Mayor' of Soweto by virtue of being the Chairman of the U.B.C. (and, after it, the Community Council). In carrying out his election manifesto to bring self-rule and self-sufficiency to the people of Soweto, he had travelled to Europe and America to raise funds. He said Soweto's economic independence, whereby its people could embark on projects like the electrification of all the houses without relying upon white finance, was a prerequisite to the political autonomy of Soweto. However, his detractors were quick to point out that a government (meaning the white government) dedicated in essence to the maintenance of the *status quo* could not have found any scheme for relieving them of their financial obligations to the people of Soweto, such as Rathebe was proposing, in any way repugnant. Rathebe went on two trips abroad and came back with a story for the newspapers to the effect that he had managed to raise a million rands in promissory notes to launch Soweto on the path to full autonomy.

Rathebe was also the owner of a large shopping complex and a petrol filling-station in the heart of Soweto. Lately he had extended his investments to GaRankuwa, a township on the outskirts of Pretoria, which had been transferred to the control of the Homeland government of Bophuthatswana upon the request of certain influential blacks. But there were many who said that Rathebe had been set up in business by wealthy Indians and whites. He became the first President of the African Chamber of Commerce when it was formed. Under its direction an African Development Bank was established. He was on its Board of Directors. Openly they encouraged investment in the Bantustans; but privately they negotiated trade concessions for themselves in the cities, like the lucrative deal involving the construction of the huge new supermarket in Soweto. They'd coined a new slogan: 'Buy Black; Buy Soweto!' Because they were such ardent supporters of government policy, both Rathebe and Chabeli had condemned the planned demonstration by the students against Afrikaans from the moment the idea was first mooted to the public.

Chabeli might be said to have been in the thick of things from the beginning. As the Chairman of one of Soweto's school boards, it was to him that the students had first brought their petition. However, he was committed to implementing government policy on education. Over the years he had gradually emerged as one of the policy's chief black protagonists.

In the early days of Bantu education, when he was still a primary school teacher, Chabeli had been among the first blacks to come out in open and full support of Bantu education. He spoke disparagingly of mission education, which the new policy was designed to replace, which he said had alienated blacks from their traditional institutions. In an article published in *Bantu-Batho*, a government-financed journal of the South African Union of African Teachers, he had propounded his views on the advantages of mother-tongue instruction in the early years of a child's education, which were based on an assignment he had written two years earlier while study-

157

ing for his Higher Primary Teacher's Diploma by correspondence with Damelin College. Two years after the publication of his article he was made Headmaster of the first Sotho/Tswana medium school in Soweto. He was already a dedicated Headmaster when the government decreed that all the students who had supported the schools' boycott organised by the Congress in protest against the introduction of Bantu Education were not to be re-admitted to government schools.

When the school boards were divided along ethnic lines he became the Chairman of the Sotho/Tswana section, a position he'd been holding for many years now. Except once as a Headmaster – when a charge of embezzlement brought against him was quashed, some people say, with the connivance of the authorities – and again in his first year as school board Chairman, no real scandal had ever touched his name. But the people of Soweto, who'll never stop talking anyhow, claimed that he was still involved in a racket of employing imaginary teachers and collecting their salaries at the end of each month, so that the Department of Bantu Education continued under the completely erroneous impression that certain schools in Soweto were better staffed than they actually were. People said that this racket in particular had enabled him to branch into private business, ultimately buying shares in the African Development Bank and subsequently in Soweto's new supermarket project.

He had turned down promotion as sub-inspector of schools several times.

Considerations of a similar monetarist nature had led him into civic politics. Very few people in Soweto ever obtain anything they desire by recourse to the procedures laid down in law. Eviction orders, long waiting lists for houses, residence permits, permits for petty traders – all need to be handled by somebody who knows his way through the corridors of Afrikaner officialdom. And given the regularity with which the people of Soweto are assailed by the most original problems of a petty-bureaucratic nature imaginable, any man with resourcefulness and contacts, who gains election to the advisory board, is guaranteed his fortune. This is not considered a racket strictly speaking, just a social service, and one's chances of re-election depend very much on one's record in manipulating the authorities for the benefit of one's client-constituents. Chabeli was consulted by people way beyond his ward, on matters ranging from passes to passports. He was understandably perturbed by the slightest hint that he might have to forego his position, from which he derived his economic leverage. So that he had given the first lot of students to come to his office with a petition against Afrikaans pure hell, despite the fact that he'd been considering transferring his own children to a school in Maseru. The students had left his office with their tails between their legs. We never forgot.

The late afternoon smoke from coal stoves had already begun to rise above Soweto in a pervasive acrid smog as we trooped towards Rathebe's house. The street lights, huge arclights hung on grotesquely tall pylons, had just come on, where they were still functioning.

It was difficult to predict what sort of reception we'd get from Rathebe and Chabeli because on the first day of the shootings they had suffered severe humiliation in the hands of certain unidentified students. Probably only Micky knew their identity, but it would have been pointless trying to find out from him. Digging for information from Micky could be as futile as trying to carry water in a bucket with its bottom removed. Whatever you said to him went in through one ear and out through the other. All we knew about what had happened was that Rathebe and Chabeli had been caught by a batch of students near Rathebe's shops and frog-marched all the way to Rathebe's house in Orlando West, two kilometres or so further up the road. We could only hope that their treatment of the night before had paved the way for some kind of dialogue and not hardened their attitudes in accordance with their reputation for intransigence.

When we arrived at Rathebe's house we noticed that security guards had been posted like shadows all around the house and outside his yard. We decided to proceed to Chabeli's house in Orlando East.

Near the Donaldson Community Centre, not far from Chabeli's house, we met his son. He was driving in his father's car and when he saw us he stopped for a chat.

Mojalefa went to school with us. He identified with us in everything we did and spoke very disparagingly of his father. He once told us that his father had wanted to send him and his sister to Maseru, but they'd told him they weren't going there. However, we preferred to keep Mojalefa in the dark about some of our activities. Not that we feared he'd sell-out, but out of a genuine regard for filial bonds. Whenever he found out that we'd kept anything away from him he became so sore at us that we always found dealing with him a problem.

'Jesus Christ! Here comes Mojalefa,' Khotso said when we spotted him.

'*Heit, majitas*!' Mojalefa said.

We returned his greeting.

'Where are you all going to at this hour of the day?' he asked. 'Not attacking the Orlando power station, are you? Because if you are I'm joining you straight away.'

We all laughed.

'Where are you going to?' I asked.

I was wondering how long we could maintain our evasiveness.

'I'm returning home from an inspection of the ruins of Soweto. It looks like the kind of sight which future archaeologists should find very interesting. The whole of Soweto is like a huge army barracks. But they've brought in the army too late. I give you my hand, chaps, you did a thorough job.' He winked knowingly at us. 'Where did you say you were going to?'

'Where have you been?'

'*Hawu*, Mazwi, why are you playing daft with me?'

It had come, what we had all dreaded.

'Why are you being so mysterious to me? You guys are always hiding things from me, as if you didn't trust me. Have I ever given you cause to be so mistrustful of me? What do you really expect me to do to . . .'

'Actually, Mojalefa, you can help us because we want to go and talk to your father,' Duke said.

'*Maar* it will be easier if we come with you,' Micky added. 'When we got to Rathebe's just now we couldn't get in because the whole place is creeping with *gatas*. We need your help in case your father has also employed bodyguards. You can tell them we're your friends.'

Mojalefa laughed as if Micky had just said something very preposterous. We waited for his laughter to die out.

'My old man and Rathebe were discussing this very idea of appealing for police protection,' Mojalefa said. 'That was last night. Today he hasn't been anywhere because his body is still aching all over after the treatment you guys gave him last night. And to think that not a single one of you told me what was afoot, despite the fact that I was with you most of the day yesterday! Yet everybody else seemed to have known what was going to happen. Everybody has been acting so mysteriously towards me I really feel insulted.'

I stopped short of telling him that some of us, even though we were in the organisation's executive, hadn't had the slightest inkling of what was going to happen until after things had happened. How could I expect Mojalefa to believe me?

'Anyway, my father dismissed the whole idea of calling in *gatas* to guard us as outrageous,' he continued. 'You know, *mos*, how much he trusts himself. But if he'd gone along with Rathebe's scheme my sister and I had already told him point-blank that we would have left home. I'd like to observe his reaction when he sees you, after the treatment you gave him last night.'

What else was there but to shrug our shoulders?

'Listen to me, Mojalefa, whatever you may think, there's no question of mistrust. We just don't want you to be involved in any of this. So if you'll keep out of the way after . . .'

'So, Mazwi, you think you want to spare my feelings? You guys should know me better by now. Come along, let's go. Some of you can hop in with me.'

'It's all right, we're already there, we'll walk,' Khotso said.

Micky got in beside Mojalefa.

'Meet you at our house then,' Mojalefa said and drove off.

We went in through the back door straight into the kitchen, where Mojalefa's mother and his sister were preparing supper. Mojalefa pulled out some chairs for us, which were not enough, so the others remained squatting on their haunches. He told his mother that we'd come to seek his father's advice on some very grave matters, and then went to tell his father in the living-room that he had visitors. He came back to the kitchen accompanied by his father.

'Well, well, well, what do I owe this singular honour to?' Chabeli asked. 'Have you come to commiserate with me or to rub *rooi* pepper into an old man's wounds?'

He was surprisingly buoyant for someone who'd been through the kind of excruciating ordeal he'd been subjected to, even though he was hobbling like an ageing gorilla.

He invited us to follow him into the living-room. 'As long as you leave your knives in the kitchen, where such instruments belong,' he added.

We left Mojalefa, his sister and their mother in the kitchen.

Chabeli eased himself into the sofa with infinite care.

'Tell me first, who are you?' he asked.

We introduced ourselves, taking the cue from Micky to give him false names.

'Do I know any of your parents?'

'Personally, I should think not,' Micky said. 'We're a new family in Soweto.'

'Where did you live before?'

'Qwa Qwa.'

That was a bit risky of Micky. But it was clear Chabeli could no longer recognise some of us as the same blokes who had brought the student petition to his office a few months back which he'd torn up even before he had read it.

What a singularly accomplished liar Micky was! And to think that the furthest he'd ever travelled down south was as far as Sharpeville near Vereeniging! His geography was generally considered to be so cock-eyed that he couldn't have told you whether Sasolburg was in the Transvaal or the Orange Free State. Qwa Qwa, my arse! He hardly knew who that Homeland's Chief Minister was.

'Yes, I can tell you're not at all like the children of the township,' Chabeli said. 'So, you want my advice on some matter of great importance to you, eh? Have they been trying to intimidate you? I can tell you this, without fear of contradiction, don't yield an inch of ground to them. People are like the proverbial camel; give them a little room for their noses, then they also want to thrust in their whole faces as well. And always remember this: Lucifer's sin, for which he was driven out of heaven in double-quick time, was insurrection. They'll reap the fruits of their insubordination, you mark my words. So, they've been trying to force you to loot and destroy, too, have they?'

'Ahem . . . Not exactly, sir,' I said.

'You must also remember, as somebody once wrote, a prophet has honour except in his own village. Stand fast on your principles. Trying to force you to act against your consciences, are they?'

'It's not quite that, sir.'

'Let's hear your problem then, put it in your own words.'

Dealing with these old fogeys was never an easy matter. They were inclined to be excitable and to let their imaginations play tricks on them. This would require tact and infinite patience or straight *kragdadigheid*. We didn't want to rough-house him, but we also didn't have until eternity to bring him back to reality.

'Actually, we're only messengers on a rather unpleasant errand,' I started again.

Noting his puzzled expression Khotso added, 'We represent the students.'

'We want you to resign your post as Chairman of the school board and as a member of the Useless – I mean, the U.B.C.,' Micky said.

Chabeli could have hit the roof with rage, only his

aching muscles held him firmly to his seat. He spoke with expansive gestures, gesticulating wildly, threateningly all the time.

'Did I hear you properly? Does anybody hear? Can the stones bear to listen to this. You come all the way from Qwa Qwa . . . Oh! no. No! You can't be from Qwa Qwa . . .'

'We live in Soweto now,' Micky said.

'Shut up! Who asked you to speak?'

His voice had risen like a prophet's at an open-air service, so that his wife came rushing into the room to find out what was happening.

'*Ke'ng, ntate*?' she asked.

'Just listen to these upstarts, these er . . . political midgets. Are my ears deceiving me? MaMojalefa *ntsipe*, pinch me; maybe I'm dreaming. Can this be true? They have the effrontery to come to my house, under false pretences, and tell me . . . me, T. J. . . . D'you know who I am, young man?'

'Calm down, *ntate*, it is not good for your blood pressure,' she said. 'What do they want?'

'They want to be flogged in public; they deserve Manthate's treatment, as a deterrent to others.'

Manthate was the leader of a group of vigilantes called *makgotla*, ostensibly formed to curb the rate of crime in Soweto. They patrolled the streets at night. If they met any young person in the streets they immediately seized him or her. They tried all their victims in an open court, resembling a tribal *kgotla*, and after finding them guilty flogged them in public, even though public floggings were illegal. The police were said to know about the existence of the *makgotla* and to condone Manthate's methods in secret.

When MaChabeli intervened, I thought here was a chance. Chabeli's choleric temper had been an obstacle to any form of discussion, where his wife's calm approach seemed to offer hope. I decided to address myself to her.

''*Me*, we're just messengers.'

'Shut up! Didn't you hear me? Yes they need to be whipped with bicycle chains until their arses are ripe, and then to have *rooi* pepper rubbed into their wounds. I never thought I'd live to see the day!'

'It's all right, *morena oa ka*,' his wife said.

She patted him fondly, fussed a great deal over him, rearranged his pillow which had slipped down his back and spoke soothing words to him all the time, calling him by all the traditional terms of endearment she could think of.

I watched Micky with the corner of my eye sneak back into the kitchen and wondered, half-hopefully, whether he had a lynching squad already stationed outside.

A few minutes later a car started outside and drove off.

'And what is your business in my house, young men?' MaChabeli asked.

'As we've been trying to say, we're merely messengers. . . .'

'Damnation on whoever has sent you here?' Chabeli interrupted me. 'What gall you have! Have you ever heard of such a thing, MaMojalefa?'

'What thing, *ntate oa Mojalefa?*'

He told her a badly garbled version of what we had said to him.

MaChabeli's face went through an interesting sequence of emotions as she tried to piece together the incoherent information from her husband. At first she seemed puzzled. Then, as a little light dawned on her, she assumed a worried expression. A deep fathomless sadness appeared to set in; her eyes had the expression of a terrified sheep's eyes before being slaughtered, lacklustre and resigned. Her face had become so pale that blood circulation to her face seemed to have stopped completely. She had a far-away look about her, which set me wondering whether she was still listening to her husband. As conflicting thoughts passed through her mind, she frowned or narrowed her eyes or looked down and so on. After a few minutes her serenity seemed to return, a smile of pure transfiguration illuminated her face, the glorious smile of a woman in the throe of inspiration. She adjusted her smile as if to dispense salvation.

'It is a big thing this you're asking of my husband, my sons,' she said after Chabeli's highly intemperate speech had run its full course. Her equanimity was now fully restored; while his exertion seemed to have left him as limp as a discharged penis. She was in full control of the situation.

'We know that, *'Me*,' I said.

'Damn it! What do they know?' Chabeli barked.

'It's all right, *ntate oa* Mojalefa; it's all right, *ngoana oa* Thesele.' She was applying his traditional praise names like an expert masseur. These verbal caresses had an amazingly lulling effect on him – for don't they say that however you may undermine a man, it is important to retain certain outward forms of propriety to cushion the man's dignity? MaChabeli was no doubt very well schooled, certainly no novice in traditional diplomacy. And with her uncanny ability for chasing with the herd-boys and running with the cattle, she spoke on with a disquieting effect upon us all. 'A matter as grave as the one you raise, my children, needs one to sleep on it. Do I speak with your voice, *ntate*?'

Chabeli groaned rather ungracefully and muttered something incoherent, his face full of murderous intent.

'Do I make myself perfectly plain to all of you, my little chiefs?' she asked.

'We hear you well, *'Me*,' Khotso replied.

As far as I was concerned that was it. I rose to leave.

'*Gents, laat ons line*,' I said to the others. 'You've all heard what *'Me*, has to say. *Ntate*, here, requires some time to digest our words.'

'I don't disagree, but might we not get a rough indication of how soon we might expect to get *Ntate's* reply? We're only messengers. Those who've sent us here will want to know.'

There was Duke, bringing up the matter all over again, just when I thought we'd resolved everything satisfactorily without much loss of face on either side!

'Hear me properly, my children,' MaChabeli said. 'I'm the first one to admit that my thought processes are now much slower than they used to be when I was your age. You've no doubt considered this matter from all possible angles. I've no reason to think that in the end we, ourselves, will not be ruled by your wise counsel. But be gracious enough, sons of the land, to give us a little time to bring our hearts, along with our minds, to learn to like the thought. We're only eccentric old dodderers, who need a little more time to discard a lifetime's habits. Do I make myself clear to you all, *bo-ntate?*'

What could we offer against a lifetime's habit of low-key diplomacy? The reasonable thing to do was to yield to MaChabeli's subtle emotional blackmail as graciously as we could.

A car came to a halt outside, and then another.

We were already all on our feet when we heard a loud knock at the front door. When MaChabeli opened the door, who should walk in but Rathebe himself! He was walking with the aid of a walking-stick, with his feet apart, like someone who'd been on an unsaddled horse the whole day. He lowered his considerable bulk carefully onto the seat next to Chabeli. The sofa groaned a little. His eyes darted about the room suspiciously.

'What puts you here?' Chabeli asked, without too much courtesy. I guess he was as surprised to see Rathebe as we were.

Were the gods smiling benevolently on our mission or was this some other fiendish plot?

We'd hardly had time to get used to this new turn of events, when I noticed Micky from the corner of my eye slinking in from the kitchen, as unobtrusively as he'd left the room. He came and stood beside me, breathing heavily down my back, and smelling of Kentucky chicken, which he was still chewing. So, while we'd been taking care of this unpleasant business he'd been stuffing himself full of Kentucky chicken in the kitchen! Really, after this business I honestly had to put Micky to order, once and for all, I told myself.

'Your son came to my house a moment ago with another young man and told me you needed to see me very urgently,' Rathebe said. 'As you can see, I came immediately. Your message shook me, man.' His eyes darted around the room like a rat's. 'I thought something dreadful had happened. Is there anything I can do for you?' He was shifting about uncomfortably in his seat.

Why did this have to happen just when I thought we'd leaped successfully over one hurdle? I've always found emotional battles, confrontations, utterly exhausting, even more so than the most demanding forms of physical exertion. I avoid excruciating emotional wrangles whenever I can; I've never relished expending my energy on unpleasant things. I'd been quite happy at the prospect of clearing out of Chabeli's house after what was, after all, a great moral victory for us. I'd already told myself that there'd be time to tackle Rathebe, but not tonight. Now, confound the fellow, here he was, looking every gram a baby elephant! Did we really have to go over the same ground again? Couldn't we simply leave him with instructions to find out from Chabeli what we'd come about?

We had another small shock coming our way. At the sight of his colleague, the old warrior spirit was rekindled in Chabeli's chest, so that even his wife had to cast her eyes, momentarily, on the ground at this new outburst.

'What!' Chabeli barked in response to what Rathebe had just said. 'The double-dealing, back-stabbing, two-faced scab! Mojalefa!'

Mojalefa's sister shouted from the kitchen that he'd not yet come back into the house, but that she could hear him driving the car into the garage.

'*Ntate*, I've already asked you not to excite yourself over such a small matter as this,' Mojalefa's mother said.

'D'you call it a small matter when a child of my own loins goes behind my back to betray me to my own enemies?' Chabeli asked.

'Hush now, *ntate*, it does your health no good. Besides, the child may have done what he did in the best interests of all concerned. What could be more sensible than to summon the only other man who can be trusted at a moment like this?'

'It's a carefully laid out plot, I tell you.'

'That may be so, but we must be grateful that now we

have the benefit of the opinion of a man like *Ntate* Rathebe on such an important decision as you've already made, for don't they say that two brains are better than one? Is that not so, *Ntate* Rathebe?'

'Ahem . . . that is indeed so, '*Me*,' Rathebe said.

She was again turning on the old magic of her craft.

'I'm glad you agree, *ntate*, it is a good thing that the child went for you, for don't they say that when a house is on fire, it is to our most trusted neighbours that we turn for help? Your presence here tonight has never been more welcomed than at the present moment. I'd have sent Mojalefa to you myself, if I'd had the presence of mind to do so. My lord's mind has been occupied with other grave matters, otherwise he'd have thought of it himself. These children you see before you here, they are our children, they've come to see us over a matter which touches very closely on our hearts.'

At another time, in another place, I should have hugged Mojalefa's mother.

She told Rathebe what we'd come about.

He was restless throughout her narrative and kept throwing furtive glances at us, but her tranquillity was undoubtedly reassuring.

'And so you see, my husband's true friend,' she concluded, 'Mojalefa's father's view, on which we'd like to have your opinion, is that he needs a little more time to chew over this matter. Is that not right, *Ntate* Rathebe?'

'Quite so, '*Me*,' Rathebe said.

I decided that if it had to be done, it just had to be done now, so I took the plunge.

'*Ntate* Rathebe, '*Me* MaChabeli has represented our views very well. What you've just heard affects you, too, as well as your colleagues of the U.B.C. We couldn't get to your house because you've planted agents of the System all around. We need to know your decision, too.'

'You see now, *Ntate* Rathebe?' MaChabeli said. 'You couldn't have come at a more opportune moment. You've already heard *Ntate* Chabeli's views on the subject, which I feel sure you'll endorse.'

It was unbelievable. I don't just mean Mrs Chabeli's

performance. Tough-talking, strutting, double-chinned Mr Rathebe himself, Soweto's own Tarquinius Superbus, giving in without a murmur of protest! Whatever medicine those students had administered, it worked like magic.

'Naturally, I shall consider this matter in the same light, too,' Rathebe said.

'And the rest of the U.B.C. will have to be dissolved too,' Duke said.

'After due consideration of the matter and if it is the people's will, yes,' Rathebe said. 'I shall, of course, raise the matter with my colleagues, as is only proper, but the ultimate decision to resign rests with each individual member.'

'Didn't I tell you, my children, that this matter would be satisfactorily resolved?' the she-fox cut in. 'Now you have the word of two men of honour, who are as concerned about the direction events have taken as we all are. Perhaps, we now want to leave *bo-ntate* by themselves to reflect on everything you told them.'

We'd hardly strung ten sentences all put together and now she was crediting us with the dubious honour of having said everything!

We took our leave of both men. The old lady very affably showed us out through the kitchen door. Mojalefa saw us to the gate and we were off.

'I guess all the members of Rathebe's family have been taught to recite all that mumbo-jumbo so that they can be allowed back into the house whenever they have to go out,' Micky said.

'What mumbo-jumbo?' Khotso said. 'What are you talking about?'

'All that stuff they call the password or something. They say it once at the gate and another time at the door, each time differently, just like at the flicks.'

Khotso shrugged his shoulders.

'Just let him be, Khotso,' I said. 'He's mumbo-jumbo himself. Micky, you still have a lot of explaining to do.'

'*Aaskies?*'

'You heard me very well.'

We walked on.

We should have known better than to think that the old quislings had meant anything they'd said. When we sent our emissaries a few days later, Mojalefa's mother told them that her husband had already relinquished his position. As the old buildings of the school board had been burnt down, it was impossible to tell how true it was that Chabeli had quit. Mojalefa, who was soon to part from his parents together with his sister, told us not to believe a word his mother said. Today, Chabeli continues to serve on both the school board and the Community Council, which replaced the U.B.C. As for Rathebe, he somersaulted and prevaricated and procrastinated for so long that the majority of us were already in exile when he announced his final decision. His trump card had been to issue press statement after press statement to the effect that he was arranging a referendum for the people of Soweto to decide whether the old U.B.C. should disband or continue (under the new banner of the Community Council), so that it could carry out its mandated function of bringing electricity and other modern amenities, so long denied us, to the whole of Soweto. The nearest thing to a referendum Soweto ever had was an opinion poll in *The World*, shortly before it was banned, which found against the Community Council and in favour of the Committee of Ten, which had been formed by then by the people to adminster the affairs of Soweto, in place of the old U.B.C. and the West Rand Administration Board. However, Rathebe has remained to the present day the unchallenged 'Mayor' of Soweto.

There remained only one task we'd set ourselves for that evening, although I just didn't relish the prospect of another confrontation. Our luck had held on this far. But wouldn't it be tempting providence to presume too much and to push ahead at this rate? Wouldn't it be wiser to put off our next task until another day? My only difficulty lay in disclosing my feelings to the others, so I trudged along. Wasn't I still the Chairman? *Vox populi; vox Dei*!

First, we wanted to touch Muntu's place to catch some

home news.

As on the previous night we had no difficulty in summoning Sindiswa outside. She told us how their house had become a beehive for SBs. They'd been raiding our homes, too, so incessantly that my parents had decided to send Vukani, fancy disguises and all, to go and stay with some family friends in Natalspruit in the East Rand. They'd taken him to Natalspruit that very same evening after returning from work. Sindiswa said Vukani had become very jumpy from answering hostile police questions about my whereabouts, after being left in the house by himself the whole day.

I had very mixed feelings about meeting my parents. Grown-ups have a way of making you feel like a baby, years after you've graduated from wearing short pants. Still, I longed to catch a glimpse of them. The others, whose parents had come for the nightly vigil that would be held at Muntu's house until the funeral, were also in two minds about meeting their parents. They were afraid that the sloppy scenes of sentimentality that were certain to result from meeting their parents would very easily undermine their morale.

Sindiswa also told us that Bella had definitely been released from police detention earlier that evening, as Bra P. had told us they'd do.

After we'd been talking to Sindiswa for some time giving her reassuring messages for our parents and so on, Micky suggested we proceed to discharge our last remaining duty for the night. '*Okay, ma-gents, ons moet nou line*,' he said.

Sindiswa asked whether we were going straight to Bra P.'s.

'No, we're going to our Principal's house first,' I said.

'But he's here. What d'you want him for? I can give him your message.'

'Nope, we've got to deliver it to him in person,' Khotso said.

'I can go and call him for you, if you like.'

'Yes, call him,' Micky said.

But Tsietsi, strongly supported by Khotso, suggested

that this was neither the place nor the occasion for such business as we had in mind. The others agreed enthusiastically.

It was one big relief to me that we didn't have to tackle our Principal that same day. But we did catch up with him a few days later. When we put our proposal to him, he showed us a copy of a letter of resignation and a receipt for a registered letter which he'd already sent to the Department. He didn't play a Rathebe–Chabeli on us either. His resignation was genuine. Because of his excellent reputation as a mathematician, he was immediately offered a lectureship in mathematics at Wits University. He was also elected into the Committee of Ten and endured long stretches of imprisonment without trial for his commitment to the struggle.

It was also largely as a result of his example that about five hundred teachers in Soweto also resigned from their posts in protest against the whole Bantu Education system.

A bombshell awaited us when we got to Bra P.'s. He and Nina were relaxing in the sitting-room, listening to records.

'*Hoe was die mission?*' he asked.

'*Die mission was grand?*' Khotso answered, giving him the thumbs-up sign for emphasis.

Nina brought our supper.

'The only good thing to have come out of all this is that I've inherited a bride and an excellent cook without popping out so much as a cent in *lobola*,' Bra P. said as we ate on.

Indeed, the food was excellent. She had cooked beans mixed with samp, called *umngqusho*, which she served with stewed mutton and an assortment of vegetables. Bra P. told us that he lived on tinned foods and only tasted vegetables when he ate out at a restaurant or at somebody else's house. He said Nina had actually forced him out of the house to go and buy vegetables, something he'd not done since his wife's death, many years ago. Nina was delighted with the compliment and blushed most charmingly.

'I've been so hungry!' Micky said, pushing his empty plate aside and patting his belly affectionately, after belching loudly and appreciatively.

'Don't be a bloody pig; say "excuse me",' Nina said.

'*Aaskies.*' Micky licked each of his fingers in turn and gave another belch of pure delight.

'*Sies!*' Nina said.

'Hungry, indeed, after stuffing yourself full of Kentucky chicken!' I said to Micky.

'It was Mojalefa who offered to buy it,' he said.

'I bet it was also his idea to fetch Rathebe!'

'*Aaskies?*'

'What are you two talking about?' Duke asked.

'Forget it.'

That was the closest I came to remonstrating with Micky and giving him a public rebuke.

After we'd eaten, Khotso and I volunteered to wash up.

'Anybody for coffee?' Bra P. asked when Khotso and I came back to the sitting room. He rose without waiting for an answer and made for the kitchen.

'I'll make it,' Duke said, trotting after him.

'You'll do no such thing, Duke Ellington; not in my house,' he said.

Duke returned to his seat.

Bra P. vanished into the kitchen and shut the door after him.

That gave us a chance to brief Nina, who'd obviously been anxious to know how everything had gone. When we had told her everything there was to tell, she asked us whether Micky hadn't blundered, as usual. But Khotso put an end to the lovers' quarrel that was brewing by telling her that Micky had been in the kitchen all the time. She complimented us on devising a perfect strategy for keeping him out of the way, but Micky refused to rise to the bait.

'Well, aren't you going to say something?' she asked him.

'They've told you everything, *mos,*' he said.

'I bet if you searched him just now, you'd most probably find some spoons from *'Me* MaChabeli's kitchen hidden in his pockets,' she said.

She told us how she'd spent her afternoon and evening, relaxing and playing records.

Bra P. came in with the coffee.

'Did you hear Bella's back at home?' he asked.

We told him Sindiswa had already told us the good news.

'Bra P., are they likely to pull her in again?' Duke asked.

'Anything's possible,' he replied.

'But, surely, they must have cleared her of all suspicion. Otherwise, they should have charged her formally.'

'I wouldn't go with you all the way there. They may have simply released her for the time being for lack of sufficient evidence.'

'Which means they may come for her again?'

'And this time they're not likely to release her after only twelve hours, even if God himself intervened.'

While this discussion was going on between Duke and Bra P., Tsietsi leaned towards me, cupped his mouth and said he had something to tell me, in private.

I wondered what other impending danger Tsietsi was about to warn us against.

'It's in my bag in our bedroom upstairs,' I said aloud.

'Excuse us for a while,' I said to the others. 'There's something Tsietsi wants from me. Come along Tsi.'

We went upstairs.

'What is it now?'

He told me that an idea had just occurred to him that perhaps we should tell Bra P. what we'd been able to accomplish that evening, just to show him how much we trusted him. I thought about his suggestion for a while and told him it was an excellent idea, but what about the others? He said he didn't think they'd object once they understood why I'd done it. I asked him if he didn't think we should wait until tomorrow, so that we could consult with the others first. He said he thought Bra P. would appreciate it better if it was done spontaneous-like. We tossed the idea backwards and forwards in this way without resolving the conflict in my own mind, so we went back to the sitting-room after I'd promised Tsietsi I'd think about it.

They were still discussing Bella's case. Micky was wondering whether it was safe for her to remain at home any longer. He wanted to go and fetch her straightaway. But Nina said she didn't think that any mother in her sane mind would allow her daughter to go out with someone like Micky at that time of the night, or at any other time for that matter. Bra P. said he thought that Bella would be safe for at least another twenty-four hours, after which anything could happen to her. He kept on emphasising the point so much that I began to suspect he meant us to go to her on the very next day before the twenty-four hours was over, when she'd had a little time to rest after her excruciating ordeal. I said as much, with my eyes glued intently on Bra P.'s face. He nodded, almost imperceptibly.

When we had exhausted the topic, I asked Bra P. if he wasn't curious to know what we'd been doing that evening. He said he wouldn't be surprised if we'd just come back from planting a bomb under the Voortrekker monument or in the Union Building itself in Pretoria. Micky asked if he thought the Union Buildings would be a particularly significant target. Khotso said it would take a raving lunatic to even contemplate taking such a step. Micky said he agreed because in his opinion the John Vorster Square was a more worthwhile target. Khotso shrugged his shoulders.

The little digression afforded me the opportunity to assess the others' reactions to what I had proposed. Only Khotso had shown some surprise, but that was enough to decide me against saying anymore. After all, I was the most vociferous critic of Micky's for taking just such liberties with us. But when I turned my eyes to Bra P., I noticed an expectant look in his eyes, so I plunged ahead without further meditation.

I narrated in detail our evening's exploits from the time we'd left Bra P.'s house. As I warmed up to my subject, the others, too, began to fill in the details I'd omitted. So, it was all right!

'D'you mean to tell me that Rathebe and Chabeli actually told you they'd resign?' Bra P. asked. 'You'll forgive me if I tell you that I don't believe a word of it, boys.'

'We can bring Mojalefa with us here tomorrow or his sister,' Duke said. 'They'll tell you exactly the same, word for word.'

'No, no, no, Duke Ellington, that's not what I mean. I'm sure it happened just as you've told me. It's just something else. Anyway, I don't think it really matters.'

Well, if Bra P. didn't really believe us, all he had to do was to wait and see.

He kept on looking at us and shaking his head, as if he thought we were the biggest yarn-spinners he'd ever met.

'Boys, I'll tell you one thing straight. I've been following African politics all my life; never before has so much been accomplished in so little a time. What more are you proposing to do, set up a National Redemptive Council, with Mickey Rooney here as military *supremo*? I wouldn't be surprised if I read in the morning papers tomorrow that you've set fire to the nuclear power plant in Phala-borwa or the oil-from-coal plant in Sasolburg. Why, if you'd been born a generation earlier we wouldn't be having collaborators like Hlubi around!'

His voice trembled a little when he mentioned Hlubi's name.

'Which brings me to something else I want to raise with you before I go to bed. As far as I'm concerned, you've now become our true and veritable heroes, *amaqhawe*, *amagora*, who should be able to take the good and the bad in their stride. I hate to be the bearer of bad news, but the world is very evil, as we used to sing at school. Evil people, who must be plucked out from our midst at all costs, torment us every day, openly. It is the way of life. But what I really want to tell you is this: some blabbering fool has been talking to that sadist of an idiotic cop called Hlubi, who must really believe his person is sacrosanct. But one of these days he'll learn that this is not Soshangange. But there I start digressing. They allege that I've been harbouring certain subversive elements in my house, who are wanted by the police in connection with various crimes against the State. Some-one has even said that the people staying in my house are guerrillas from abroad.

'You've seen it fit to confide some of your operations in me, I'm not unmindful of the compliment. But Mazwi, next time you want to divulge information of a confiden-tial nature to an outsider like myself, be sure to consult with all your comrades in advance, and not just with Tsietsi. Ha! ha! ha!'

'I don't mind telling you, boys, that I have many enemies, who would rejoice to see me put in the can for good. But I'm clean; I'm probably smarter than they, anyway. But I don't think I'm inviolable, like that Hlubi bum. So I stay with my eyes open all the time. As a black man in this country, particularly in this city, you've got to stay awake in order to keep alive. I take nothing for granted, except what my granny who brought me up left me. Anyway, the word is out. I've taken the initiative to clear my name of this awful smear campaign. The police will be here to search the house at eight a.m. tomorrow. You understand what that means, boys. You've got to be out of this place before they come. After that they'll keep half the force trailed on this house. There's immediate promotion for any of them who can nail me down. So, if you wish to stay out of their hands, don't come anywhere near this house again. I'm only sad because I'm being deprived of my new *makoti*, barely twelve hours after I've inherited her. But I know Micky Rooney will take good care of her, so I needn't really worry on that score. I only want to add that I've contacts all over the country and across the borders. If you ever need my assistance, though I hope it never comes to that – one Sharpeville was enough! – if you ever need any help, you only have to send word . . . I guess that beats anything Fr. Molale could have dreamt up in a month of Sunday sermons, wouldn't you say?'

It was clear in these troubled times there was a limit to

the influence even of a man like Bra P. However, we already felt sufficiently heartened, especially by his reference to us as *amaqhawe* and *amagora*. We gave him our firm assurance that he needn't really worry about us; there was still some fighting spirit left in us.

'Wonderful!' he said. 'That puts my mind at rest.'

'There's one thing we should bring up before Bra P. retires,' Tsietsi said. 'Don't you think so?' He turned his sweet, cherubic expression at us.

'*Maar*, how the hell should we know what's on your mind?' Micky asked.

'Listen, who's talking!' Nina said. 'Whoever knows what goes on in that *pampoen* head of yours?'

'I wasn't talking to you, *wena. Nx!*'

'Are you saying "*Nx*" to me, Micky?'

'Just hold your tongues you two,' Duke said.

'Pay no attention to them, Tsi,' Khotso said. 'Just tell Bra P. what's on your mind.'

'I mean, it might be important, don't you think?'

'*Ja!*' several of us said together.

'Bra P., what I really wanted to know is this: Do you think it would be advisable for us to attend the funeral on Sunday? I mean, maybe the *gatas* don't even know our faces.'

The question rocked us a little. It hadn't occurred to us that our close buddy might be buried without any of us being able to attend the funeral.

'I'm going,' Micky said.

'Nobody's asked you anything,' Nina said.

'What a lot of spirit my bride has!' Bra P. said. 'Tsietsi is right to worry about the matter. But I'd agree with Mickey Rooney there. I'd go if I were you. Nobody would have the guts to touch you during the actual funeral service, not even such a godless creature as Hlubi. But if you're still around after the funeral, make sure you're better armed than the South African Defence Force . . . Well, I must be going to bed now. See you in the morning.'

We didn't stay up for long after Bra P. had gone to bed. We needed to make an early start. We discussed the matter at length and agreed to call on Bella first thing in the morning.

The morning mist and chimney smoke rose like a canopy over Soweto. A stream of people, completely wrapped up in thick overcoats with their collars turned up, poured out of their houses and rushed to catch the early morning transport to work. Scavenging township mongrels, returning from their night's adventures, pressed cautiously against the fences, away from the murderous kicks of foul-tempered township residents. Soldiers in armoured cars, shaped like fierce hippos, patrolled the streets. Helicopters flew low over the matchbox houses on an early mission of reconnaissance. Pedestrians scuttled for the safety of ditches and *dongas*, catching the usually vigilant dogs completely by surprise and causing them to shriek in terror. The cold morning breeze cut with biting savagery into our skins.

We stood huddled together at the corner of Bella's street, waiting for Micky, who had taken a devious route to Bella's house.

Micky eventually returned, walking daringly up the street, with a message from Bella's mother that we could walk straight up to their house, as it was not being watched. In this the people of Soweto have a truly marvellous gift. By some unerring instinct they can smell a cop a few blocks away.

We walked up to Bella's house without a trace of fear.

We filed into the kitchen. Bella's mother was getting ready for work. She offered us coffee and fatcakes, which Bella served with the help of her kid sisters. She asked us to stay as long as we liked and left for work. We found the old lady's warm reception most heartening, if somewhat extraordinary, because we had expected her to be resentful of her daughter's association with an organisation which had led her daughter into serious trouble with the police.

We sat around the table, slowly sipping coffee, our eyes fixed intently on Bella's face, while she told us of her gruelling experiences with the police. Her esteem had been raised immeasurably in our eyes. Among us police detention confers a new status and authority. Henceforth she could pontificate on all political matters because all she needed to say was – 'when I was in detention', and old men would sit up and listen. Her eyes seemed withdrawn, distant and introverted. She might have been one of the early Christians, tortured and persecuted for righteousness sake. She was a true witness of the struggle. And, like the Pauline traveller on the road to Damascus, she had been transfigured, metamorphosed, utterly transmuted. Gone was the Bella of yesterday. She had crossed the threshold. She had undergone the supreme test; she had been baptised by fire. She had spiritual superiority conferred upon her by her gruesome prison experiences. She spoke without self-pity or bitterness, with the great dignity that was the special mark of the Mohlakoane women.

The police had raided her home very early on Thursday morning, when there was only the sound of township dogs barking half-spirited messages to their brethren scattered all over the backyards of Soweto. Her whole family was woken up by the sound of loud persistent knocking on the windows, on the front and at the back door, all at once. She showed us where the police had peeled off the paint from the door with their heavy boots and thick batons. Inside the house they were doing the June–July. Their only consoling thought, which mollified their morbid apprehensions a little, was that it couldn't possibly be thieves or robbers, because thieves and robbers never knock. Perhaps it was some neighbouring family in desperate need of help or come to summon their mother, the midwife, they thought. But when their mother opened the door, the police budged in and went to work straightaway, without producing a search warrant. When Bella's mother pointed this out they were very arrogant to her. The rest of the family was dragged out of bed most unceremoniously. Searchlights raked their naked unprotected contours, through thin flimsy night dresses, with the thoroughness of fine toothcombs, while the police made lewd anatomical jokes. They ran-

sacked the place thoroughly, flinging everything careless-
ly about. The house was completely surrounded by fully
armed men, as though they'd come to raid a barracks full
of combat-ready enemy troops.

They made Bella dress in their presence, while they
painted lurid and lascivious scenes of how she would
taste in bed. Then they drove her to the police station at
Protea.

At the police station she was given over to two white
officers. One was a tired-looking, extremely bored man
in his mid-fifties, who yawned all the time; the other was
a much younger man, a boy almost, robust and athletic-
looking.

'*Wat is jou naam?*' the old man at the reception desk
enquired.

'Bella Mohlakoane.'

He scanned through a long list on the desk, yawned
several times over it, until he came to her name. 'Bella
Jojo Mohlakoane?'

'Yes, sir.'

'Yes, what?' the younger man asked.

'Yes, *Meneer.*'

'*Meneer is 'n kaffir predikant, jong*! Yes, what?'

'Yes, *Baas.*'

'Why have they brought you here?' the old man resumed.

'Don't know, sir.'

'Don't know, what?' the younger man asked.

'Don't know, *Baas.*'

The younger constable turned to his colleague, who
was old enough to have been his father, and told him that
the younger ones were more cheeky. He'd been brought
up by a *kaffir* maid of the old generation, he said, who
could have been older than his mother. But she had
called him *klein baasie* from about the time he was five.
But what happened with the younger ones? They went to
school and considered themselves as good as the white
man. Where was the sense in that? It all came out of
educating them, he said. He'd heard that they were even
taught mathematics at school. In a way, it served the

authorities right, this burning down of schools.

The older guy again yawned over the papers on the desk. After fidgeting with them for a while, he declared that he could not find the rest of the papers relating to whatever charges had been brought against her.

'*Sy's net een van hulle kaffir kommanissie hoer-meide*,' his young associate said helpfully.

The old man raised indolent eyes at Bella, asked her two questions and then washed his hands of the case.

'Were you part of the illegal demonstrations against the government in Soweto yesterday morning?' he asked.

'No, *Baas*.'

'Are you a member of the S.R.C. or the A.N.C.?'

'No, *Baas*.'

'This one will just have to wait for Koos,' he said.

Bella was left standing in the middle of the room where she'd been standing since they'd brought her in. They simply ignored her and talked of other matters. The younger man prattled on incessantly while his listener hardly bothered to suppress his frequent yawns. The older man kept glancing at his watch.

An hour passed, perhaps more, before the one called Koos appeared. With him was Hlubi. Between them they were kicking and swearing at a young man, walking in front of them. The young man's face was a pathetic sight. He was swollen all over, like a dumpling, so badly his own mother might not have recognised him. Narrow slits, which would have made Lee Chong's eyes look like marbles, showed where his eyes should have been. His lips were so thick that a doctor's first reaction would have been to treat him for elephantiasis. He staggered into the room, obviously punch-drunk and looking every cubic inch a ravaged remnant from a serious car-wreck.

'This one should be ready to talk now,' Koos said to his two white colleagues.

Koos had the appearance of a Springbok scrum-half. He towered over everybody else in the room, including the young man whom Bella had thought huge. His shirt-sleeves were rolled up to his shoulders to display his immense arms, the size of small tree-trunks. His hands were like shovels. His neck was as thick as an Afrikander bull's, with jugular veins jutting out. He sported a Kallie Knoetze moustache and had the ruddy appearance of a person accustomed to a vigorous outdoor life.

'Now, you *blerry skelm*, will you tell the *Oubaas* who your student leaders are?' he asked.

It was impossible to tell what the reaction of the student with the bloated face was. It was inconceivable how anyone in that condition could have been expected to talk. Bella had seen many badly beaten people in her life, in the hands of thugs; they were a common township sight. But the mere sight of this man drew tears from her eyes.

The younger of her interrogators came closer to the man with the swollen face, so as to miss as little of the sport as possible.

'*Jou donder se kaffir, kan jy nie praat nie*?' he asked.

But the beaten student only groaned and said nothing.

Koos walked round the room. He yawned loudly and stretched his tree-trunk limbs lazily. He did not look at the battered student; he did not walk directly towards him, but at an angle, as if to bypass him. When he was abreast of the student, he suddenly struck with the swiftness of a *mamba*. Squarely on the head of the groaning student his truncheon crashed, and the student collapsed like a sack of potatoes.

The younger of Bella's interrogators roared his appreciation.

'Now you watch us go to work on him,' Koos said.

He called for cold water and Hlubi trotted out of the room, like a surgeon's assistant, and came back with a bucketful of water. He emptied the bucket on the face of the student.

The wounded student stirred a little, then moved his head from side to side.

Koos estimated his distance carefully, like Gary Player preparing to hit a drive. He took a well-aimed swipe with his truncheon, which landed flush on the student's shoulder as he was trying to rise. They went to work on the man coldly and methodically. Koos worked from the shoulders downwards and Hlubi took the feet first. The man howled and spun and twisted and rolled. He grovelled on the floor before them. Despite his deafening screams, the beating continued. The screams grew weaker and weaker until the student passed out.

Koos called for more iced water, but the old man at the desk said, '*Dit is genoeg.*'

Koos ordered Hlubi to tear off the man's shirt.

The old man at the desk turned his face the other way.

The man's welts were like hosepipes. Koos handed Hlubi a packet of *rooi* pepper to rub into the unconscious man's raw wounds.

They carried him out of the room, more dead than alive.

Koos returned, looking as self-satisfied as a rugby player after a glorious test match, with Hlubi tagging along behind him like an autograph hunter.

'Let's see if he's not ready to talk when he wakes up!' Koos said.

The other young white constable's laughter rang weirdly through the room.

'Koos, we have a small problem here,' the old man said, yawning and turning to his papers. 'This lassie you see before you is Bella Mohla-something. Her name's on your list. We don't have the details. What's she in for?'

Koos came up to the desk and peered at the list.

'The ones on this list,' he said, pointing with his wet truncheon, 'all twenty-five of them, are the ring-leaders.'

He approached Bella and walked round her, inspecting her with wanton eyes. Then he went back to the desk and picked up the list.

'Isn't she a dish?' he said to the younger constable, who winked. 'Are you Bella Jojo Mohla . . . – Ag, these *blerry* native names, they so difficult! How do they ever manage to pronounce them? – Is that your name?' he asked.

'Yes, *Bass*.'

She was trembling uncontrollably, after having been treated to a free and masterful display of systematic sadism.

'How many men have you slept with?' he asked.

The question caught her unexpectedly. '*Baasie?*'

'They're taught sex from the cradle,' he told the others. 'You're an office-bearer of the S.R.C., is that right?'

'No, *Baas.*'

'We've not come here to play marbles, understand?'

'Yes, *Baas.*'

'What's your position in the S.R.C.?'

'None, *Baas.*'

Hlubi came towards her and told her in Zulu that the white man wasn't there to play. If she didn't want to shit on her bloomers, he continued, she'd have to tell the white man everything he wanted to know and to answer his questions positively. He told her that what she'd seen them do to the stubborn young man was just a small thing compared with what they'd do to her. He asked if anybody had ever rubbed *rooi* pepper into her vagina.

They examined and cross-examined her, but she stuck to her story. Whoever had alleged that she was in any way associated with the student demonstrations, she told them, was just bent upon discrediting her and besmirching her name. Not only was she in no way connected with the S.R.C., but on the very morning of the students' demonstrations she'd been at the clinic in Orlando, as the police could confirm for themselves.

It wasn't her gamble which saved her. Several factors saved her from receiving the beating of her life. To begin with, the staff on duty, who were the night staff really, had already had as much sport as they wanted. They were fatigued, after all the physical exertion of the night they'd been through. What had started as a delightful game of striking terror into the hearts of young African students had gradually lost its novelty and excitement as the night wore on. It had been a busy night, indeed, with the students pouring in faster than they could tackle them. Inevitably many of the new arrivals had had to be shunted aside to wait their turn. The time for the night staff to go off duty was approaching and they were looking forward to a well-deserved rest. Their victims could wait until they came on duty again. All these things the officers discussed, as they burrowed their heads in the papers on the desk. Another factor which saved her was that she was a frail-looking girl, so that when Hlubi raised his hand to strike her the old man at the desk ordered him to stop.

She was kept standing for perhaps another hour afterwards, and, before her interrogators could go off duty, they instructed Hlubi to lock her up until the evening.

Hlubi led her to a cell, which already had two girls. She knew them both.

Sonti had been taken from Baragwanath on Wednesday afternoon, after receiving treatment for a bullet wound in her leg. The police had made her stand on her bad leg until she could support herself no longer. Still they picked her up from the floor and made her stand on one leg all over again. She passed into a delirious state and woke up to find herself in that cell. Gangrene had begun to form on her injured leg. She was moaning softly and repeatedly from the unbearable pain.

Bella's other cell-mate was a buxom girl called Dithole. Dithole was pretty even when she was crying, but they also said that she could be as stubborn as a mule and had the temper of a wild cat. Her kid sister had been shot by the police, right in front of her. She attacked the police, single-handed, pelting them with stones and any other missile she could lay her hands upon. The police had then grabbed her – still kicking, biting, scratching and screaming – and pushed her into a waiting police van. She kept kicking and clawing at the sides of the police van all the way to Protea. There they tried every trick to break her, but she might just as well have had twelve skins, each one as thick as a hippo's hide, for all the effect their brutality had on her. The mere sight of a policeman moved her into such a violent tantrum that they'd still not been able to get through to her. In the evening one police officer, who must have been Koos from the description, had called for her in his office and asked to be left alone with her. After he'd locked the door, he told her that he knew she was only faking her hysteria. He suggested that if she allowed him to do her, right there, he'd see to it that she came to no harm. He approached her with a drooling mouth, but the moment he laid his hands on her she sunk her nails so deeply into his bull neck that he screamed with pain and knocked her to the ground with a stinging slap that made her ears sing. He cursed her loudly, eloquently and anatomically. Hearing the fracas the other policemen rushed to the door. He opened the door, still mouthing heavy unprintable insults. His eyes were glowing like two red hot embers. He gave instructions for her to be locked up until he could make up his mind how to deal with her. They'd still not visited her in the cell since bringing her in on the night before.

The police wanted to know from everybody they interrogated who were the student leaders. The detained students were repeatedly told that the police already knew the names of all the people they wanted. All they wanted to test from the other students they questioned was their truthfulness, they said. They'd be released as soon as they'd confirmed what the police wanted to know. In the case of Sonti and Dithole, the carrot had been dangled and removed, dangled and removed until both girls lost interest.

At one stage, before Bella was brought in, there'd been a dozen girls in that cell.

Bella had been in that cell for what seemed like a whole glacial age when her name was called out. A policeman, his whole expression surprisingly amicable and genial, came to unlock the door and escorted her to the reception office. On the way to the reception he told her that she had a visitor. She could only think of her mother. But it was Bra P.

Her sunken hopes rose a little.

He told her not to worry, that everything would be fine, because the police had already assured him that everything would be just fine, they'd release her that very same evening when their investigations had been completed.

But how could she not worry? What were they still

keeping her for? Why wouldn't they allow her to go with Bra P.?

Bra P. could explain no further.

He'd brought her fish and chips, with bread rolls, vienna sausages and a can of coke. She had no appetite and wrapped the parcels to take back to the cell so that she could share the food with her cell-mates, who had told her that they'd not been given food since they'd been locked up the previous night.

He told her that she was not allowed to take food into the cell.

She nibbled a little and then pushed the food aside. He coaxed her to eat a little more. She could only drink the coke.

She told him about Sonti and Dithole. But Bra P. told her he was powerless to do anything for them.

She returned to their cell with just a flicker of hope glowing in her heart.

On her way back to the cell she overheard the new Afrikaner constable at the desk muttering something to Bra P. about the whole affair having been a mistake and the work of certain over-enthusiastic upstarts.

Later that afternoon they brought them their supper of cold, soft porridge, without sugar, which was served in heavy enamel plates.

Sonti spewed after the first spoon. Thereafter they could only glare at the nauseating stuff.

At about 7.00 p.m. she was again called to the office. At the reception desk the same Afrikaner constable who had spoken to Bra P. told her that she was now free to go. Just that. No explanation. He told her that she'd be driven home, that was all.

Could this be another of their tricks, she wondered. Did they perhaps want to break her by making her chase mirages? She had not really believed Bra P. But now her hope was rekindled. Her heart leapt with expectation.

They dropped her outside the gate of her home.

There was jubilation in the house. Her eldest sister, who was married in Dobsonville, had come home the moment she heard of Bella's arrest. They were simply elated at this new turn of events. They fussed over her and treated her like an invalid, like royalty, like the incarnation of a miracle. Their ecstasy was contagious, so that soon the ice inside her began to thaw.

After Bella had finished her story we remained silent for a while.

At length I raised the problem of her safety while she remained at home. As it turned out, she'd already discussed the matter with her mother. Bra P. had told her mother that Bella had only been granted a temporary reprieve. They were bringing in new men of the crack anti-riot squad, instead of the regular police, to handle the situation in Soweto. A new brigadier, who was still to assume duties, had already been appointed. From what Bra P. had heard, the new brigadier and his supporting staff all belonged to the new school, graduates of the military academy, with academic degrees and learned treatises on the native problem to their credit. Such new brooms, with more zeal than experience and no regard for tradition, were known for their ability to upset established relationships. As Bra P. saw it, these over-innovative guys would most certainly want to institute their own investigations when they took charge of operations and Bella's name was likely to pop up again. Bra P. had advised Bella's mother to remove her daughter from home as soon as possible, within the next twenty-four hours. Her mother had then suggested that she should go and stay with relatives in Atteridgeville near Pretoria until things could simmer down a little. Bella's own view on the matter was that she'd helped to precipitate the crisis, along with her colleagues in the S.R.C.; she'd not abandon the ship at that stage simply to save her own skin. Her mother had understood. Instead they'd agreed that she could go and live with friends, right there in Soweto, who were not immediately under suspicion. In that way she could continue to serve in the S.R.C., without abdicating her responsibilities at a critical stage in the struggle. If a reassessment of their positions within the S.R.C. ever became necessary, it would have to be done orderly without creating a leadership vacuum.

We discussed our own positions in the light of what Bella had said. Her own predicament highlighted the general predicament; her cherished ideals were our own. It became manifestly clear that we'd have to divide into smaller groups and meet every night at some pre-arranged rendezvous. We would sleep at the homes of school friends, never staying long enough at any place to attract notice. We agreed it was best to move in groups of two. Until the funeral we would meet every night at Muntu's.

The discussion then veered into other matters. We still had other functions to perform before the day was over, the most important of which was to collect all the funds which had been raised so far, so that they could be distributed accordingly. Khotso and Bella, as Treasurer and Deputy respectively, would remain behind to receive all the funds that were brought in. The rest of us would round up our various cell leaders in our respective areas. When we'd completed our errands, we'd reassemble at Bella's place, after taking the usual precautions to make sure that we weren't being followed, with all the money we'd managed to collect. The process of distributing the money would follow the same procedure in reverse. When the money had been divided among all the bereaved families, according to their relative needs from the reports of our field workers, we'd send the contributions through our usual functionaries.

As the organisation's Chairman I had no specific area, so it was agreed I should cover Khotso's. And so we set out in groups of twos to scour the townships in the discharge of our duties, inspired by a new civic consciousness.

Everywhere we passed, signs of devastation wrought by the children of Soweto stared us in the face. Every public building lay in ruins, razed to the ground; all the despicable symbols of authority had been reduced to ashes.

In an obvious show of strength army planes periodically flew low over Soweto. Crowds of pot-bellied, mucus-stained children clambered out of the ditches and the *dongas* they used as playing grounds to wave at the aeroplanes and to shout, 'Aeroplane bring me back a child!'

In the streets soldiers paraded the length and breadth of Soweto, shooting on sight any gathering of more than two people. The sound of machine-gun fire soon became familiar to the ears of Sowetans.

At some street corners sporadic fights broke up between the soldiers and stone-throwing youths, enraged by some new provocative action of the authorities. The police unleashed dogs on a gang of youths, lounging outside Rathebe's shops, but the youths retaliated by knifing the Alsatians and burning them with paraffin from Rathebe's shops. A police car with four whites opened fire on a group of youths playing soccer at the Phefeni football ground. And near Phefeni station another car with no registration plates in which two whites were travelling shot a young man and left an axe lying by his side. A policeman was dragged out of his car outside the Dube Y.M.C.A., beaten up and tied at the wrists to the steering-wheel with his own handcuffs before army reinforcements came to his rescue. In certain cases unidentified snipers, hidden beyond the reach of the army, retaliated by opening fire upon the soldiers and the police. These incidents increased as more police and army detachments were surprised by their attackers and disarmed. Sophisticated weapons exchanged hands in the backyards of Soweto. The people confined all direct confrontation with the authorities to the back alleys of Soweto, where their supremacy over the state forces was unchallengeable. By and large they ducked any kind of notice and conspicuosity – which is perhaps why none of their triumphs were reported in the news media, which, however, continued to give prominence to all the news about our own vanquished.

It was incredible, the vast sums of money our people had managed to raise! There couldn't have been a single pocket in Soweto which they'd not tapped.

We drudged along late into the night, so that when we parted, after concluding all our business at Bella's place, we were all ready to drop from sheer exhaustion.

I was to go with Khotso to Shakes' home, with whom I had already concluded arrangements earlier in the day. Bella was to go with Nina, after the latter had refused Micky's offer of the Nazarene tower.

We arranged to meet the following night at Muntu's place during the wake. Until then we could do as we pleased with our time. I planned to catch up on my sleep.

The wake was like a combination of some big religious revival, political rally and major social event. All over the twenty-eight townships which comprise Soweto similar wakes were being held for the other children of Soweto who had fallen in the struggle.

The coffin, brought in from the mortuary in Phefeni earlier that evening, lay in the main bedroom, supported on benches and draped with a white velvet pall. Mattresses had been spread on the floor. At the head of the mourners sat Muntu's mother, flanked by his maternal and paternal aunts.

In the sitting-room Fr. Molale of the local Anglican church led the congregation in prayer and in the singing of hymns. They sang 'Abide with me', 'Through all the changing scenes of life', 'Peace, Perfect Peace' and other favourites. Fr. Molale announced the hymns in Xhosa, Tswana and English. A former Methodist woman, who had married into the Anglican church, shouted the hymn numbers as found in the Xhosa Methodist hymnal for the benefit of Methodists. Another woman, who sang in the church choir, started the first line of each hymn in a strong vibrating soprano voice and the congregation joined in from the second line onwards. At the end of each line a verse-feeder read out the words of the next line in a lilting tenor voice for the benefit of those without hymn books, and each hymn proceeded in this anti-phonal manner to the end. With brilliant extemporisation, which would have done credit even to an *imbongi*, Fr. Molale broke into a prayer to fit the occasion and the family's special circumstances. A hymn followed, 'Fight the good fight', a short impromptu sermon, another hymn, followed by yet another prayer.

After the last prayer the people squinted and rubbed their eyes to get used to the light again.

At the end of his contribution Fr. Molale announced what amounted to a programme for the rest of the wake. He still had other wakes to attend in his parish that same night. He relinquished the Chair to an appointed successor to mark the end of the formal opening ceremony.

When he stepped down, the church elder identified for the purpose, a lay preacher in the Anglican church, rose to take his place. Thereafter there'd be no strict rules of precedence, although in general seniority by age and church rank, the numerical superiority of each denomination represented would all be accorded special status. The older men would come before the younger ones, the lay preachers before members of the women's *Umanyano* and so on, all in strict vigil protocol. The Methodists, the Lutherans and members of other denominations, according to the strength of their numbers, would all await their turn after the Anglicans whose territory, as it were, this was, as Muntu's parents belonged to their *ibandla*. But in the end neither their numerical strength nor territorial advantage would be allowed to interfere in any way with the sense of fair play, the communal feeling, the ecumenical spirit, which are the special marks of all African wakes. So that before long the *umshumayeli* who had taken over from Fr. Molale would yield his place to the leading member present of the Methodist church. '*Sizakucela ibandla laseWisile khe lizokubhedesha nalo*,' he would say, and then efface himself as soon as the Methodists, whom he had just invited, were ready to start their *umbhedesho* or contribution to the wake.

Immaculately clad in their red waist coats, the *amadodana* of the Methodist church would mount their denominational offensive. Their senior *umvangeli* would rally them with a spirited rendition of 'Noyana, Noyana!'; now humming the tune like the muted sound of a trumpet, now rising again to a full crescendo; beating his bible and stamping on one foot to keep time. The exuberant, effervescent Methodist forces would hold the fort for as long as their ammunition lasted or until a relief force of Lutherans was ready to replace them.

As the night wore on, the denominational approach would be replaced by individual effort and contributions, when a free-for-all, as it were, would be declared. A man of no special status, except that he also belonged to the community, would rise and speak off the cuff, paying a moving tribute to the sterling qualities of the deceased; not to be outdone, another would quickly take the floor and tell an anecdote, with a dozen possible morals. Every speech would be punctuated by a hymn of the speaker's own choice. Sometimes an experienced speaker, a veteran of many wakes, whose Saturday nights were always fully occupied in similar business, would spread his hymn throughout his address by singing one verse at a time and then speaking on, only to break his speech with another verse again and so on until the end. Someone else, for the benefit of any strangers, would give a life history of the deceased, with the dates all badly muddled up. Straight on his heels another would rise and confess frankly to never having set her eyes on the face of the deceased, and then give a stirring message of encouragement to the family of the deceased. Relatives, family friends, neighbours, casual acquaintances, strangers, professional wake-goers, township and traditional philosophers would all have their chance to deliver their obituaries and convey their messages of condolence. In this way the dead man's life would be tossed backward and forward, from relevant to irrelevant and, sometimes, to an intoxicated speaker, too. Qualities would be discovered in him which, if he were present, he'd have been surprised to know he possessed. When the speakers had run out of things to say they'd sing hymns, so that even those who didn't possess any powers of oratory could, at least, bawl out their favourite hymns, until daybreak. Everyone's full democratic right to console the bereaved, air their grievances and generally let off steam would be fully catered for.

An old man, a close relative or trusted family friend, with a pen, an exercise book and a small dish for a cash register, sat at a table in a corner of the tiny sitting-room nearest to the door to receive contributions.

At regular intervals tea would be served with scones, which the women in the kitchen were baking all the time. Neighbours would also come with dishes of whatever they'd been able to bake to augment the supply.

Some people would leave; others would arrive and so on, until dawn.

Outside, a group of old men sat around a burning log, telling stories to pass the night, to blunt death's painful sting and to relieve the congestion inside the matchbox house. They spoke of their youthful days, when a good suit used to cost £2 10s. Someone else mentioned the miners' strike of '46 because he used to know somebody who had fallen in the strike. A general discussion of strikes ensued. Somebody else came very close to the subject in everyone's mind by alluding to the recent bus boycott in the township of Kwa-Thema; another one steered the discussion to the Alexandra bus boycott of the fifties. They hedged around the subject, telling minor stories in order to avoid the main one; building up to it gradually, delicately, reluctantly. And when they could no longer avoid it, an old man sighed and said, '*Ja*, things have only changed for the worse!'

Another asked, 'Did you hear what happened to all three of MaMthombeni's sons? That was a sad story. She's that epileptic woman whose husband we buried last month. And now for this to happen to her again! It's simply too much.'

They received the news with appropriate groans.

'If there's a God, why does he allow this?' an old man with atheistic inclinations asked.

'Keep God out of this,' another said.

They exchanged information about the latest atrocities with corrosive self-pity.

'What monster is this our children have unleashed upon us?' someone else asked.

'And now they want to bite the hand that feeds them!' another said.

'Did you read the circular they've issued?'

The talk accordingly turned to the strike which had been called for the following week. A note of vexation, aggravation, dejection and resignation crept into the conversation. Many expressed themselves in the most pessimistic terms possible and said the whole thing would never work. They said the only certain outcome of the strike was going to be a loss of jobs for most of them, while workers were brought in from the Homelands to replace them. They complained that without their jobs they could neither keep their houses nor remain in Johannesburg in terms of the influx control regulations.

At least once during the night each one of them would go into the house, pay his respects and retire to the fire outside in order to give room to late-comers and women.

A cow and two sheep were being slaughtered in the yard near the peach tree, on which a bright gas lamp had been hung. Men in their middle ages skinned the beasts while the older men round the fire directed the operations, passing critical remarks all the time about the lack of skill of the younger men. A general discourse on the shortcomings of the *simanje-manje* generation, as they called them, followed. The old men were full of contempt for the ways of the new generation, who purchased all their meat from butcheries. One told the story of a child who was once asked where milk came from and had replied, 'From a bottle.' The rest expressed their scorn in high-pitched guffaws. They were full of condemnation for the vices of urban youths; they were full of lamentation for the passing of the old ways.

Portions of meat from the slaughtered beasts were pierced with spikes or simply placed on the logs to be grilled over the fire. The ripe pieces of meat were passed round to be shared among all the men. One of the men who'd been involved in the slaughtering tasted the meat and complained that it had no salt. He went to the kitchen for salt. An old man with a halo of white hair and no front teeth jeered and said disdainfully that it confirmed everything they'd been saying about the decadence of the new generation. He called for the gall-bladder of one of the slaughtered sheep and sprinkled a little gall on his meat. The younger men squirmed as he swallowed.

As the fire died down, the youngest in the group would fetch another log in a corner of the yard to rekindle the dying embers.

Women boiled water and cooked meat and *umngqusho* in huge black three-legged pots over open fires. Now and again they called on the men to shift the pots.

In another section of the yard a group of students sat huddled together round a brazier, singing freedom songs:

> *Izokunyathel' iAfrika*
> Afrika is going to trample you under.
> *John Vorster, shoot! Uzakwenzakala.*
> John Vorster, shoot! Or you're in mortal
>     danger.
>> *Hey, John Vorster! Hey! Uzakwenzakala.*
>> Hey, John Vorster! Hey! You're in
>>     mortal danger.
>> *Hey, Pasopa! Uzakwenzakala.*
>> Hey, Look out! You're in mortal
>>     danger.

It was a daring song, a challenge and a warning to the forces of oppression. Boys' voices droned in heavy mournful tones, full of sorrow and menace.

A girl from the same group started another song, more convivial than the first, in a high-spirited swaggering voice. Other voices picked up the chorus:

> *(Thina) Thina silulutsha.*
> (We are) We are the proud youth.
> *(Asi . . .) Asinakubulawa.*
> (We won't) We won't succumb to death.
> *(Aso . . .) Asoze sabulawa ngu Jimmy Kruger,*
> (We won't) We won't be liquidated by
>   Jimmy Kruger,
>> *Sisebatsha . . .*
>> We are the youth . . .

Their defiant voices carried deep conviction in the ultimate triumph of the forces of liberation for which they
stood. In their voices were the suffering of generations
and the hope of millions.

Around the fire of the burning logs an old man, afraid
the young ones were courting trouble, voiced his opinion.
A few others grunted as an expression of mutual feeling,
but otherwise held their tongues. Another old man
shrugged his shoulders and said, '*Sizothini*? It is a sign of
the times.'

A few of them hummed the songs very softly under
their breaths.

In another corner of the yard a small motely crowd
had gathered around Aunt Bessie and Zandie, both of
whom had long since reconciled their differences. They'd
been drinking together like kindred spirits since sunset,
as if to seal their alliance, and had managed, through
sheer magnetism, to draw like-minded people around
them. These were relatives from afar, as dehydrated as
the Kalahari sands, and chronically thirsty uncles, who
had come from other townships on the Reef. They all
made profuse attestations of their gratitude to Zandie for
relieving them from the drought of Soweto. They treated
him like one of the family and, following Aunt Bessie's
example, he was already calling them '*Malume*'. He and
Aunt Bessie had taken an early initiative, as if by tele-
pathy, to sound the feelings of all arriving relatives about
contributing to a refreshment fund. They worked separately at first and then as a team, once a feeling of mutu-
ality mixed with expediency had superseded the initial
animosity each had felt for the other. Each time enough
money was raised through *gazaat*, Zandie took the contributions and went to buy alcohol from a shebeen which
only he knew about, since all the shebeens had already
been ordered to shut down. Nor did he permit anyone to
accompany him.

Behind the lavatory a drunken couple, completely
oblivious of their surroundings, performed a familiar
ritual in *staan-staan* fashion. A dog came, sniffed at their
legs and went on its way.

That same evening I met my parents. There was nothing really spectacular about our reunion. None of the demonstrative scenes I'd imagined. The disagreeable sermons I'd expected, the distasteful scenes of remonstration and recrimination just did not take place. When Sindiswa brought me to the bedroom where they were waiting to see me, my mother's first question was whether I'd eaten, as if I'd just returned from watching a football match at Orlando Stadium. Without waiting for my answer she told Sindiswa to bring me food, despite my protestations that I'd done nothing but eat and sleep the whole day. Except for her eyes, which sparkled in a certain sorrowful, affectionate and compassionate manner, she evinced very little emotion.

My father, too. He was never a man of many words. He asked me whether I was well. And when I told him, with as much nonchalance as I could muster, that I just felt fine, he said that was good to hear. Then in as few words as possible he exhorted me to bear it like a man.

It was always impossible to tell what was behind that mask of imperturbability. He was as composed as a song. In a world of insecurity and instability, that expression of equanimity had always represented the only constants in my life. I'd never known chinks to show in his armour. And now in my greatest hour of need I was truly grateful for the stoicism instilled in me by my encounter with him in his usual inscrutable but unflappable manner.

Still I could feel an undercurrent of anxiety and turmoil beneath the placid surface and atmosphere we all tried to cultivate.

Sindiswa brought me a ridiculous helping of *pap* and *boerewors*, enough for several famished people. I forced myself to eat while my parents stared at me as if I'd just come from outer space.

Not a word about taking my politics with me to hell!

They gave me news of Vukani's departure for Natalspruit the night before. I told them I'd already heard the news from Sindiswa, so they filled in the details. He was staying with old family friends, the Mzizis, who also had boys about our age. My parents said they'd left him feeling considerably cheerful after a discomposing day in which he'd had to answer several knocks from highly saucy and pushy policemen in search of me. They had even threatened him that if they failed to locate me they'd most probably haul him in, in my place, until I could give myself up.

When things settled down, my mother said, they'd fetch him. Since the Minister had already announced the predicted closure of schools only that morning, a week earlier than we were scheduled to close, there was no hurry for him to get back.

She also spoke of the insecurity in Soweto, which had intensified over the last two days.

I waited for the inevitable. But first they seemed determined to feel their way around the subject, to allay all my suspicions and misgivings first, to build up an atmosphere of normalcy.

They spoke of a few other families we knew who had also taken their children away from Soweto.

An awkward silence followed, that stillness that preludes a plunge.

Finally my mother came to the point delicately, soothingly, persuasively. She asked me what I proposed to do with myself. When I told her I didn't know, she hastened to add that my welfare was their only concern.

Another silence followed.

Then she pleaded with me passionately to take a powder. She reminded me how the wisest generals always sounded a retreat at the exact moment when the odds appeared heavily loaded against them, only to pounce back with renewed vigour at a more auspicious time with the speed and fury of a leopard.

They wanted me to go and live among my father's people, at least until things simmered down a little. She said it sweetly, inoffensively, as though going to the Transkei was no different from going to Natalspruit. I could have told her that going to the Transkei was like a child playing hide-and-seek, burrowing her head under a chair, with her buttocks up in the air, and shouting, '*Andikho*!' But I only looked up at the roof and affected to give the matter some very deep thought.

She steered the conversation away from the subject, imagining no doubt that she was giving the idea time to sink in. She asked me whether I felt warm enough without my overcoat, whereupon my father immediately offered me his, but I protested gently and said I'd go home on the sly and fetch myself something warm to wear.

I asked them how much longer they intended to remain at Muntu's place because I wanted the key to our house to go and change, and maybe take a nap. My mother thought that was an excellent idea but urged me to be careful of being tailed. I winked. She said I could have the key because they'd be at the wake until early in the morning, as long as I left it at the usual place.

I went to rejoin my colleagues outside where they had congregated around the brazier.

They were discussing the form our contribution to the funeral should take, after having been approached by one of Muntu's uncles responsible for the programme. We rejected the notion of electing a speaker to represent us because a straightforward oration was likely to lead to the victimisation of whoever we chose to speak on our behalf. We knew the funeral would be buzzing with informers. Eventually we opted for poetry, which would be read in church and perhaps at the graveside. That was a better gamble because members of the police force in general do not stay at school for long. Even if their informers taped the poetry the police were likely to dismiss it as some obscure prayer, one of those with 'thees' and 'thous' and 'thines'. So it was agreed we approach Mandla, a young and accomplished poet of the black consciousness movement, to compose an appropriate poem for the occasion.

A further suggestion from Micky was that instead of the usual hearse we should request Zondo, the coal merchant, to lend us his horse-drawn cart or carry the coffin ourselves. Because of the distance to Doornkop cemetry we agreed instead that Micky and Duke should approach Zondo with our request in the morning.

Micky asked what we intended to do with Zondo's horse, if he refused. But Khotso told him that there was only one bloke in our outfit who thought along those lines and that the whole question of retribution had better be left to him.

'*Se dit weer, Jack?*' Micky asked, but Khotso simply refused to repeat his statement.

When we discussed the idea with Muntu's uncles of substituting the hearse with a horse-drawn carriage, at first they were all filled with consternation. 'It's just not done,' one of them said flatly. They told us that, besides, the hearse had already been hired. We told them that it didn't matter even if they'd already hired transport because the other mourners who had no transport of their own could squeeze into the hearse. We haggled a bit, trying to point out that we detested the notion of anyone making capital gain out of the tragic situation in Soweto and that at a later stage we might have to deal with any African funeral undertaker who exploited the situation. The discussion was brought to an end by a senior uncle from Queenstown who said,

'*Enyanisweni, ngumsebenzi wabo, bayekeni abantwana benze ngeyabo indlela* – In truth, the ceremony is theirs, let the children do as they see fit.'

We asked if we could be allowed to act as pall-bearers and the *malume* from Queenstown promised he'd arrange it.

When Muntu's uncles left us, after we had agreed on our part in the programme, we discussed the question of transport for the many mourners expected at the funeral. We decided to shelve the question until the following morning.

Shortly before dawn I left Muntu's place.

I approached our house from the direction of Ntate Sebotsane's yard. Somebody had untied his vicious dog. I nearly jumped on its back as I prepared to scale the fence. So I skirted round his yard until I reached home.

I hoped I wasn't being followed, even though I'd taken the necessary precautions.

After unlocking the door, I left the key under the

coal-box and pulled the door after me, which locked itself.

There were still a few hours before the funeral, which wasn't due to start until around midday. So I went straight to bed. They'd have to break in to get me. I slept the sleep of the dead.

Although I didn't know it at the time, that was to be the very last time I slept at home.

We buried Muntu on Sunday. There were several other funerals being held all over the township, funerals of other students who had died in the police shootings.

Despite the chill of a vicious high *veld* morning, people started to arrive for the funeral in large numbers from about ten in the morning. They lounged about or sat on benches in the yard.

Women, many of them without having had so much as a wink of sleep all night, were still busy peeling potatoes, cooking rice and more meat over the open fire in the yard and preparing salad for the expected crowd.

Bra P.'s analysis had been correct. The police were making themselves scarce in the townships that morning. There wasn't a single police van on sight. What with people's tempers on edge and emotions running so high! It only needed a single police uniform to inflame the people and precipitate a vast conflagration, which would engulf us all. The people were, indeed, in a mean mood. You could see it in the grim, set expressions on their faces, in the knitted furrows on their foreheads and in the way their eyes narrowed as if to take in every little detail and impress it indellibly on their souls. But if uniformed policemen had been temporarily withdrawn, we had no illusions about the fact that the place was crawling with SBs and other informers, poised like lice in a prison cell to receive new inmates.

We came out stealthily at first, like rats from a hole, and then boldly took our places beside the other mourners.

A horse-drawn cart moved slowly up the road towards Muntu's home. As it drew nearer, wer recognised the squat figure of Zondo, looking like an Afro-American slave chariot-driver of old, dressed up according to his master's instructions for some special occasion. Seated beside him were Duke and Micky.

Some dogs a few houses away chased the cart a few yards up the road but were soon discouraged by the haughty indifference of the horse. They hesitated and withdrew completely as they approached the large gathering of people.

The cart stopped outside the gate.

Duke and Micky came to where we were standing in the yard, leaning against the fence.

Tsietsi suggested we ask Zondo to move the cart up to the church and park it as near the door as possible, as we only needed it to transport the coffin from the church to the cemetery.

Micky volunteered to accompany Zondo. They rode up to the church. We didn't see Micky until much later.

We asked Duke how he and Micky had fared with Zondo.

Zondo's attachment to his horse was proverbial in our township. People spoke of him and his horse as if they were talking of David and Jonathan. He usually left it to graze in the open space between Elkah Stadium and the dam, while he kept watch over it from some distance. Actually, he spent his time chasing after township urchins, who persistently took potshots at the horse with their slings just for the fun of having Zondo after them. Otherwise, if he wasn't driving round in his cart, selling firewood and coal, he was trimming his horse's bushy mane or brushing its glossy skin until he could almost see his reflection on its flanks. He would only pause to feed the horse out of his own hand. He was inordinately fond of that horse and so we wondered how he'd reacted to our request.

Duke told us how he and Micky had gone straight from the wake to Zondo's house as soon as morning light came.

'*Hawu, majita!*' Khotso exclaimed. 'You mean, you couldn't even wait for him to wake up?'

'I did suggest that. But Micky kept asking: What if Zondo should wake up, harness the horse and take off before we arrive? You can't argue with Micky, *mos*.'

We all knew how early Zondo went out on his morning rounds.

So Duke and Micky had woken Zondo up very early that morning, knocking at his door as if they'd break in if he didn't open. At first he thought it was some early customers come to buy wood and coal.

'Round! Take your buckets round the house,' he shouted from somewhere inside the house. 'I won't be long.'

'Bab' uZondo, we've come to consult you on a very grave matter,' Duke hollered back.

Zondo opened the door and admitted them into the sitting-room.

His shock came in stages as they explained their business. At first he was completely mystified, so that they had to repeat themselves twice over. And then, as a little comprehension dawned on him, his mind searched in panic for other alternatives.

'What's wrong with a car or a lorry?' he asked. 'I could let you have my lorry. Other people use lorries.'

Zondo owned a lorry, which was also used to deliver wood and coal. He had hired a driver for the lorry, because he preferred to drive the cart himself.

It was clear that Zondo only thought there'd been some difficulties in procuring a proper hearse and that maybe in our modesty we thought even a horse-drawn cart would do. It was with some difficulties that Duke and Micky managed to explain to him how we thought a true son of the soil should be buried.

A great fear assailed him.

'What if they should shoot my horse?'

'Then we'll pay for it,' Micky said.

Zondo laughed without amusement.

'Have you any idea how much a horse costs?'

'How much?' Micky said.

'R150 for an ordinary horse; for a special pedigree like mine . . .'

'It's all right, we'll pay,' Micky said.

Again that laughter that was like the sound of a car engine misfiring.

'When you can't even pay for a hearse!'

'On the contrary, we'd rather support honest, hard-working traders like yourself rather than any of those money-grabbers who operate as undertakers, some of whom are mere fronts for white businessmen, at any rate,' Duke said.

'We've collected some money,' Micky said.

Zondo was not sure what to make out of all this. For the first time he appeared to give the matter some serious thought.

His wife walked into the sitting-room and asked, 'What's the matter, *Baba*?'

'Nothing,' he said. 'Go back to the bedroom.'

She did as she was told.

'Look, Bab' uZondo,' Duke said. 'You know Muntu's people, *mos*. Well, *sithunywe yibo*.'

Zondo leapt at the opportunity. He spoke with the deliberateness of someone who had finally found a way out of a very tricky dilemma.

'If, as you say, Muntu's people sent you here and if they want this funeral conducted in the way you say they do, how come they didn't mention it to me last night, when I was with them at the wake? Why haven't they come to see me themselves? Why have they left everything until now?'

He was barely able to conceal the note of triumph in his voice.

'*Maar* they can't think of everything at once or do everything on their own, can they?' Micky asked. 'What are relatives and family friends for? Anyway, we only thought of this matter last night.'

This seemed to puzzle Zondo even more and to dampen his spirit completely.

'Bab' uZondo, this is the only favour we're ever likely to ask of you,' Duke said. 'If you grant us just this one request, we promise, nobody's ever going to touch your property. Please, Bab' uZondo.'

It was a rash promise.

Zondo's heart sank. He appeared to weigh the odds very carefully.

'I'll have to drive the cart myself,' he said at length.

'That's okay,' Micky said. 'You needn't even wait for us, Bab' uZondo, you can ride straight back home after you've dropped us at Doornfontein.'

'Doornfontein!'

'He means Doornkop, Bab' uZondo.'

'I mean Doornkop. How much d'you charge Bab' uZondo?'

'How much are you able to pay?'

'But, my children,' he continued without waiting for an answer, 'why do you make things so difficult for us, as if we weren't your people?'

'On the contrary, Bab' uZondo, if everybody developed this spirit of *masibambisaneni*, let's pull together, which we're trying to cultivate, our burdens as black people would become that much more lighter,' Duke said. 'For, *Baba*, don't you in your wisdom teach us that one hand cannot wash itself, it needs another?'

With that clincher, it was then left to Zondo to back down without much loss of face.

Duke and Micky stayed on to help him clean the cart, brush the horse and feed it. When they left he appeared quite gay and considerably reassured.

They returned at eleven a.m., as arranged, to find the horse already harnessed to the cart and the stocky figure of Zondo in tails, chalk stripes and a black top hat waiting beside the horse and stroking it affectionately. They rode up to Muntu's house.

Students in their school uniforms had already started to pour in. They lined the street on both sides from Muntu's home right up to the church door, some half a kilometre or so further up the road.

A lay preacher in a faded black cassock and a slightly torn surplice arrived to lead the procession to the church.

Soon after, the coffin came out amidst incantations of holy sayings from the preacher who was walking in front: 'I am the resurrection and the life; he that believeth in me though he were dead yet shall he live . . .'

Muntu's mother appeared, walking immediately behind the coffin, at the head of the mourners and flanked by two of Muntu's aunts on either side who were holding to her elbows.

The pall-bearers put the coffin into the hearse parked just outside the gate. All the chief mourners got into some of the waiting cars. The rest of the congregation followed on foot.

The students, who had formed a guard of honour, right-hand fists raised to the air, burst into a funeral dirge of the African resistance movement. A voice began in a high tenor that was more like a cry of anguish, and the chorus picked up the song: 'Senzeni na? Senzeni na maAfrika?' (What fault have we committed? What fault have we Africans committed?)

The procession slowly wound its way to St Francis further up the hill.

Many people had already preceded the cortège to the church to enable them to get seats, so that only the first four rows or so had been left unoccupied for members of the family.

The church was filled to capacity. The very doors were blocked with people trying to take a glimpse inside; others had climbed on the windows. The rest spilled into the church yard and further on to the streets.

The service itself was brief and simple. It had been arranged so that most of the speeches could be made in church and all the wreaths read there, too, to cut down on the time we'd spent at the cemetery.

The new Anglican Dean of Johannesburg, Fr. Mpilo Tutu, the first black man to be appointed to the post, delivered a stirring sermon that went to the guts. He began by reading out a text from the Bible: 'The people that walked in darkness have seen a great light . . .' He moved on to pay homage to all the saints who had died, he said, so that we might live. He said the people of Soweto had indeed seen a great light; that their hearts and minds had been truly illuminated by mere school-children. Signs of divine providence that mere school-children should outstrip us in the end! What could God's message be in this miraculous event of our time? he asked. He said that the Christian message was essentially a gospel of deliverance from bondage of all sorts. 'Blacks in this country do not want their chains made more comfortable,' he said, 'we want them off.' He built up steadily by piling question upon question, observation after observation – something he called 'the testimony of our time' – to a rousing climax, an unorthodox finale to the run-of-the-mill sermons we'd become accustomed to.

'I have felt God's grace,' he said. 'I have felt God reigning over the stand taken by these children of Soweto. I look at these little ones, now departed, as having fallen like true soldiers, our veritable heroes, *amagora ethu okwenene*', he repeated emphatically. 'They have set us on the path to freedom, as Moses once set the children of Israel on the road to the promised land. Children are proclaiming the gospel of social relevance all over the streets of Soweto. The children are seeking that Kingdom on earth of which the prophet Isaiah spoke when he said, "Violence shall no more be heard in thy land, wasting nor destruction whithin they borders." And, by God, we shall attain unto that kingdom, for victory is ours. Freedom in our life-time! *Amandla!*'

The congregation roared back, '*Amandla!*'

The other major address was delivered by our Headmaster, Mr Kambule Mathabathe. If we had thought before that he was a System man, his speech that day dispelled all our suspicions. He lambasted the authorities for committing what he called 'Herod's sin'. He publicly denounced Bantu Education as education for servitude. He said that for two decades they, as teachers, had dithered about whether to operate within the System so that a few African children could at least pick up some little crumbs of knowledge or to boycott Bantu Education altogether and deprive their children of the little benefits which accrue even from a system as malevolent as apartheid. 'The children have finally resolved our dilemma,' he said. 'Their answer has been quite categorical: there can be no real meaningful choice between slow poisoning and outright starvation.' He called on the authorities to reconsider their whole attitude towards blacks. 'Black people,' he said, quoting an eminent black South African author, "are on the march in the direction of freedom, in the direction of determining their own fate and destiny in their own way.' He said blacks rejected every policy based on 'amelioration' as being 'cosmetic and so much white-wash'. The people were not interested in the Bantustanisation of the townships so that a privileged few could be given a few political spoils and some economic incentives in exchange for maintaining the structure of apartheid, running the townships and generally lording it over us. Then he alluded to some Roman emperor called Nero and a French queen named Marie-Antoinette (but I forget now in what context he mentioned these names as my notes taken at the time are not very explicit on the matter). Finally, he issued a strongly-worded ultimatum to the authorities and ended with the words of some famous playwright. 'Take warning, my masters,' he quoted, 'we'll scorch you in the end.'

Our Principal's address had contained so many issues we'd often thought about ourselves, all the concepts we'd often grappled with, without being able to articulate them half as clearly.

Next, Mandla was called upon to read a poem, which he did to the soft mournful background of *malombo* drums and voices humming an African martial tune, '*Sizobadubula ngombayimbayi*' (We'll bombard them with cannons). The audience was spellbound throughout the reading, their thoughts and emotions floating along with the rhythm of the music and the words of the poem:

> To those who've caused
> The little ones to weep
> To those who've betrayed their brethren
> To those who've given false testimonies
> To those who've brought about the
>     existence
> Of widows widowers orphans and refugees

To those who've turned away the hungry
Divested the cripples of their crutches
Flaunted gaudy robes before the unclothed
Denuded the cold and cast them into
    darkness
To those who've brandished handcuffs
Set dogs loose to go for our vitals
Pulled triggers and hurled grenades at the
    unarmed
To those who've raped with a serrated
    penis
Like an electric saw and caused us
The whole nation to hang our heads in
    shame
To those . . .
Let it not be forgotten
That our anger will endure forever
Our lust for freedom is more lasting than
    all the gold
In the Witwatersrand
And our vengeance will transcend eternity
To those . . .

At the end of each line people groaned and their groans
increased as Mandla read on in his clear bass voice
which boomed through the church. People took out their
handkerchiefs and dabbed their faces. Others, from force
of habit, looked around nervously.

At the end of the church service, after all the wreaths
had been read out – they were so many that only messages of the immediate members of the family were read
out in full; as for the rest only the senders' names were
read out – Bra P., who was the M.C., announced the
order of the pall-bearers. From the church to the hearse,
he said, the coffin would be carried by Muntu's colleagues. When we reached the cemetery, members of the
family would carry him to his final resting-place.

Six of our strongest chaps, who had been selected for
the purpose, walked up to the front of the church. They
lifted the coffin and carried it down the aisle and out of

the church, their free hands raised in clenched fist salute.

The rest of the students also raised their fists. Other members of the congregation also did likewise.

I caught Sindiswa with the corner of my eye, walking behind her mother, with her fist raised to the air.

Behind Muntu's people walked some students carrying wreaths.

The congregation flowed out of the church.

Outside, thousands of students waited, carrying placards and singing freedom songs. They had also been distributing SRC pamphlets along with the funeral programme.

Other students helped the lone traffic cop to control the traffic.

Two half-empty PUTCO buses, on their way to Nancefield station, approached the circle outside St. Francis and were stopped. The students hopped in and motioned to some of the funeral crowd to follow suit. These were people who didn't have their own transport and depended on the transport which is traditionally provided by the bereaved family. The passengers caught in this way in the buses resigned themselves to the inevitable. One bus driver, who tried to escape through the thick crowd, was quickly apprehended, brought back and instructed to drive in the direction he'd come, to Doornkop.

I approached another group of younger students, fiercely remonstrating with a couple in a car. The couple, in mourning attire, was desperately trying to explain to the students that they were not going on a pleasure trip, but to another funeral right there in Soweto.

'How can we tell?' a student asked.

'D'you think we've put on these clothes for fun, eh? Can't you tell, man, from the way we're dressed?' the man in the car asked.

'Are you trying to hoodwink us?'

The man lowered his head over the steering wheel.

The students recognised me as I came up to them. I asked what the problem was. They said the couple was trying to pull wool over their eyes. I asked them to let the couple pass. They stared at me but did as I had asked.

'Okay, mister, move on.'

I waited until the car had driven off and then called the group of students together for a quick word. I told them that in order to cultivate mutual trust and respect between ourselves and our people, so that we could be certain of their maximum support and co-operation at all times, we had to show good faith and to take them at their word, unless there was irrefutable evidence to the contrary. Otherwise we had to give them the benefit of the doubt.

They told me that they had strict instructions from Micky not to fall for any 'bourgeois' tricks. Some of the people, they said, were only dressed in black in order to fool everybody. Otherwise they were just about their 'reactionary' business. (I made a mental note to check the terms. Whoever had taught them that? I mean, they were only in Form I and I was in Form V).

I told them that everything Micky had told them was true, but that certain cases had to be treated on their own merit.

A pretty, plump girl from our street, Monica, who was with the gang, told me, in her usual loquacious way, of a family friend of theirs she'd overheard openly boasting to her parents that the only way of moving about un-molested in Soweto these days was to go about in mourn-ing clothes. I listened patiently with a smile and then drifted off.

More transport was commandeered as it approached the circle outside St. Francis. Buses, taxis, lorries, vans and private cars.

An eminent township doctor and his family were found with a picnic basket in their car. The doctor was in bermuda shorts, a striped T-shirt and a golf cap. They were ordered to join the cortège.

The pall-bearers lifted the coffin into Zondo's cart, parked just outside the church door, and climbed after it. A few other students clambered after the pall-bearers. But Duke, who was sitted beside Zondo, held them back.

The horse trotted gently on towards Doornkop, with the hearse immediately behind, carrying myriads of wreaths. Behind the hearse were the family cars and behind them the rest of the mourners.

Small children we passed, too young to be at the funeral, stopped their play and sat down beside the road as the cortège passed them.

The procession was several kilometres long. So that those who were among the first to reach Doornkop had to wait a full forty-five minutes for the rest.

At the cemetery we found several other crowds burying their dead, most of them students.

Virtually all the families had resisted our move to hold a mass funeral for all the victims of the police shootings. Out of deference to their sensitivities we'd decided not to press our idea any further. Grief is essentially a private affair, even though custom gives others the right to mourn with you. The family must bury their dead as they see fit. But many of us also felt that these narrow cleavages among our people, the tendency to care only for one's immediate relatives, had to be overcome. Soweto needed a new sense of family, blood-ties based on our common destiny.

We'd also tried to urge our students to distribute themselves more evenly by attending the funerals nearest to their homes. But they tended to gravitate towards the funerals of the most popular and those they'd known more intimately.

As we waited at the graveyard for the rest of the mourners, I caught a glimpse of Micky – I'd been wondering where he'd disappeared to. He pulled two students aside who were carrying wreaths. They waded through the crowd and headed for the smallest of the funeral congregations. When they came back they were no longer carrying the wreaths.

The congregation sang hymns until all the people had gathered in thick concentric circles around the grave.

Before Fr. Molale, who was officiating, could proceed with the interment service, the M.C. called for a student representative. Another of our brilliant young poets, Lefifi, who had approached us shortly before the service started, with a poem he wished to read (Bra P. had no objections to slotting Lefifi into the programme), ascended the mound of earth beside the grave and recited in a sharp piercing voice:

> Our spears are immersed in blood
> We are on the warpath
> Of Blood River
> The distance is long
> The distance is strenuous
> But the courage is thriced . . .
> We are the elephant
> We are the warrior
> Transformed into a guerrilla
> The spirit of Sharpeville
> Emerges from the past
> And haunts the present
> Wearing a new mask
> Soweto Soweto Soweto
> History repeats itself
> We are the elephant
> We move the way of no return

As the coffin was being lowered into the grave, the church choir of St. Francis sang 'Hamba, hamba kahle' (Farewell, farewell).

The family filed past the grave and dropped in little sods of earth from a shovel. Then the men began to fill up the grave, taking quick turns with the shovels.

After the grave had been completely covered and some extra soil piled up to identify it, the M.C. called on Muntu's uncle from Queenstown to say a few words on behalf of the family.

Speaking in Xhosa, with Bra P. himself translating into Sesotho, the uncle told the crowd of mourners how the people and the children of Soweto had taught him a lesson he'd never forget, one he'd take back home with him. He thanked everybody for their individual and collective contributions, material and otherwise, and ended his speech with the usual expression of gratitude, 'Nangomso!'

216

Fr. Molale called upon Dean Tutu to pronounce the blessing:

> God bless Africa,
> Guard her children,
> Guide her rulers,
> Grant her peace,
> And may the grace of our Lord . . .

Led by the students, the whole gathering, fists raised high,burst into a rendition of our national anthem and sang in a manner I'd never heard it sung before or since. They sang it alternately in Xhosa and Sesotho. My voice choked with tears. I can never sing when I'm in the grip of emotion. People, with tears streaming unchecked down their faces, sang:

> *Nkosi sikelel' iAfrika.*
> God bless Afrika.
> *Maluphakanyisw' udumo lwayo.*
> Raise high her fame and esteem.
> *Yiva imithandazo yethu.*
> Heed Ye our supplications.
> *Nkosi sikelela, thina lusapho lwayo.*
> God bless us, we her progeny.
> > *Woza moya, Woza moya oyincwele.*
> > Come o spirit, Come o spirit divine.
> > *Nkosi sikelela, thina lusapho lwayo.*
> > God bless us, we her progeny.
> *Morena boloka sechaba sa heso.*
> May the Lord preserve our beloved nation.
> *U felise lintoa le matsoenyeho.*
> And terminate all hostilities and sufferings.
> > *U se boloke, U se boloke,*
> > Preserve it, Preserve it,
> > *U se boloke morena,*
> > Preserve it, oh Lord,
> > *Sechaba sa heso,*
> > This our nation,
> > *Sechaba sa heso,*
> > This our nation.

An old Congress warrior from our street, old man Kumalo (everybody called him ANC), who had marched in the Defiance Campaign, called 'Afrika!' and the people responded, 'Mayibuye!' (May it come back). Another old man, a veteran of the anti-pass campaign, which had led to the Sharpeville massacres, also shouted, 'Ilizwe!' (The land!); and the crowd roared back, 'Elethu!' (It's ours!). Then there was a spontaneous outburst from several students who asserted, '*Amandla*!' (Power); thousands of tiny voices piped, '*Awethu!*' (To the people!!)

As the people prepared to disperse, the police, unobserved, crept behind the crowd. Suddenly the voice of their commanding officer came through the loudspeaker and ordered the people to clear out of the cemetery in five minutes.

A real stampede ensued.

Other funerals, not sure if they were included in the general directive, broke up in pandemonium, too. People left their business half-finished an scuttled away like rats. The priests pronounced hasty benedictions, tucked their cassocks above their knees and cleared out.

A hijacked bus driver jumped off his bus and took off on foot in the direction of Zola.

The police sprayed teargas on the crowd.

A shot rang out from somewhere in the centre of the crowd.

All hell broke loose.

The police fired into the thick crowd.

A funeral undertaker from Phefeni, who had hired out his cars for Muntu's funeral, was shot dead as he was gathering his equipment.

An African photographer for *Die Beeld* was hit on the shoulder, shot in the left arm, twice in the stomach, once on the back and on his buttocks.

He crumpled and collapsed like an empty sack of potatoes.

Several people sought cover from the empty graves.

Mourners who had managed to reach their cars drove back like racing aces to the homes of those they'd come to bury, to wash their hands and eat.

At the cemetery the police asked a few remaining people, mainly members of the bereaved families who'd been left in the lurch, at gunpoint, to carry the bodies of the dead and injured into the waiting police vans.

Fortunately, Zondo's horse was not harmed. Instead of riding back, as we'd proposed, he had decided to stay on for the rest of the funeral service. When Duke and Micky went to his house in the evening to thank him and to offer him payment, he told them that he wouldn't accept any payment from them for doing what was, after all, his duty to the dead. Instead he asked them to promise him one thing only, never to come to him with a similar request again. They promised. But how could they have known that his cart and his horse would be in such great demand in the months to come in the other student funerals which followed? The pattern had been set; a new tradition had been established. Zondo was to solve the problem himself by buying a scraggy beast, specially for 'Black Power' funerals. And he charged nothing.

Daylight slowly receded from the streets of Soweto. The matchbox houses, pale sand-coloured silhouettes of uniform ugliness, were just visible. A heavy pall of smoke from braziers and coal stoves hung like a cloud and covered everything else.

As early as 4.00 a.m. on Monday, students assembled, as arranged, at all the thirteen stations or so which served Soweto.

The winter chill cut mercilessly through the skin. The streets were deserted, except for packs of hounds reluctant to take leave of one another.

At Mzimhlophe Station, where I'd gone with a group of other students, police and soldiers in armoured cars turned up in large numbers. They stood high up on the stairs crossing into the platform, shining their torches so as to be visible from a distance. They had also left the lights above their squad cars flashing.

We kept to the shadows, on either side of the station.

A few straggling workers with faulty passes or without passes at all simply turned back the moment they noticed the police, even before we could confront them.

A scattered number of other workers from the Mzimhlophe hostel strutted defiantly towards the station. As they came abreast of us, we emerged from the shadows and intercepted them, catching them completely by surprise.

Our conversation with the first man we stopped set the tone for the rest:

'*Uyaphi mfowethu?*'

'To work, of course. Why?'

'In defiance of the people's call?'

'What call?'

'Against going to work.'

'I don't know of any such call.'

'And yet you live here in Soweto!'

'I've been on leave. I came back last night.'

'Didn't the others at the hostel tell you anything about the strike?'

'No.'

'Well, we're asking you now, please, go back home; don't go to work. All our people must stay at home until whites learn to treat us as people.'

'But I'll lose my job!'

'Not if we all withdraw our labour. They'll soon be on their knees. Can't you see?'

'No.'

'Look, *mfowethu*, they've been shooting our people out there; we need your support. Won't you pledge your solidarity with your people?'

'Look here yourselves. I left my wife and children in Mahlabathini to come and work here, not to . . . not to . . . *angizanga ukuzoganga lapha!*'

'Why should you think *we* are trifling? Besides, there are thousands of others in your position, but they've heeded our call. D'you want to be known as the man who betrayed them, the Judas of Soweto?'

'What they decide to do with their own lives, whether they decide to throw away their jobs or not, is their own *indaba.'*

'Is it none of your business, too, when they get chucked out of work because of you?'

'I've a wife and three children.'

'Wouldn't you like them to come and live with you here in Jo'burg, where you work? Don't you desire an end to all the laws which prohibit your family from joining you here?'

'We've our own place in Mahlabathini. This is no place for women and children.'

'We're wasting time. Are you going to comply with our request or not?'

Depending on each person's response to the latter question, we either cheered the person on his way back home or used less subtle methods of persuasion to turn him or her back.

There were other students operating in different parts of Soweto.

An early morning train caught fire between Merafe and Inhlazane.

At New Canada, the main junction into Soweto, the rail track was dismantled and a signal installation destroyed, causing a complete disruption of rail services. The service was only restored in the afternoon.

With the police and their hippo-like tanks all clustered around the stations, we had the rest of the territory to ourselves.

We mounted roadblocks on all the major roads of Soweto. All traffic going to town was turned back by students chanting, 'Renegades, careerists and sell-outs, who want to take a back seat in the struggle!'

By the time the police had got wise to what was happening, we had already withdrawn. At any rate, as daybreak approached, it became increasingly risky to operate in the open.

That same day a major propaganda offensive was mounted by the Transvaal Chamber of Industries, the SABC, the police and some newspapers.

Pamphlets were dropped from helicopters all over Soweto, carrying the following message:

## TO: THE BLACK WORKERS
## FROM: THE TRANSVAAL CHAMBER OF INDUSTRIES.

The Transvaal Chamber of Industries is the place where your employers meet to talk about the problems of their factories. All the things that worry them are talked about there; that is where they discuss together what can be done to make things better for their factories and for their workers.

The Transvaal Chamber of Industries wants to tell you what will happen if you listen to agitators!

Firstly: There are many factories which for some time now have not been as busy as they used to be. Some factories could even close down or work short time, but they are trying to keep going so that you can keep earning your pay.

Secondly: Therefore, if you stay away from work you are harming yourself as well as your employers.

Thirdly: You know that there are many black people who do not have jobs and who could easily take your place.

Fourthly: If you stay away from work it is your family and your children who will suffer.

You must be strong and come back to work so that you can earn money for your family and children to buy food, clothing and other necessaries. Your well-being depends on your working with us; listening to the agitators will not improve your position or help you in anyway.

## WE REPEAT
## KEEP YOUR JOB AND IGNORE THE AGITATORS

Other pamphlets were slipped in under the door of each house in an attempt to sow further confusion among the workers. Printed in English, Sesotho and Zulu, they read: WORKERS PLEASE NOTE: OUR BIG STRIKE FOR THIS WEEK IS NOW POSTPONED UNTIL FURTHER NOTICE. WE WILL CALL ON YOU AGAIN.

The SABC, on all its language services, repeatedly told its listeners that the police would provide 'protection to all law-abiding citizens who wished to go to work'.

The police went from house to house to ask why people hadn't gone to work. They ordered them to go or face arrest. But the people produced their season tickets and said that there were no trains. Besides, PUTCO, which had by now become as expert at reading the townships' barometer as a meteorologist, had withdrawn its buses at the first signs of trouble. Initially the police pretended that the operation was not connected with the strike but was what Colonel Fierce described as 'a crime preventative operation aimed at flushing out criminals and layabouts'. But later the Colonel admitted to *The World* that it was 'a clean-up operation, aimed at protecting those who wished to go to work and rounding up agitators'.

The newspapers, in general, projected the official view. But it was also noticed that those English language newspapers with a large black readership were becoming more and more wary of supporting the authorities.

In many parts of Soweto water supplies were cut periodically and brought back.

Despite our precautions many workers did manage to slip through our picket lines. Several workers had slept at their places of work the previous night and for a whole week thereafter, without once being raided for night passes and special permits. Moreover, we had no way of preventing workers from the East Rand and the West Rand, who flock into Johannesburg each morning. However, even *The Star* acknowledged that among Soweto residents the strike had been 90% successful.

Certain people, with little kids to look after, who'd been to work that day, returned home in the evening. We sent round groups of students to tell them not to go to work the following day and for the rest of that week. But, for reasons which should soon become clear, it became increasingly difficult to maintain our picket lines.

With the schools closed and most of the students becoming increasingly restive, we had also sent out word to the effect that they could make themselves useful by cleaning up the litter which had been accumulating in Soweto since the previous Wednesday. Dustmen were not working. We also told the students to run away when they saw the police because the government had already imposed a ban on all gatherings, save those of a religious nature.

They took to their chores with bubbly spirits.

Parents and children worked side by side to clear their backyards. Washing, which would otherwise have been attended to on Saturday, was brought out. There was general spring-cleaning in many homes.

Ash piles, papers, fruit peels, discarded tins and bottles, refuse, stinking garbage, rotting bodies of cats and dogs were cleared from the streets and dumped in the *veld*.

It was in such high spirits that a group of young boys and girls bumped into Ntate Sebotsane on his bicycle near the Stands in Rockville, one of the few electrified areas of Soweto. Since he worked in the township, he hadn't thought that the stay-away also affected him. He thought it only applied to people who worked in town and so was on his rounds, reading meters from house to house, when the students met him. They charged at him. He dropped his bicycle and, with his books firmly tucked under his armpits, took to his heels. The students chased him without really putting in much effort to catch up with him. He tore across the open sports fields and disappeared around Tirisano higher primary school in Moroka central.

For three months after this episode, long after the strike had been called off, Ntate Sebotsane firmly refused to venture anywhere near anybody's meter. As the schools' boycott went into October and November with a new call against exams, he came to rely more and more on Vukani, who had since been brought back from Natalspruit, when trouble broke up in that township as well. Vukani used to hop across the fence to his house each morning to help him cook the books. Consequently the average water and electricity bills in Soweto fell below a fifth of their pre-June level.

If the West Rand Administraion Board (WRAB), which administers Soweto, thought there was anything fishy about these figures, they never let on what they truly felt.

The information had somehow leaked that we were planning a march to John Vorster Square. Very early on Tuesday morning, when we left to board the city-bound trains, we were met by the police at the stations. We were easily identifiable in the thin traffic because of our school uniforms. But it was an important part of our strategy that we should wear our school uniforms, because we didn't want to be mixed up in anybody's mind with any other organisation. The view taken by some people that agitators were behind our actions was a deliberate ploy to sow discord and to side-track people's attention from our real grievances. And so we'd decided to dress in our full school uniforms for all our public appearances.

There was a more steady flow of traffic than on the day before. And the police had kept their promise to 'protect the law-abiding citizens'. They'd turned up in full force to man not just the railway stations but the bus stops and the taxi ranks as well. They told the people to go to work and beat up the children stopping them. The *Rand Daily Mail* reported that morning that the government, maybe in pursuit of its hard-line policy against the students, was considering extending official recognition of Manthate's *makhotla* vigilantes, after earlier denouncing their methods as savage and brutal.

We had another problem coming our way. Hostel-dwellers from Mzimhlophe retaliated when students tried to prevent them, as on the day before, from going to work. Walking with concealed weapons, they fell unexpectedly upon unarmed students. The students could only fight back with stones.

The news media reported these incidents between students and the hostel-dwellers in a very triumphal light. The authorities and the police could scarcely conceal their glee at what they described as a 'backlash by responsible elements'.

There'd been efforts made, of course, to mobilise these supposedly responsible elements against the students. Some students, who had visited the hostels on the previous day, had definitely seen and heard Hlubi and other cops at Mzimhlophe hostel talking to groups of migrant workers. 'Eat and drink well,' Hlubi told one group of Zulu migrant workers. 'So that you can kill on full stomachs.'

The hostel-dwellers fell upon the students mercilessly in the streets.

After such violent confrontation, in which the students got the worst of the exchanges, the men from the hostel proceeded on their way to work. But some students set fire to a portion of the hostel later in the day.

We'd hardly had time to analyse these events, when that very same evening hordes of hostel-dwellers from Mzimhlophe went on the rampage through the streets of Soweto, in the neighbouring townships of Meadowlands and Orlando East and West. Zuly migrant workers, brandishing dangerous *knobkierries*, *assegais* and *pangas*, unleashed a brief reign of terror, reminiscent of the *lifaqane* wars. They broke into innocent people's homes. They robbed everybody within sight of money. They molested old men and women, raped young girls and murdered most of the men they found.

At MaVy's house, where some of them used to drink in former times, some men broke in and confiscated all her stock of alcohol. Then they held her husband pinned to the wall while others raped Violet and her mother before his very eyes, taking turns with the women. When they had finished they clubbed him to death, burnt MaVy's house and left. Her other five kids were saved by running away the moment the invaders entered the house.

But once the hordes of Zulu marauders started burning down houses, an official of WRAB was sent to talk to them. 'We didn't order you to destroy WRAB property,' he told them. 'You were asked to fight people only. You are warned not to continue damaging the houses because they belong to the WRAB. If you damage houses you will force us to take action against you to prevent this. Now get this into your heads once and for all: you have been ordered to kill only these trouble-makers.'

Township gangs like the Hazels offered disorganised and ineffective resitance.

The police stood by and watched.

When he was later asked to comment on police connivance on these attacks on innocent township residents, Colonel Fierce said, 'I have no knowledge of these rampaging Zulus, but if it is happening, I am not surprised. If people want to organise themselves into resisting *tsotsis* we can't stop them. People are getting very fed-up with the things that are happening in Soweto.'

Minister Parkes also told Parliament that, 'People are allowed to protect themselves against intimidation. The situation will calm itself once people realise there is a strong backlash.'

Early editions of the evening paper, *The Star*, carried banner headlines on the 'SOWETO BACKLASH KILLINGS'. The paper recounted an event of the previous night, when two students picketing the station near Mzimhlophe hostel were beaten to death by hostel-dwellers returning from work. In fact, there were never any such killings on Monday. But on Tuesday night, after *The Star* had reported on the killings of these students by hostel-dwellers, the long-predicted and already reported 'backlash' actually happened.

Then Bra P. jumped into his Mercedes and headed for Naledi township.

In next to no time, multitudes of blanket-clad Basotho 'Russians' in lorries, vans and private cars, poured into Meadowlands and Orlando.

The army, which had been placed on the alert at the outskirts of Soweto, was galvanised into action. Tanks roared into Soweto like hippos. They moved in against the 'Russians' and the re-organised gangs of township youths.

A fierce battle raged on all night, leaving about a hundred dead and numerous others injured.

The war continued furiously for days, with the hostel-dwellers being mercilessly punished.

It was a wasteful war of retribution, which clearly had to be stopped. Moreover, the authorities and their *agents provocateur* were on the receiving end.

Chief Gatsha Buthelezi was flown from KwaZulu to Soweto.

In a very widely publicised address, he asked the people of Soweto for forgiveness (I can't remember now for what). He said that although he supported the students' just demands for the abolition of Bantu education – our demands had by this time evolved to encompass the abolition of the apartheid system itself, including Bantustans, but Buthelezi never referred to this – he could not condone the burning of schools and other public buildings. He asked the students not to cut off their noses to spite their faces. He deplored what he called 'police excesses'. But he exhorted the students to work within the framework of the law, even if it hurt.

He also visited Baragwanath hospital to see the victims of the township disturbances.

Before leaving Soweto he announced that his movement, called Inkatha kaZulu (a movement with a strong Zulu ethnic base), would boycott the forthcoming elections for the new Community Councils to replace the defunct UBC, unless the government released the detained students and other community leaders, who had by this time been arrested for siding with the students.

In a conciliatory move the government had recently announced new measures to scrap the UBC (which we'd already rendered ineffective, anyway) and replace it with a new Community Council, with increased powers over roads, housing allocation and other social amenities. But, as I explained shortly before I went into exile in an interview with Aggrey Klaaste, the political columnist of

*The World*, who, together with his new editor, Percy Qoboza, had become our most vociferous supporters, the people didn't want cosmetic concessions or to be in charge of roads and rubbish. They wanted organic change to rule their lives outside the system of apartheid.

Rathebe identified himself with Chief Buthelezi's call for the boycott of the Community Councils and announced his membership of Inkatha. He was to disassociate himself later, when it became manifestly clear that Chief Buthelezi's tribal organisation had no grassroots support in Soweto, except among Zulu migrant workers in the hostels and among a few dyed-in-the-wool Zulu tribalists like Dr Nyembezi, Buthelezi's representative in Soweto.

It is now history that few students, if any, were released as a result of Chief Buthelezi's intervention. Many still languish in South African prisons to this day. Among our arrested parents, they did release those who were the most prominent members of our community, like Dr Nthato Motlana of the Black Parents' Association, formed in the wake of the Soweto uprisings and later Chairman of Soweto's governing interim committee, popularly known as the Committe of Ten, which had no government recognition but was backed by the SRC and the people of Soweto.

Immediately after his release from Modder Bee prison Dr Motlana was clandestinely taken to a secret rendezvous with officials of WRAB, together with Dr Nyembezi and Rathebe. In a subsequent press release Dr Motlana announced that he refused to be bought with his own freedom, while thousands of black children and their parents suffered. Dr Nyembezi, with the apparent blessing of Buthelezi, said that Inkatha members could contest the Community Council elections in their individual capacities.

The elections which were held shortly afterwards were a farce. Rathebe himself won a resounding victory in his own ward with ninety-seven votes in a 4.4 per cent poll, one of the highest in these elections. He retained his position as 'Mayor.'

Apologists for the System blamed the low percentage poll in the elections on several factors. First, they attributed the fact that the vast majority of the people had stayed away to the weather – after the severe winter it rained cats and dogs in Soweto, as if God was wringing out his dirty underwear. Next, they blamed the low turn-out at the polls to intimidation and adverse publicity by *The World* – for which Aggrey Klaaste, Percy Qoboza and a few of their colleagues were quickly clamped behind bars. Finally, they pointed out that the majority of blacks had still to learn the intricacies of democratic procedures like voting instead of being saddled with hereditary chiefs.

During the same round of peace initiatives sparked by the Battle of Soweto, another prominent member of Inkatha, Credo Mutwa, an eminent author of tribal lore, told reporters that we should all be grateful for the timely intervention of the police and the military in Soweto. He praised them, especially for defending the minority rights of people like the hostel-dwellers. (Not so long ago my mother wrote to me to say that Credo Mutwa's palatial house in Diepkloof had been razed to the ground by a mysterious fire.)

I believe that when the history of Soweto in those few weeks is written (and I don't mean the white-inspired accounts which have been hastily churned out by white analysts, putting their stamp, as always, on the interpretation of our struggle), our struggle will be shown to have been plagued by fratricide, senseless carnage and considerable duplicity. But none of these things were ever intended by us.

It was at a much later stage, after my time, that an understanding was ultimately reached between the students and the hostel-dwellers. A student delegation went on a mission of conscientisation to each of the hostels in Soweto. They met representatives of the hostel-dwellers to explain our position; they scoured every hostel room like faithful Watch Towers. The hostel inmates listened and discussed. So that when the students subsequently called another strike towards Christmas, they received a near-perfect support from the hostels. Together with the hostel residents, the students formed impenetrable picket lines during the rest of the boycotts which followed: against Christmas shopping, rent increases and so on. If anything, the students had to explain to their hostel comrades that it wasn't always necessary to crack the skulls of those who defied them in order to sink their points in the minds of the opponents.

This time the army moved in and indiscriminately cracked everyone's skull.

It was a chilly Wednesday morning towards the end of June.

We were marching through the city of Johannesburg when we encountered them. They stood across the road blocking our way. We had been marching resolutely through the city with children from other schools, gathering yet more others as we proceeded. The protest march was designed to demand the release of our detained comrades.

Looking back in time, we can usually tell everything; when and where certain things started to go wrong; what things we left undone which we should have done; in exactly what way we should have approached this and that issue. With the wisdom of hindsight there are, oh, so many things we could say . . .

After our planned march to John Vorster Square had been frustrated the day before, we devised a new strategy before taking off again that Wednesday morning.

We put on workers' clothes over our regular uniforms: overalls, dustcoats and so on. We folded our placards and carried them in paper bags. We wielded sticks about, as if carrying them for personal protection. We left with the early morning traffic.

There were more people going to work than on the previous two days. And, no doubt, they must have been surprised that nobody made any attempt to stop them. Without officially calling off the strike, we'd reckoned that a certain number of morning commuters was necessary if we were to pass through all the police cordons without focusing all the attention on ourselves. However, I also realise now that, much as considerations of a purely strategic nature had forced us into that position, our failure to call off the strike clearly then and afterwards, when it was already showing all the signs of fizzling out – if only we'd listened to Bra P.! – was a mistake because it also served to sow discord and confusion among our people. But then much of what occurred in those days was done very much on an *ad hoc* basis.

When we passed the police patrols on our way to the station, we were greeted with remarks which were meant as an encouragement to the workers: 'Good show, use your sticks on them . . . Foil their blerry communist ploys . . . *Ja*, they only want to destroy your families . . . That's right, because they've no families of their own . . . Bunch of shittish homosexuals and perverted arseholes who fuck their women in gang-bangs!'

We'd planned to leave Soweto from different stations and to converge at a fixed time in Commissioner Street.

We'd also taken the extra precaution of leaving the little ones behind – all those who'd not yet reached J.C.

At eight a.m., along Commissioner Street, we dropped our top clothes and threw them into our paper bags, unfolded our placards and pinned them on our sticks. The messages read: 'Vorster release our leaders . . . Charge or Release . . . *Asikhathali noma bayas'bopha.*'

The rays of the winter sun struggled ineffectually through the gloomy clouds and the thick smog of Johannesburg. Pedestrians, puffing smoke, pulled up their collars and walked briskly through the morning traffic.

As the city opened its curtains to the early morning shoppers, it was greeted by the unusual sight of black children marching resolutely through its streets, waving placards, chanting slogans and singing freedom songs.

A few shopkeepers in the vicinity, mainly Indians, quickly sensed trouble, shut their shops and closed business for the day, notwithstanding the signs on their doors which read: 'Back in ten minutes.'

White shopkeepers came and stood at the doors of their premises, arms akimbo, as if watching a Cape-goon carnival.

Cigar-smoking executives glanced curiously for a brief second only from their offices in the upper storeys of the tall buildings we passed through.

The black workers we met shot up their arms in the clenched-fist salute; others downed their tools and joined in the march.

A guy, who'd been cleaning windows as we marched past, dropped his rag, jumped down the ladder and followed us as surely as if someone had said, 'Put down your rags and follow me.' His boss came out and saw him disappearing into the crowd. He shouted after him in Fanakalo: '*Hey, Jim, yini wena yenza manje? Buya back lapha or wena cabanga this country lo-communist Zambia, eh!*' (Hey, Jim, what the hell are you up to? Come back here or d'you imagine you're in Communist Zambia, eh!') But Jim barely condescended to look back. He grinned most happily and sang with great gusto.

'*Jim, uyakubiza umlungu wakho, awuzwa?*' someone said.

'He can call until his voice is hoarse, for all I care,' the man replied. 'Besides, my name is Ginyibhunu, not Jim!'

A woman in green kitchen overalls, a white apron and a green nanny's *kappie* marched briskly beside me and said, '*Batla ikutloa kajeno* (today let them see to finish), we'll see who they'll be shouting "Anna this . . . Anna that" to!'

As word about our demonstration spread round, we were also joined by a few whites, hippie-looking Hillbrow types, always tuned in to the slightest nuances of deviationism and nonconformity. It turned out they were students from Wits, who had been about their Rag activities in the city when they were attracted by our demonstration. Nobody tried to stop them. They were good insurance.

With the crowds came the first batch of policemen, who charged at us like enraged bulls.

We had indeed expected brutal assault, which is the standard treatment meted out to black demonstrators. But we were determined not to counteract their violence. I realise now that armed, as we were, with only a high morality we couldn't have been much more than cattle fodder for them.

In some respects we had calculated correctly. In their own backyard they were disinclined to shoot first and enquire afterwards.

No shots were fired – something seized upon and highly commended by the country's news media, as if it was perfectly acceptable to outrage black demonstrators in every other conceivable way short of gunning them down.

They charged at us like infuriated bulls, their truncheons raised like horns.

As I ducked under a delivery van parked nearby I saw a white student, wearing a Wits T-shirt and a multi-coloured, badly mutilated, dirty pair of jeans, which looked as if they'd been picked up from a painters' jumble sale, confront a white cop and ask, 'What moral right have you? This is a peaceful demonstration.'

The cop, his bull neck bulging with thick veins, turned from the black student he was about to pursue and beat the Wits student until he was as red in the face as a beetroot. The policeman was furiously shouting all the time, '*Jou blerry kommanissie . . . Kafferboetie!*'

I was praying that the driver of the van under which I was hiding, taking an underview of the fighting, as it were, shouldn't get back just then.

Some black workers, many of them innocent bystanders who'd been assaulted along with the rest, stood their ground and fought back furiously.

Another black worker, in a khakhi dustcoat, stood up to a white cop admirably. The cop charged in with his truncheon. But the guy drew a knife and waited. In close combat ghetto youth are simply marvellous. By the time the stupefied policeman thought of reaching for his revolver, the guy had already carved a deep wound on his arm and disappeared into the crowd. The policeman was left holding his badly wounded arm, blood oozing freely. Some of his colleagues rushed to his side and quickly drove off with the wounded policeman.

A few pickpockets with magnets for fingers who happened to be in the vicinity took to picking people's pockets with impunity. An elderly white lady hobbling down Commissioner Street had her bag snatched by a guy who hardly bothered to run away but instead approached a second victim. Another white chap, an executive type, was just locking his car when he was confronted by two township thugs. They held him against his Jaguar Executive. One went through his pockets while the other stood glaring at him and grinning from ear to ear like a complacent Cheshire cat, with the glittering blade of his scotch knife pointing at the white man's throat. When they'd finished with him they dragged another passer-by to the same spot and repeated the operation, before deciding to move in an opposite direction to the marchers.

Those businessmen who'd not been sharp enough to close their shops at the first signs of danger had a few shocks coming their way, not enough perhaps to rock their business premises to their foundations but certainly of enough strength to send a small tremor down the corridors of the Johannesburg Stock Exchange. When the first batch of policemen came, a notorious shoplifter, who always received an escort from the manager himself any time she entered one of the city's large chain stores, dashed into a nearby shop, selling ladies clothes. She emerged with a bundle of new clothes, which weren't even wrapped up, still in their hangers. Hot on her heels was the squat figure of the furious Jewish shop-owner, mouthing obscenities and imprecations which must have made the shoplifter's ancestors squirm in their graves. He didn't go far because a black youth came from behind him and tripped him. The Jewish shopkeeper landed flush on his face, still shouting and pronouncing damnation on the whole black race.

A young policeman, chasing a student, tripped and fell insensible to the ground, after his fleet-footed target dummy-ran him into an electric pole. He was driven away in a police van.

More and more police arrived and mounted a baton charge. They chased the students up and down the streets. Many students were hit with truncheons and thrown to the ground, then thrust into the waiting police vans.

I waited under the delivery van, meditating. When I was absolutely certain the street was clear of cops, I picked myself up from under the van and brushed myself a bit. Passers-by glanced at me curiously. Blacks walking up and down the street shouted greetings of '*Amandla!*' I got into a pair of denim overalls I was carrying in my mother's overnight bag and headed for Park station.

Once again a peaceful demonstration had been ruthlessly suppressed, though not as ruthlessly as on the previous Wednesday. Thanks to our white hostages! Still, that was small consolation. Micky's words came flooding back to my mind: 'Jack (Micky had the uncanny habit of calling everybody "Jack"), 'strues God I'm telling you, I heard this from my late grandfather, that whenever our people have tried to influence government thinking through peaceful means such as demonstrations, from Bulhoek through the Defiance Campaign right up to Sharpeville and Langa and now Soweto, the results have always been the same. Niggers never learn. Otherwise, everyone would be knowing by now that Boers are impervious to reason. That's the simple fact. Me, I'm through with tokenism (his choice of words was sometimes truly astounding for one whose English was as indifferent as Micky's). It's like bumping your head against a granite wall, Jack.'

Micky had been mistaken in one important respect: it wasn't like bumping one's head against a granite wall at all. It was more like charging headlong into a herd of hippos, unarmed.

We found our way singly and in pairs to Soweto, most of us nursing very badly bruised scalps.

The late evening edition of *The Star* carried a report of a knife attack on five whites in the afternoon near John Vorster Square by a black man shouting, '*Amandla!*' and 'Revenge for the children of Soweto!' After a chase, he was wounded by police bullets and taken to John Vorster Square. Minutes later he plunged to his death from the fourth floor of the Security Police building. It was alleged that he died while attempting to escape.

The editorial of *The Star*, a newspaper which had consistently claimed that agitators were at work in Soweto, grudgingly acknowledged the existence of our organisation – for the first time the SRC was referred to by name – and alluded to some of our grievances. Although it did not completely drop its claim that instigation and intimidation were rife in Soweto, it urged the government to drop its intransigence and give serious attention to our demands for the release of detained students. The paper went on:

> It is essentially a call for peace based on two conditions: that all students still held in detention should be charged or released and that police harassment of students should end . . . The SRC request seems to us a reasonable starting point for some sort of township detente . . . The SRC may not speak for all the township's youth, may have resorted to abhorrent means even for the redress of their grievances, but it is the only visible organ of a key sector of black opinion.

In fact, at this time our relations with the press were not all uniformly bad. *The World*, for one, had already made a complete *volte face*. What with the vast majority of its reporters being actually resident in Soweto! There was, indeed, a great deal of meaningful 'township détente' taking place between the students and all sectors of the black community in Soweto. As a result, *The World*, adopted a new position which was to lead to the internment of many of its leading journalists, including its editor and its political commentator, and eventually to a total government ban on the newspaper about a year later. Following our abortive march to John Vorster Square, *The World* became unequivocal in its support of student demands. Its journalists began to articulate our grievances, very often more eloquently than we were able to do ourselves. Moreover, they could put across our views to the community in an adult language, which our parents could more readily understand. *The World* thus became an important channel of communication between the SRC and Sowetans at large, and obviated the need for us to be always asking people like Bra P. and others who worked in offices where there were duplicating machines to print circulars for us each time we wanted to communicate important messages to our people.

Following our attempted march through the streets of the city, *The Financial Times* reported a precipitate rise in the sale of firearms of every description, from heavy calibre revolvers to semi-automatic rifles, to all sectors of the white community in Johannesburg. 'The favourites,' *The Financial Times* reported, 'are shotguns, preferably automatic, revolvers and automatic rifles. The little weapon is out, and the large calibre automatic and the magnum revolver are in.'

In Soweto there were also backrooms and sheds that were beginning to look more and more like the storerooms of a small armaments factory.

They came for Hlubi on Wednesday night.

An earlier attempt on his life had failed. A crude petrol bomb planted at his home in Rockville had exploded on Sunday night, bringing down his garage only.

However, on Wednesday night they made no mistake. He had gone to a shop in Diepkloof to demand his *diza* or *tjotjo*, his dues, from one of numerous small businessmen and petty traders in Soweto, who had to pay Hlubi a small fortune in bribes in order to stay in business. What with all the statute book being like a huge rat trap for blacks! It was simpler for such small businessmen to make advance payments on the Hlubi instalment plan in lieu of any future statutory offences for which Hlubi could pull in any one of them with whom he was displeased. And, like all bullies, the only predictable thing about Hlubi was his sadism. To keep on the right side of

his intemperate nature and explosive temper, petty traders in Soweto preferred to pay him a considerable prop-
ortion of their small profits. Besides, there was always
the matter of having to renew one's business licence
annually, depending on a favourite report from the police
to the licencing board. All in all, Hlubi and other cops
like himself were sitting on a gold mine.

They came for him that very same Wednesday night.

When he came out of the shop in Diepkloof, sipping a
coke he hadn't even paid for, an accurate shot fired from
a fast-moving car hit him squarely on the forehead and
killed him instantly. Two other bullets grazed the walls
of the shop and another sank in at the back of the shelves
in the store just above the shopkeeper's head.

At that time of the evening in Soweto, before the shops
actually close, there must have been dozens of eye-
witnesses when Hlubi was shot. But when the police
came round to conduct a very thorough investigation
that took them to every house in the neighbourhood,
there wasn't a single witness willing to step forward.
Random arrests were made and the police tried to pin
the case on several people on whom the charge just
wouldn't stick. Consequently the case against all the
individuals picked up in connection with Hlubi's murder
was dropped and the crime was never solved, so that the
police quickly linked it to the insurgents of the ANC.

But word making its rounds in the township had it
that the shots had been fired from a Mercedes Benz.
Others hotly disputed this and said the shot had been
fired from a BMW. The only point on which the people
were in complete agreement was that the assassin's
bullet had been fired from a car of German make.

As this narrative of our struggle draws to a close, it only
remains for me to try and give a brief summary of events
to the end; to list our achievements, such as they were,
and draw whatever lessons we learnt in those days.

For us the single most important lesson of events in
those days was that we might have benefited a great deal
from a more intimate knowledge of the history of our

people's struggle. Not all of us possessed the kind of historical perspective shown by our poets laureate, like Lefifi, in their poetry or imparted to Micky by his grandfather. So that cut off, as we were, by an endless list of bannings, banishments, arrests, deaths in detention and flights into exile, from any knowledge of what our predecessors in the struggle had accomplished or where they had failed, we could not help but repeat the mistakes of an earlier generation, the most glaring of which had been our tendency to offer ourselves as cattle fodder to the police and the army.

We were what our poet laureate, Mandla, has described as 'the children of the hour', with all the organisational spontaneity, dependence upon fortuitous occurrences, and our reliance upon the sensational and spectacular to produce the desired effects, which the phrase implies.

Our major limitation, of course, was that we were not a political organisation, as such, with a blueprint for political change and a series of fall-back positions from which we would recoup our forces. We had no grassroots, country-wide support; no effective communication network with our people we could call our own; no finances and all that goes into effective organisation at this level. In a word, we were ill-equipped for a protracted struggle against the most ruthless and efficient machine of total control and repression ever devised by man. We had little more than morality on our side.

For the people of Soweto as a whole, the events of those days taught us, as nothing else had ever done before, to organise effectively at all levels, from shebeens to clerics, among laymen and professional groups. People were also jerked out of their previous apathy and complacency, and the lines of battle drawn more distinctly. Political attitudes crystallised more clearly and people learnt that in our situation, where even neutrality had the effect of condoning certain practices, one was either for or against the System.

The events of those days also helped to diffuse the Black Consciousness ideology among all our ranks. So that even children of kindergarten age could be heard shouting, 'Powder!', in the streets and garbage heaps of Soweto, which they used as playgrounds; drunkards, enjoying looted alcohol from WRAB bottle stores, talked of '*Utshwala bePower*'.

There emerged a proliferation of organisations, all subscribing in broad terms to the Black Consciousness Movement (BCM): the Institute of Black Studies, the Union of Black Journalists, the Azanian Poets and Writers' Association, the Black Parents' Association, the Azanian People's Organisation and even a people's interim government of Soweto, the Committee of Ten.

Lawyers, doctors, teachers and businessmen, for long isolated elitist entities in our struggle, divorced from the true needs and aspirations of the people, suddenly came to the fore and formed a united front with the people. There were, no doubt, many jolly riders on the BCM bandwagon, especially among our commercial and professional classes. But many others were genuine in their commitment, as their staying power has proved. It was, indeed, a splendid example of the altruistic spirit and selflessness of a community; of what can be accomplished through dedication and solidarity.

It is equally true that many of the organisations formed during this period did not, in fact, survive their inaugural conferences. In some cases the nerves of some people snapped under pressure, a process which brought about some very peculiar behaviour. The Director of the Institute of Black Studies did a most unlikely thing and fled to the Transkei, shortly after the IBS's inaugural conference, to escape police harassment, thus earning the dubious distinction of being the first person to seek political asylum in the newly independent state of the Transkei. Not so long ago he was shown who is the true master in the Transkei, when the Transkei government threw him out, back to Johannesburg. In the majority of cases the government moved against existing organisations and incarcerated many of their leaders, as it had done after Sharpeville. But each time these organisations were banned and their leaders incarcerated, the same organisations re-emerged under different names and under new leadership. So that the SRC, banned in October, re-emerged in November as the Soweto Students' League; the Union of Black Journalists became the Writers' Association of South Africa and later the Media Workers' Association of South Africa. These 'new' organisations now had more clearly defined long-term objectives, carefully drawn-up programmes of action and strategies, with the kind of inbuilt safety valves and fall-back positions I mentioned earlier.

Many supporters of the System, from members of the police force to members of the UBC (or the Community Council, as it had become), were put in their right places, at least for a while. And when they did ultimately rear their ugly heads, their credibility and influence had sunk to an all-time low from which they were never to re-emerge. So that people like Rathebe and Chabeli have become something of a bad joke in Soweto.

Developments in other parts of the country seemed to augur well for a popular uprising. Less than a week after the outbreak of the uprisings in Soweto, students from Langa, Kagiso, Alexander, Gugulethu, Nyanga, New Brighton and other townships all over the country also flared up in an ever-widening spiral. Headlines announced: TOWNSHIPS BLAZE ALL OVER THE REEF, VAAL, AND PRETORIA COMPLEXES, THE CAPE PENINSULA AND THE EASTERN CAPE . . .

The police and the army became desperate, frantic and over-stretched. They were airlifted from one part of the country to go and help quell rebellion in a different part of the country, only to find that disturbances had flared up anew in the places from where they'd been airlifted. Deaths in detention increased. In most cases official reports said the people concerned had committed suicide with their belts or slipped on a small bar of soap under the shower; others, it was said, had plunged like human torpedoes headlong through the windows from the upper floors of the offices where they were being interrogated. It was a last-ditch stand by the authorities to stamp out insurrection and turn back the clock.

As for us, well, we were expendable cogs in the wheel; only, the wheel would keep on rolling, with or without us, and grinding everything on its path.

When things started to hot up unbearably for the leadership of the SRC, our own safety became a matter of some concern. We lived in mortal fear of the police and their agents; we lived like Scarlet Pimpernels, never sleeping at the same place twice. For three months we fled and ducked the police, directing the affairs of Soweto from our hide-outs, meeting our friends and parents clandestinely. One big advantage in South Africa is that the residential areas are segregated, so that wherever we went we were still among our people.

Things took a turn for the worse when they cracked down on Micky, who'd always been the toughest and the most elusive cookie among us. It became quite apparent that we could not evade the Security Police for ever.

Micky was taken from the Nazarene tower, where he was conferring with a group of students from Kagiso in the West Rand. They were all charged under the Terrorism Act.

A price of R500 was placed on my head. I was wanted in connection with the murder of several whites who had died in Soweto. Unable to comprehend what had hit them, the authorities were clearly going for blind shots. The important thing was to identify some enemy, real or imaginary, to sustain the myth of white invincibility.

My parents became very agitated; I was also jittery, though quietly determined to face the worst.

They were so importunate that I eventually promised to clear out. But not to the Transkei!

Following a meeting with Bra P. at some secret rendezvous, we decided to skip the country. But not before we had arranged for a smooth transition. A new executive was elected, which was to keep a lower profile than we had done. Our outgoing executive was mandated to open an office in exile, responsible for mounting a diplomatic offensive on the international front and for liaising with other exiled liberation organisations.

Khotso and I were the first to go. We drove with Bra

P. at night part of the way and walked the rest of the distance, sleeping by day and walking by night, through Boer-infested country and the heavily patrolled district of the Marico, where over a century before the armies of the great Mzilikazi, son of Mashobane, had retreated before the Voortrekker invasion, until we reached Botswana.

Duke, Tsietsi, Bella, Nina, Micky himself (when he was released for lack of sufficient evidence, and before they could nab him again on some other pretext), Mojalefa and his sister, and a host of others soon followed.

Bella's kid sisters, Tshidi and Queen, were also hounded out of their home and followed her to exile. Queen, ten years of age, was the youngest among us and we called her the 'Queen of the Exiles'. They had walked more than four hundred kilometres from Soweto on foot. (Their other sister, who had been a student at Turfloop, was appearing in a trial, along with eight other leaders of the South African Students' Organisation, charged under the Suppression of Communism Act.)

Sindiswa also followed, but not before the police had broken her nose when they took her in for interrogation for the third time.

We were the children of the new diaspora, we, the children of Soweto, germinating everywhere we went little new seeds of vengeance, hatred, bitterness, wrath, on the fertile soil of our hearts, watering our cherished seeds with our own blood, sweat and tears and that of our people.

How sweet it is to sit on the balcony of the President Hotel, protected from the steaming tropical heat, sipping cold Castle lager, and watching pretty Batswana women with their well-padded buttocks shaking to a sensuous rhythm, with their breasts like watermelons and some of the most fabulous legs I have seen, walking up and down the Mall below, on my lap a copy of *God's Bits of Wood*!

I've been catching up on my reading in the time I've been here. Every book I can lay my hands on which is banned in my country.

I've also been struggling to finish our book.

Four years have passed since the Soweto uprisings. Four long years! We've had time to ponder over a wide range of issues connected with the events.

I stand up and press the buzzer to summon the waiter, and resume my seat.

I have also been memorising chunks of passages from my favourite authors, Ngugi wa Thiong'o:

> Whenever any of us is degraded and humiliated
> even the smallest child, we are all humiliated
> and degraded because it has to do with human
> beings . . . For as long as there's a man in
> prison, I am also in prison: for as long as there is
> a man who goes hungry and without clothes,
> I am also hungry and without clothes.

The waiter arrives and I call for another Castle. I've not yet grown accustomed to this Prinz Brau that's drunk here.

The others arrive and each places an order.

We drink for a while in silence.

I'm fighting an almost overwhelming lethargy. But I've got to finish our book.

Four bloody long years!

The heat in this country!

Very soon a hubbub of conversation and laughter starts around me. But I can't participate fully . . . Whenever any of us is degraded and humiliated . . . Something deep inside me, something quite irrepressible, is screaming for expression.

The words of the poet flash across my mind; from up, up there in the sky:

> Peace will come.
> We have the power
> the hope
> the resolution
> Men will go home.

## MAYIBUYE! ILIZWE!! AMANDLA!!!

# Hungry Flames and other Black South African Short Stories

## Edited by Mbulelo Mzamane

From the bare concrete of the crowded prisons to the carpeted drawing rooms of the new African middle class, these fifteen short stories by South Africa's finest Black writers paint an urgent and vital picture of contemporary South Africa.

These stories rank with those of Steinbeck and Hemingway in their honest portraits of working men and women in all their strengths and in all their weaknesses — all of them living in the shadow of the apartheid state.

Over fifty years of Black South African writing in English is represented in this collection. A critical introduction describes the evolution of writing from the pioneers, such as R.R.R. Dhlomo and Sol Plaatje, through the urban 'jazz' style of the fifties to the more politicised Black Consciousness writers of the Sharpeville and Soweto eras.

The editor, Mbulelo Mzamane, is himself a distinguished writer of short stories and is the author of *My Cousin Comes to Jo'burg* (1982) and of *The Children of Soweto* (1982). He now teaches in the Department of English, Ahmadu Bello University, Zaria in Nigeria.

ISBN 0 582 78590 1